THOMISTIC PHILOSOPHY

BY

Rev. HENRI GRENIER, Ph.D., S.T.D., J.C.D.
Professor of Philosophy, Laval University

———

Translated from the Latin of the original
CURSUS PHILOSOPHIAE (Editio tertia)
by
Rev. J. P. E. O'HANLEY, Ph. D.

———

IN THREE VOLUMES

——

VOLUME II
METAPHYSICS

———

First English Edition

—

Published by
ST. DUNSTAN'S UNIVERSITY
CHARLOTTETOWN, CANADA

——

1948

Nihil obstat:

Gavan P. Monaghan, Ph. D., Paed. D.,

Censor deputatus.

Die 20 Julii, 1948

Imprimatur:

† Jacobus Boyle, D.D.,

Episcopus Carolinapolitanus.

Carolinapoli, die 2 Augusti, 1948.

To

ST. DUNSTAN

Scholar Statesman Saint

TABLE OF CONTENTS

INTRODUCTION

I

GENERAL METAPHYSICS
OSTENSIVE PART

BEING IN GENERAL
THE ONLY BOOK

—— ——

II

GENERAL METAPHYSICS
DEFENSIVE PART

BOOK I

THE FIRST PRINCIPLE

BOOK II

TRUTH

III

METAPHYSICS OF FINITE BEING

Book I

FINITE BEING

BOOK II

CAUSES

IV

METAPHYSICS OF INFINITE BEING

Book I

EXISTENCE OF GOD

Book II

ESSENCE AND ATTRIBUTES OF GOD

Book III

GOD'S OPERATION OUTSIDE HIMSELF

METAPHYSICS

METAPHYSICS

INTRODUCTION

––––

486. Origin of Metaphysics. — In Philosophy of Nature we studied mobile being in as much as it is mobile, and also its principles and properties. There remains for our consideration being, not as mobile, but simply as being, and also its principles and properties (¹). This consideration of being is the origin of Metaphysics, a science which is distinct from Philosophy of Nature. Philosophy of Nature, in as much as it deals with being as subject to motion, does not abstract from sensible matter; Metaphysics, in as much as it deals with all beings considered simply as beings, abstracts from sensible matter.

487. Names of Metaphysics. — This part of Philosophy is designated by the following names:

a) Metaphysics. This name, according to its etymology (from the Greek μετὰ τὰ φυσιχὰ), signifies *after Physics*. The term, it would seem, owes its origin to Andronicus of Rhodes, who, in classifying the works of Aristotle, placed the books dealing with immaterial being after the books of Physics (*Philosophy of Nature*).

b) First Philosophy. It is given this name, because it deals with the first causes of things. The other parts of Philos-

––––

(1) . . . Antiqui enim non opinabantur aliquam substantiam esse praeter substantiam corpoream mobilem, de qua physicus tractat. Et ideo creditum est, quod soli determinent de tota natura, et per consequens de ente; et ita etiam de primis principiis quae sunt simul consideranda cum ente. Hoc autem falsum est; quia adhuc est quaedam scientia superior naturali: ipsa enim natura, idest res naturalis habens in se principium motus, in se ipsa est unum aliquod genus entis universalis. Non enim omne ens est hujusmodi: cum probatum sit in octavo Physicorum, esse aliquod ens immobile. Hoc autem ens immobile superius est et nobilius ente mobili, de quo considerat naturalis. Et quia ad illam scientiam pertinet consideratio entis communis, ad quam pertinet consideratio entis primi, ideo ad aliam scientiam quam ad naturalem pertinet consideratio entis communis; et ejus etiam est considerare hujusmodi principia communia. Physica enim est quaedam pars philosophiae: sed non prima, quae considerat ens commune, et ea quae sunt entis inquantum hujusmodi. — *In Metaph.*, l. IV, l. 5, n. 593 (Cathala).

ophy, as Cosmology and Psychology, deal with the causes of things in the first degree of abstraction.

c) Theology (science of the divinity). Aristotle uses this name, because Metaphysics ultimately attains God and separated substances.

488. Real definition of Metaphysics. — Metaphysics, according to its real definition, is *the science of being as being,* i.e., *the science of all beings considered simply as beings.*

From this definition we can deduce the material object, the formal object *quod,* and the formal object *quo* of Metaphysics.

1) The material object of Metaphysics is all beings ([1]): substance, accident, God, possible being, and being of reason.

Substance is the principal object of Metaphysics, for it is the material object in which is most perfectly realized that aspect of being which is the formal object of Metaphysics ([2]). Metaphysics deals with accidents as beings which pertain to substance, for an accident is a being of a being, rather than a being.

Metaphysics deals with God as the common cause of being. God is the material object or subject of greatest excellence of Metaphysics, i.e., the subject of highest dignity.

Metaphysics deals with possible being in as much as possible being has relation to being existing in reality.

---

(1) ... Quaecumque communiter unius recipiunt praedicationem, licet non univoce, sed analogice de his praedicetur, pertinent ad unius scientiae considerationem: sed ens hoc modo praedicatur de omnibus entibus; ergo omnia entia pertinent ad considerationem unius scientiae, quae considerat ens in quantum ens, scilicet tam substantias quam accidentia. — *In Metiph.,* l. IV, l. 1, n. 534 (Cathala).

(2) Hic ponit quod *haec scientia principaliter considerat de substantiis,* etsi de omnibus entibus considerat, tali ratione. Omnis scientia quae est de pluribus quae dicuntur ad unum primum, est proprie et principaliter illius primi, ex quo alia dependent secundum esse, et propter quod dicuntur secundum nomen; et hoc est ubique verum. Sed substantia est hoc primum inter omnia entia. Ergo philosophus qui considerat omnia entia, primo et principaliter debet habere in sua consideratione principia et causas substantiarum; ergo per consequens ejus consideratio primo et principaliter de substantiis est. — *Ibidem,* n. 546.

Being of reason comes under the material object of Metaphysics, not in as much as it has foundation in real being, as a second intention,— as such it pertains to Logic,—but in as much as it is opposed to real being. It is under this aspect that Metaphysics deals with being of reason. Opposites are treated by the same science: medicine is concerned with health as well as with sickness, and grammar with what is grammatically correct as well as with what is grammatically erroneous. (¹)

2) The formal object *quod* of Metaphysics is being as being, i.e., being common to the ten predicaments, substance and the nine accidents.

3) The formal object *quo* of Metaphysics is the positive immateriality of real being which abstracts from all matter. Metaphysics is thus distinct from Logic, whose formal object *quo* is the negative immateriality of being of reason, in as much as being of reason has its foundation in real being; and from Philosophy of Nature, whose formal object *quo* is the immateriality of mobile being, which abstracts from singular matter, but not from sensible matter.

489. Metaphysics is science and wisdom.— 1° *Preliminaries.* *a*) Science is certain knowledge through causes.

b) Wisdom is used to signify either a moral habit or an intellectual habit.

A man is said to have wisdom as a moral habit, when *by inclination* he makes a correct judgment as regards what he ought to do; v.g., a man who has a particular moral virtue makes a correct judgment in regard to the things which ought to be done in accordance with this virtue, in as much as he is inclined to these things

Wisdom, as an intellectual virtue, has a *wide meaning* and a *strict meaning.*

In its *wide meaning,* wisdom signifies any kind of perfect knowledge; v.g., a man may be described as wise in his art.

---

(1) *In Metaph.,* l. IV, l. 3, n. 564 (Cathala).

In its *strict meaning*, wisdom is certain knowledge which speculates on all things according to their highest causes and first principles.

Hence science may be understood specifically, and as such is distinct from wisdom; or it may be identified with wisdom.

A science, in the specific sense, is one which judges according to the first principles and ultimate causes in a particular order only.

A science which is wisdom is one which judges according to the first principles and ultimate causes in every genus.

2° *Proof.*—Certain knowledge through highest causes and strictly first principles is science and wisdom. But Metaphysics is certain knowledge through highest causes and strictly first principles. Therefore Metaphysics is science and wisdom.

The *major* is clear from the preliminaries.

Minor.—The causes and principles of being considered simply as being, are the highest and strictly the first. But Metaphysics deals with and knows the causes and principles of being as being. Therefore Metaphysics is certain knowledge through highest causes and strictly first principles.

490. Division of Metaphysics. — Metaphysics is formally only one science: it is specified by the immateriality proper to being as being. But it can be divided into several material parts.

We divide it into four parts.

In the first part, we deal with being in general and with what results from being. This part may be called ostensive general Metaphysics.

In the second part, we study the first principle which is derived from the notion of being, i.e., the first principle of all human knowledge, for the purpose of explaining and defending it. This part may be called defensive general Metaphysics.

In the third part, we treat finite being; and in the fourth part, the first cause of finite being which is infinite being.

Hence the four material parts of Metaphysics are as follows:

General Metaphysics, ostensive part.
General Metaphysics, defensive part.
Metaphysics of finite being.
Metaphysics of infinite being.

POINTS FOR REVIEW

1. Explain why substance is called the principal material object of Metaphysics, and under what aspect God is its material object. Does being of reason come under this object? Explain.

2. Name the formal object *quod* and the formal object *quo* of Metaphysics, and explain what is meant by being in general.

3. Explain why Metaphysics is called First Philosophy, and why it is science and wisdom.

4. Is Metaphysics formally one science?

TEXTUS. — Sicut docet Philosophus in Politicis suis, quando aliqua plura ordinantur ad unum, oportet unum eorum esse regulans, sive regens, et alia regulata, sive recta. Quod quidem patet in unione animae et corporis; nam anima naturaliter imperat, et corpus obedit. Similiter etiam inter animae vires: irascibilis enim et concupiscibilis naturali ordine per rationem reguntur. Omnes autem scientiae et artes ordinantur in unum, scilicet ad hominis perfectionem, quae est ejus beatitudo. Unde necesse est, quod una earum sit aliarum omnium rectrix, quae nomen sapientiae recte vindicat. Nam sapientis est alios ordinare.

Quae autem sit haec scientia, et circa qualia, considerari potest, si diligenter respiciatur quomodo est aliquis idoneus ad regendum. Sicut enim, ut in libro praedicto Philosophus dicit, homines intellectu vigentes, naturaliter aliorum rectores et domini sunt: homines vero qui sunt robusti corpore, intellectu vero deficientes, sunt naturaliter servi: ita scientia debet esse naturaliter aliarum regulatrix, quae maxime intellectualis est. Haec autem est, quae circa maxime intelligibilia versatur.

Maxime autem intelligibilia tripliciter accipere possumus. Primo quidem ex ordine intelligendi. Nam ex quibus intellectus certitudinem accipit, videntur esse intelligibilia magis. Unde, cum certitudo scientiae per intellectum acquiratur ex causis, causarum cognitio maxime intellectualis esse videtur. Unde et illa scientia, quae primas causas considerat, videtur esse maxime aliarum regulatrix.

Secundo ex comparatione intellectus ad sensum. Nam, cum sensus sit cognitio particularium, intellectus per hoc ab ipso differre videtur, quod universalia comprehendit. Unde et illa scientia maxime est intellectualis, quae circa principia maxime universalia versatur. Quae quidem sunt ens, et ea quae consequuntur ens, ut unum et multa, potentia et actus. Hujusmodi autem non debent omnino indeterminata remanere, cum sine his completa cognitio de his, quae sunt propria alieni generi vel speciei, haberi non possit. Nec iterum in una aliqua particulari scientia tractari debent: quia cum his unumquodque genus entium ad sui cognitionem indigeat, pari ratione in qualibet particulari scientia tratarentur.   Unde restat quod in una communi scientia hujusmodi tractentur; quae cum maxime intellectualis sit, est aliarum regulatrix.

Tertio ex ipsa cognitione intellectus.   Nam cum unaquaeque res ex hoc ipso vim intellectivam habeat, quod est a materia immunis, oportet illa esse maxime intelligibilia, quae sunt maxime a materia separata.   Intelligibile enim et intellectum oportet proportionata esse, et unius generis, cum intellectus et intelligibile in actu sint unum.   Ea vero sunt maxime a materia separata, quae non tantum a signata materia abstrahunt, « sicut formae naturales in universali acceptae, de quibus tractat « scientia naturalis », sed omnino a materia sensibili.   Et non solum secundum rationem, sicut mathematica, sed etiam secundum esse, sicut Deus et intelligentiae.   Unde scientia, quae de istis rebus considerat, maxime videtur esse intellectualis et aliarum princeps sive domina.

Haec autem triplex consideratio, non diversis, sed uni scientiae attribui debet.   Nam praedictae substantiae separatae sunt universales et primae causae essendi.   Ejusdem autem scientiae est considerare causas proprias alicujus generis et genus ipsum: sicut naturalis considerat principia corporis naturalis.   Unde oportet quod ad eamdem scientiam pertineat considerare substantias separatas, et ens commune, quod est genus, cujus sunt praedictae substantiae communes et universales causae.

Ex quo apparet, quod quamvis ista scientia praedicta tria consideret, non tamen considerat quodlibet eorum ut subjectum, sed ipsum solum ens commune.   Hoc enim est subjectum in scientia, cujus causas et passiones quaerimus, non autem ipsae causae alicujus generis quaesiti.   Nam cognitio causarum alicujus generis, est finis ad quem consideratio scientiae pertingit. Quamvis autem subjectum hujus scientiae sit ens commune, dicitur tamen tota de his quae sunt separata a materia secundum esse et rationem.   Quia secundum esse et rationem separari dicuntur, non solum illa quae nunquam in materia esse possunt, sicut Deus et intellectuales substantiae, sed etiam illa quae possunt sine materia esse, sicut ens commune.   Hoc tamen non contingeret, si a materia secundum esse dependerent.

Secundum igitur tria praedicta, ex quibus perfectio hujus scientiae attenditur, sortitur tria nomina.   Dicitur enim scientia divina sive theologia, inquantum praedictas substantias considerat.   Metaphysica, in quantum considerat ens et ea quae consequuntur ipsum.   Haec enim transphysica inveniuntur in via resolutionis, sicut magis communia post minus communia. Dicitur autem prima philosophia, inquantum primas rerum causas considerat. Sic igitur patet quid sit subjectum hujus scientiae, et qualiter se habeat ad alias scientias, et quo nomine nominetur. — *In Metaph.*, Prooemium s. Thomae.

GENERAL METAPHYSICS
OSTENSIVE PART

THE ONLY BOOK

Being in general

Prologue. — The ostensive part of general Metaphysics deals with being in itself and with what is most closely connected with being. This part will contain only one book; and in it we shall study: first, the nature of being; secondly, the properties of being; thirdly, the division of being into potency and act. Hence there will be three chapters in this book.

Chapter   I. Nature of being.

Chapter II. Properties of being.

Chapter III. Division of being into potency and act.

NATURE OF BEING

Prologue. — In this chapter, we shall treat first the notion of being; secondly, the transcendence of being; thirdly, the analogy of being. Therefore the chapter will contain three articles.

Notion of being
- Being cannot be defined or properly described
- Improper description of being
- Being, as signifying that which is, is an essential predicate of all things to which it is attributed
- Being, as signifying existence, is an essential predicate of God
- Being, as signifying existence, is not an essential predicate of creatures
- Being, as it is first known, is not known as metaphysical being

Transcendence of being
- Statement of the question
- Thesis: Being is transcendent with respect to all things
- Being is the ontologically first concept
- Being is the most general and simplest of predicates

Analogy of being
- Statement of the question
- Opinions
- Thesis: The term *being* with respect to infinite being and finite being, substance and accident, is neither equivocal, nor univocal, but analogous by analogy both of proper proportionality and of attribution
- Definitions
- Abstraction of the analogous concept
- Difficulties

NOTION OF BEING

491. Being cannot be defined or properly described. — Being cannot be defined, because every definition is composed of a genus and a differentia. But there can be no genus above being; nor can being have a differentia properly so called. Therefore being cannot be defined.

Being cannot be properly described. Every description, properly so called, of a thing or a notion is made from notions that are clearer and better known than the thing to be described. But being is the best known of all notions: if a person does not conceive being, he conceives nothing. Therefore being cannot be defined or properly described.

492. — Improper description of being. — Grammatically, being is the present participle of the verb *to be*. But the verb *to be* is used in two ways:

1° To be signifies *to exist* in reality; v.g., God is, i.e., exists.

2° To be is a *copula* verb in a proposition; v.g., man is mortal; man is a species.

Being, as a copula verb derived from *to be*, is anything of which an affirmative proposition can be formed, even though that thing is nothing in reality. Under this aspect, privations and negations may be called beings; v.g., when we say: blindness is in the eyes.

Being, derived from the verb *to be* as signifying existence, is predicated of *that which is*. Under this aspect, only things that have or can have existence in reality may be called beings([1]).

(1) Sciendum est quod, sicut in V Metaphysicae Philosophus dicit, ens per se dicitur dupliciter. Uno modo, quod dividitur per decem praedica-

Being which has existence in reality implies two things:

1° that from which the noun being is derived, namely, *existence;*

2° that to which the noun being is applied, namely, *that which is* (¹).

Hence being which has existence in reality can have two meanings:

a) Being may be understood as *signifying existence*, that is to say, as signifying that from which the noun being is derived.

b) Being may be understood as *signifying that which is,* that is to say, as signifying a subject which has existence, i.e., an essence which has existence.

Hence, being, as signifying that which is, is a compound that contains essence and existence.   Essence is a part of being i.e., a subject which connotes a relation to existence, but not in as much as it implies existence or non-existence (²).

Being, as signifying that which is, is the object of Metaphysics.

493. Division of being. — 1° Being, in its broadest meaning, is divided into *real being* and *being of reason.*

---

menta.   Alio modo, quod significat propositionum veritatem.   Horum autem differentia est, quia secundo modo potest dici ens omne illud, de quo affirmativa propositio formari potest etiam si illud in re nihil ponat: per quem modum privationes et negationes entia dicuntur; dicimus enim quod affirmatio est opposita negationi, et quod caecitas est in oculo.   Sed primo modo non potest dici aliquid quod sit ens, nisi quod in re aliquid ponat.   Unde primo modo caecitas et hujusmodi non sunt entia.   Nomen igitur essentiae non sumitur ab ente secundo modo dicto; aliqua enim dicuntur hoc modo entia, quae essentiam non habent, ut patet in privationibus; sed sumitur essentia ab ente primo modo dicto.   Unde Comment. in eodem loco dicit: Ens primo modo dictum, est quod significat substantiam rei. — *De Ente et Essentia*, c. 1.

(1) Sed in Entis nomine duo aspici possunt, scilicet id a quo nomen Entis sumitur, scilicet ipsum esse, quo res est; et id ad quod nomen Entis impositum est, scilicet id quod est. — CAJETANUS, *in De Ente et Essentia*, c. IV.

(2) ... Ens, ut infra dicetur, significat *id quod habet esse:* id autem quod habet esse, comprehendit in se essentiam: essentia vero significat id quod importat definitio, ut dicetur, quae non importat esse vel non esse, ex primo posteriorum.   Ens ergo ita se habet ad essentiam, quod complectitur in se utrumque, essentiam scilicet et esse; essentia vero alterum tantum, et ideo ens appellatur compositum respectu essentiae. — CAJETANUS, *in De Ente et Essentia*, Prooemium, sub fine.

Real being is being which has existence in nature.

Being of reason is being that has objective existence only in the mind, and can have no existence in reality; v.g., species, genus (n. 117).

2° Being is again divided into *actual being* and *possible being*.

Actual being is being which has existence in reality.

Possible being is being which has not, but can have, existence in reality.

In possible being, a distinction must be made between two things: *a*) the thing, i.e., essence; *b*) the state of possibility.

As regards the state of possibility, possible being is being of reason, because the state of possibility does not admit of actual existence (¹). Therefore in possible being there is a blend, so to speak, of real being and being of reason. Hence possible being sometimes may be said to be real being, sometimes non-real being: real being as it is opposed, in virtue of its essence, to fictitious being; non-real being as, in virtue of its state possibility, it does not admit of actual existence and is opposed to actual being.

3° Actual being is divided into *infinite being* and *finite being*.

_____

(1) ... Status possibilitatis in creaturis non est aliquid reale formaliter positive illis conveniens, et actu in illis inventum: licet res quae tali statui subditur sit realis, non actu exsistens, sed solum objective, id est, cum non-repugnantia terminorum. Et illud dicitur non habere repugnantiam terminorum, quando praedicatum convenit subjecto sicque potest habere rationem entis, quod autem implicat contradictionem et habet repugnantiam terminorum, ideo est, quia involvit aliquid de ratione non-entis in non conveniendo praedicatum subjecto. Hoc ipso autem quod aliquid est participabile a primo ente, seu objective habet rationem entis et non-repugnantiam terminorum, dicitur contineri in ratione omnipotentiae et participat ab illa denominationem possibilis seu statum possibilitatis: qui est status excludens exsistentiam actu, non tamen repugnantiam ponens in ipsa re: et ideo ex parte ipsius rei objective dicitur aliquid reale licet ex parte status ut excludit actualem exsistentiam nihil exsistentiae sit, est tamen aliquid essentiae objective, seu non-repugnanter. Unde licet ex parte exsistentiae positive et actu non sit aliquid, et ex hac parte dicatur ens rationis, sed tamen objective dicitur aliquid reale in quantum id cui convenit talis status est objectum potentiae realis, et non habet repugnantiam seu implicationem ut fiat a potentia reali. Id autem quod est pure nihil et ens fictum, nec positive nec objective dicitur ens reale, quia habet repugnantiam seu incapacitatem ut sit ens. — JOANNES A SANCTO THOMA, *Cursus Theol.*, t. II, p. 373b (Sol.).

Infinite being is the first cause of finite being; it is that which is in no way limited as being.

Finite being (actual and possible) is divided into the ten predicaments.

4° Actual finite being, as an actual whole, is divided into its entitative parts, i.e., into essence and existence, which are related to each other as potency and act.

As a result of this division, we have the division of being into complete being, which is a compound of essence and existence, and incomplete or partial being, i.e., essence and existence taken separately.

494. — Being, as signifying that which is, is an essential predicate of everything to which it is attributed. — 1° *Preliminaries.* — a) An essential predicate is a predicate which signifies the essence of the thing of which it is predicated, not something distinct from this essence.

b) An essential predicate may be either proper or common.

A proper essential predicate is a predicate which is found in the definition of a thing, for it signifies either its genus, or species, or differentia.

A common essential predicate is a predicate which signifies the essence of a thing, but is not found in the definition of the thing, for it does not express either the genus, or the species or the differentia of the thing.

Being is not a proper essential predicate, but rather a common essential predicate.

2° *Proof of proposition.*

a) A predicate which signifies essence is an essential predicate. But being, as signifying that which is, signifies essence: being signifies that which connotes a relation to existence, i. e., a subject which exists or can exist. Therefore.

b) If being were not an essential predicate, it would signify something added to the thing of which it is predicated. And since this addition would have its own essence, the same ques-

tion would recur in regard to it, and so on into infinity ([1]) Therefore, to avoid this recurrence of the same question into infinity,
we must conclude that being, as signifying *that which* is, is an
essential predicate of everything to which it is attributed.

**495. Being, as signifying existence, is an essential
predicate of God.** — A predicate which signifies the essence
of the thing to which it is attributed is an essential predicate.
But being, as signifying existence, signifies the divine essence,
for God's existence is His essence: there is no real composition
of essence and existence in God. Therefore.

**496. Being, as signifying existence, is not an essential
predicate of creatures.** — 1° An essential predicate is a
predicate which designates the essence of the thing of which it
is predicated. Hence an essential predicate of a thing cannot
be denied without destroying the concept of the essence of that
thing.

Being as signifying existence, is not an essential predicate
of creatures, because creatures are beings by participation
(entia ab alio), i.e., beings which receive their existence from
another. Hence they participate existence, and therefore have
it by participation, not essentially.

2° Being, as signifying existence, is an accidental predicate of creatures, in as much as existence is a contingent predicate of the creature, that is to say, a predicate that can be
denied the creature without destroying the concept of its essence: for a creature can be conceived as existing or as not
existing. The definition of the creature makes no reference to
existence or non-existence.

---

(1) ... Quod autem ens et unum praedicentur de substantia cujuslibet
rei per se et non secundum accidens, sic potest probari. Si enim praedica-
rentur de substantia cujuslibet rei per aliquod ens ei additum, de illo iterum
necesse est praedicari ens, quia unumquodque est unum et ens. Aut ergo
iterum de hoc praedicatur per se, aut per aliquid aliud, iterum esset quaestio
de illo addito, et sic erit procedere usque ad infinitum. Hoc autem est impossibile: ergo necesse est stare in primo, scilicet quod substantia rei sit una
et ens per seipsam, et non per aliquid additum. — *In Metaph.*, l. IV, l. 2,
n. 555 (Cathala).

Nevertheless, a creature's existence is determined and specified by its essence. Examples: the existence of substance is assigned to the predicament of substance; the existence of quantity, to the predicament of quantity; the existence of man is human existence, and distinct from the existence of the horse. Hence, from this point of view, existence may be considered as a property of the creature of which it is predicated; but, in as much as it belongs to the creature only contingently, it is an accidental predicate, i.e., it is an accident, according to the meaning of accident as the fifth predicable.

497. Being, as it is first known, is not known as metaphysical being.— Being as first known is being abstracted by negative abstraction, as the most general and confused of notions which is predicable of all things. Metaphysical being is being which makes abstraction from all matter; it is the object on which Metaphysics speculates, and whose principles, properties, and first cause metaphysical speculation attempts to discover. Hence being as first known is not metaphysical being.

POINTS FOR REVIEW

1. Explain why being cannot be defined.

2. What is the derivation of the word *being*? State two meanings of the word as derived from *to exist*.

3. What is the difference between being and essence? Is possible being real being or being of reason? Explain.

4. Show whether being is an essential or an accidental predicate of creatures.

5. Does existence belong to the predicament of substance? Explain.

6. Explain how being as first known differs from metaphysical being.

TRANSCENDENCE OF BEING

498. Statement of the question. — 1° The problem with which we are concerned at present may be stated as follows: on the one hand, being is a most indeterminate predicate; on the other hand, the things of which being is predicated are determinate, and do not admit of the indeterminateness of being; v.g., when we say: *Peter is a being,* Peter is a determinate person, but being signifies something indeterminate. Hence it would seem that being is a pure abstraction, i.e., a purely logical notion, which attributes nothing to the thing of which it is predicated. This is the conclusion at which Hegel arrives ([1]).

But yet we must affirm that being is something real, and that being excludes non-being, because being and non-being are in contradictory opposition to each other.

2° But if we hold that being signifies something real, we are confronted with another difficulty.

If being is something real, there exists only one being, for being is predicated of all things. Things are not distinct from each other as beings, for being is not distinct from itself. Hence we must conclude that the principle of distinction between things is something which is not being, that is to say, *non-being,*

---

(1) Being, pure being, without any further determination. In its indeterminate immediacy it is similar to itself alone, and also not dissimilar from any other; it has no differentiation either within itself or relatively to anything external; nor would it remain fixed in its purity, were there any determination or content which could be distinguished within it, or whereby it could be posited as distinct from an other. It is pure indeterminateness and vacuity. Nothing can be intuited in it, if there is any question here of intuition, or again it is merely this pure and empty intuition itself; equally there is in it no object for thought, or again it is just this empty thought. In fact, Being, indeterminate immediacy, is Nothing, neither more nor less. — *Science of Logic* (Translation of *Wissenschaf: der Logik* by W. H. Johnston B.A. and L. G. Struthers, M.A., 1928), p. 97.

i.e., *nothing*. But such a conclusion is merely another way of saying that things are not distinct from each other, because things whose sole principle of distinction is non-being are not really distinct.

3° The solution of our second problem can be reached very easily, if we know that being is transcendent.

That is transcendent which is found really, intrinsically, and formally in all things. Therefore a transcendental is found not only in everything by which things are similar, but also in everything by which they are distinct. In other words, whatever is found in a thing, whether it be a principle of similarity, or a principle of distinction, is formally being.

499. Statement of the thesis.

THESIS. — Being is transcendent with respect to all things.

Everything which exists is either infinite being or finite being; and finite being is either substance or accident. But infinite being, finite being, substance, and accident are intrinsically and formally beings, for they exist in as much as they have relation to existence.

Moreover, the principle of the distinction between infinite being and finite being, and between substance and accident, is intrinsically and formally being, for otherwise it would be non-being, which cannot possibly be a principle of distinction. Therefore being is transcendent with respect to all things.

500. Being is the ontologically first concept. — a) The ontologically first concept is that concept which is found in all things, and into which all other concepts are resolved.

b) The ontologically first concept is distinct from the first ontological. The first ontological is the first being, i.e., the first existing thing which is the cause of all other beings. The first ontological is God.

c) Being is the ontologically first concept, because it is the most transcendent of all concepts. Hence it is found in all other concepts; and all other concepts are resolved into being, because they are derived from addition to being.   Substance is *being* of itself; accident is *being* in another; the true is intelligible *being*, etc.

501. Being is the most general and simplest of predicates. — 1° *Preliminaries. a)* Being is used here as signifying *that which* is, not as signifying existence.

b) The most general of predicates is that predicate which is predicable of all things.

c) The simplest of predicates is that predicate which not only signifies a simple essence, but expresses it in the simplest manner, abstracting in so far as possible from all determinations whatsoever.   In other words, the simplest of predicates is that predicate which is composed of the least possible number of notes.

2° *Proof.—a) Being, as signifying that which is, is the most general of predicates.*—That predicate which is predicable of all things is the most general of all predicates.   But being, as signifying that which is, is predicable of all things, because being is a transcendent, i.e., is transcendent with respect to all things.   Therefore being, as signifying that which is, is the most general of predicates.

b) Being, as signifying that which is, is the simplest of predicates.—The most general of predicates is the simplest of predicates.   But being, as signifying that which is, is the most general of predicates.   Therefore being, as signifying that which is, is the simplest of predicates.

Major.—The comprehension and extension of a predicate, i.e., of a concept, are in inverse proportion to each other.

The minor is evident from the proof of the first part.

POINTS FOR REVIEW

1. What is a transcendent notion ?

2. State what is meant by the most general of predicates, and the simplest of predicates.

ANALOGY OF BEING

502. Statement of the question. — 1° We have already learned that being is a transcendent, i.e., something real which is found in all its inferiors, not excepting their differentiæ. Now we shall treat the question of how being, as a common term, is predicable of its inferiors: whether univocally, i.e., as a genus, or equivocally, or analogously. Hence we are at present concerned with the second intention of the notion of being.

2° An equivocal term is a term which does not signify an objective concept common to the things designated by it, but has totally different meanings as applied to different subjects; v.g., dog as applied to an animal and a star.

Therefore things designated by an equivocal term have nothing in common except a mere name, so that it is only the name that is equivocal.

A *univocal term* is a term which signifies a single objective concept (perfection, nature), and is distributively applicable to many subjects (one in many); v.g., the term man as predicated of Peter and Paul; animal as predicated of man and the brute.

An *analogous term* is a term which signifies an objective concept (perfection, notion) which is absolutely different, but in a particular respect, i.e., proportionately, — for analogy means proportion, — the same in the subjects of which it is predicated; v.g., the term *healthy* as applied to animal, food, and color. Hence an analogous term is a mean between an equivocal term and a univocal term.

3° An analogous term can be such either by analogy of attribution or by analogy of proportionality.

a) Analogy of attribution (of proportion) obtains when the same term is applied to several subjects only because of the relation they have to the principal analogate, in which alone the perfection signified by the term is found formally and intrinsically; v.g., the perfection which we call health is possessed formally and intrinsically by an animal, and it is used with reference to medicine, food, and color, only because it has the relation of cause or sign to the health of the animal.

The subject in which the perfection signified by the analogous term is found formally and intrinsically is called the *principal term, supreme analogate,* or *principal analogate;* and all the other subjects are called *secondary terms, minor analogates,* or *secondary analogates.*

Since analogy of attribution is the proportion of one or several subjects to a single term, it is called simple analogy, simple proportion, or even analogy of simple proportion.

Analogy of proportionality obtains when the same term is applied to several subjects, because the perfection (form) signified by this term is found in them *intrinsically,* but according to a mode that is only proportionately the same; v.g., a point and an efficient cause are called *principles,* because the relation of a point to a line is, in a certain proportion, similar to the relation of an efficient cause to its effect.

The essential condition of analogy of proportionality is as follows: the perfection (objective concept) signified by the analogous term is found *intrinsically* in all the analogates, i.e., subjects, to which the term is applied, but according to an essentially *different mode* in each of them. Therefore the analogates have each a different relation to the perfection expressed by the analogous term. And it is this different relation to a same perfection (form) that is foundation of the proportional similarity of the several subjects.

Therefore analogy of proportionality is a compound proportion, i.e., a proportion of proportions (5 :10 : : 10 : 20), and always requires, either formally or virtually, at least four terms of comparison.

b) Analogy of proportionality is of two kinds: *metaphorical* and *proper*.

Analogy of proportionality is *metaphorical* when the perfection signified by the analogous term is in one subject in its proper sense, and in another in an *improper*, transferred, or figurative sense (¹).

Thus, for example, the dignity of king is found properly in man, and figuratively in the lion. This proportionality is expressed as follows: the lion is to beasts as a certain man is to his countrymen, that is to say, is king(²).

Analogy of proportionality is *proper* when the perfection signified by the analogous term is found *intrinsically* and *properly* in each of the subjects to which the analogous term is applied. (³)   This, indeed, is true and fundamental analogy of proportionality.

503. Opinions. — 1° Moses Maimonides holds that the term being is equivocal. Nominalists and Agnostics support this opinion, at least implicitly.

2° Monists, all pantheists, both ancient, as Parmenides, and more recent, as Spinoza, presuppose that being in univocal. For, if being were univocal, the differentiae by which being would be contracted would be extraneous to it, and therefore would be non-being, i.e., nothing. Therefore the only being that could exist would be a unique and infinite being.

Anthromorphists, who conceive God as a human person, agree with this opinion, in as much as they implicitly presuppose a certain univocity of being.

3° Scholastics commonly teach that being in analogous, but disagree on the kind of analogy by which it is analogous.

a) Scotus affirms that being is not a genus, and therefore is analogous, but analogous in such a way that it is, in a certain sense, univocal too.

---

(1) *De Veritate*, q. 2, a. 11, c. — I, q. 13, ad 1 et 3.
(2) I, q. 13, a. 6.
(3) *De Veritate*, q. 2, a. 11.

b) Suarez maintains that being is analogous by analogy of attribution. He teaches that in analogy of attribution the perfection signified by the analogous term is found intrinsically not only in the principal analogate, but also in all the other analogates.

c) Thomists teach that being with respect to infinite being (God) and finite being (the creature), substance and accident, is analogous by analogy which formally is analogy of proper proportionality, but virtually is analogy of attribution. Being, according to this opinion, is virtually analogous by analogy of attribution in this sense: if by impossible hypothesis finite being were not formally being, it would, nevertheless, be denominated being on account of its relation to infinite being. The same would be true of accident in its relation to substance.

504. Statement of the thesis. — The importance of this thesis must be evident to all ([1]). For, if being is analogous, it expresses inferiors with essentially distinct modes of being. If it is univocal, every being has the same mode of being, and there can be only one being, a unique being. If it is equivocal, infinite being cannot be known from finite being, nor can substance be known from accident; and this is agnosticism.

> **THESIS.**—THE TERM BEING WITH RESPECT TO INFI-
> NITE BEING AND FINITE BEING, SUB-
> STANCE AND ACCIDENT, IS NEITHER
> EQUIVOCAL, NOR UNIVOCAL, BUT AN-
> ALOGOUS BY ANALOGY OF BOTH PROPER
> PROPORTIONALITY AND ATTRIBUTION.

First part. — *The term being...is not equivocal.* A term which signifies a perfection common to the subjects of which it is predicated is not equivocal. But the term *being* signifies a perfection (objective concept) common to infinite being and finite being, to substance and accident. Therefore the term

---

(1) Ens quod denominatur ab esse, non univoce de Deo et creaturis dicitur, nec tamen prorsus aequivoce, sed analogice, analogia tum attributionis, tum proportionalitatis. — *Thesis* IV s. Thomae.

being with respect to infinite being and finite being, substance and accident, is not equivocal ([1]).

The *major* is evident from the statement of the question.

Minor.—Being signifies a subject that connotes a relation to existence. But infinite being and finite being, substance and accident, are denominated beings, because they connote a relation to existence. Therefore.

Second part.—*The term being . . . is not univocal.* If being is not a genus, the term being is not univocal. But being is not a genus. Therefore the term being is not univocal.

Major.—If being were univocal, it would signify a perfection which is one and the same in subjects which are contracted, i.e., made determinate, by differentiae which are extraneous to being.

Minor.—The differentiae by which being is contracted are not extraneous to being, for otherwise they would be nothing. Therefore being is not a genus.

Third part.—*The term being . . . is analogous.* A term which is neither equivocal nor univocal is analogous. But the term being is neither equivocal nor univocal. Therefore the term being is analogous.

Fourth part.—*The term being . . . is analogous by analogy of proper proportionality.* A term which signifies a perfection which is found properly and intrinsically in the subjects of which it is predicated, but according to a mode that is only proportionately the same, is analogous by analogy of proper proportionality. But the term being signifies a perfection which is found properly and intrinsically in infinite being and finite being, in substance and accident, but according to a mode that is only proportionately the same. Therefore the term being with respect to infinite being and finite being, substance and accident, is analogous by analogy of proper proportionality.

---

(1) *De Potentia*, q. 7, a. 7.

The *major* is evident from the statement of the question.

Minor.—The subjects of which the term being is predicated are infinite being and finite being, substance and accident. But these subjects are properly and intrinsically beings, because they connote a relation to existence, although according to modes that are only proportionately the same: infinite being is being whose essence and existence are identified, whereas finite being is being whose essence and existence are really distinct; substance possesses its existence in itself, whereas accident only possesses existence in a subject: accident has existence dependently on the subject in which it inheres.

Fifth part.—*The term being is virtually analogous by analogy of attribution.* If by impossible hypothesis finite being were not analogous by analogy of proper proportionality, it would be analogous by analogy of attribution. But being which is analogous in this way is virtually analogous by analogy of attribution. Therefore...

Major.—If by impossible hypothesis finite being were not properly and intrinsically being, it would be such by extrinsic denomination, because of its relation to infinite being, i.e., as an effect and sign of infinite being, just as, v.g., color, though not properly and intrinsically healthy, is denominated healthy in as much as it is a sign and an effect of health. The same is to be said of accident in relation to substance. Therefore...

NOTE.—Therefore the analogy of being presupposes identity of essence and existence in infinite being; and, in finite being, a real distinction between essence and existence, and between substance and accident.

505. Definitions. — *Univocal* things are defined: things which have a common name which signifies one and the same perfection in all of them.

Equivocal things are defined: things which have a common name which signifies an essentially different perfection in each of them.

Analogous things are defined: things which have a common name which signifies a perfection that is essentially different, but proportionately the same, in each of them.   There are two things in these definitions which we should observe:

a) Perfection (formality) signifies that which is conceived of a thing, i. e., the objective concept of the thing.

b) Thus are defined univocated univocal things, equivocated equivocal things, and analogated analogous things, i.e., things of which univocal, equivocal, or analogous names are predicated.

506. Abstraction of the analogous concept. — We shall obtain a better understanding of analogous things if we compare the mode by which the analogous concept is abstracted from its inferiors with the mode by which the univocal concept and the equivocal concept are abstracted.

a) In the case of *equivocals*, there is abstracted not one concept, but several essentially distinct concepts.   The term (name) only is equivocal.

b) In the case of *univocals*, we have one complete concept, perfectly prescinded, i. e., completely abstracted, from its differentiae, which it contains not actually, but only potentially, as notions extraneous to itself.   Therefore the univocal concept is contracted *by composition*.   Thus, for example, *animal* is perfectly prescinded from *rational* and *irrational*, and is only in potency to them, in as much as it can be contracted by them as by notions extraneous to itself.

c) In the case of things which are *analogous by analogy of attribution* and by *analogy of metaphorical proportionality*, we have several concepts which have a certain unity of comparison; v. g., healthy as predicated of its supreme analogate, i.e., of animals, is properly univocal; and it is analogous only in as much as its secondary analogates, v.g., food, color, are compared to the supreme analogate, i.e., to animal, as healthy.

d) In the case of things which are *analogous by analogy of proper porportionality*, we have one concept, but a concept that is incomplete, not perfectly prescinded from its differentiae, but containing them in *confused act* (*actu confuso*), i.e., actually, but in a confused manner, as notions intrinsic to itself.

Hence a concept that is analogous by analogy of proper proportionality is not contracted by composition, but by a *more express* concept. Thus, for example, the differentiae by which being is contracted are not extraneous to being.

507. Difficulties. — 1° A term which represents a concept abstracted from several subjects is univocal. But the term *being* represents a concept abstracted from several subjects. Therefore the term *being* is univocal.

Major. — Perfectly abstracted, *I concede;* imperfectly abstracted, *I deny.*

Minor. — Imperfectly abstracted, *I concede;* perfectly abstracted, *I deny.*

The objective concept of being is not perfectly abstracted, because what still remains is being.

2° But the term *being* represents a perfectly abstracted concept. Therefore the difficulty remains.

A term which expresses an objective concept common to several subjects represents a perfectly abstracted concept. But the term *being* expresses an objective concept common to several subjects. Therefore the term *being* represents a perfectly abstracted concept.

Major. — An objective concept that is absolutely the same, *I concede;* an objective concept that is only proportionately the same, *I deny.*

Minor. — An objective concept that is absolutely the same, *I deny;* proportionately the same, *I concede.*

3° But the term *being* expresses an objective concept that is absolutely the same in all the subjects of which it is predicated. Therefore the difficulty remains.

A term which does not express the differentiae by which the concept signified is contracted expresses an objective concept that is absolutely the same in all the subjects of which it is predicated. But the term *being* does not express the differentiae by which the concept of being is contracted. Therefore the term *being* expresses an objective concept that is one and the same in all the subjects of which it is predicated.

Major. — Which does not express the differentiae, because it represents them only potentially, *I concede;* in confused act, *I deny.*

Minor. — Does not express the differentiae, because it represents them in confused act, *I concede;* in potency, *I deny.*

4° But the term being does not represent its differentiae in confused act. Therefore the difficulty remains.

If being represents its differentiae in confused act, it includes all things. But if being includes all things, it cannot be predicated of a particular being, v.g., of man, which is absurd. Therefore being does not represent its differentiae in confused act.

Major. — It includes all things materially, *I concede;* formally, *I deny.*

Minor. — Being cannot be predicated of a particular thing materially, *I concede;* formally, *I deny.*

Being *materially understood* is used to designate all things of which it is predicated. Since all things which exist or can exist participate the general notion of being, being materially understood includes all things in confused act, i.e., actually, but in a confused manner. But being formally understood, i.e., according to its formal signification, signifies a subject which connotes a relation to existence. Hence the proposition: man is a being, signifies: *man is a subject which connotes a relation to existence.*

POINTS FOR REVIEW

1. Distinguish between: the analogy of being and the transcendence of being; analogous term and equivocal term.

2. Explain what is meant by each of the following: analogy of attribution, analogy of proper proportionality, supreme analogate.

3. What is the teaching of Suarez on the analogy of being?

4. Explain the statement: being is analogous by analogy of attribution.

5. Distinguish between contraction of a notion by composition and contraction by a more express concept.

CHAPTER II

———

PROPERTIES OF BEING

Prologue. — First, we shall consider the properties of being in general. Since unity, truth, and goodness (the one, the true, and the good) are the principal properties of being, we shall study each of them in particular. After that we shall discuss beauty, which pertains to goodness and truth. Hence this chapter will contain five articles.

Properties of being in general	Statement of the question Thesis: The properties of being are five in number Formal constituent of property of being Distinction between the properties of being Order of the properties of being
Unity	Comprehension of unity Extension of unity Division of unity Notion of multitude Transcendental multitude, predicamental multitude Opposition between unity and multitude
Truth	Notion and division of truth Transcendental truth does not consist in external denomination Derivation of the transcendental truth of things Formal constituent of the transcendental truth of God Formal constituent of the transcendental truth of finite being Transcendental truth as a property of being Extension of transcendental truth Truth of artificial things Truth of speech Falsity in things

Goodness

{
Comprehension of goodness
Extension of goodness
Goodness consists formally in mode, species, and order
Division of goodness
Absolute being and absolute goodness
Axioms
Evil is not a nature
Subject of evil is a good
Good is the cause of evil
Evil is caused by good only accidentally
Evil accidentally derives from good in two ways
}

Beauty

{
Definition of the beautiful
Formal beauty, and objective beauty
Extension of beauty
Powers which apprehend beauty
Opposite of beauty
}

PROPERTIES OF BEING IN GENERAL

508. Statement of the question. — 1° A property *in the strict sense* is an accident which necessarily results from the constituent principles of an essence; v.g., risibility is a property of man; the intellect is a property of an immaterial substance.

Hence there are two requisites of a property in the strict sense:

a) a necessary connexion with the essence of a thing;

b) a real distinction between the property and the essence from which it results.

2° Since being is transcendent, nothing real can be distinct from being. Hence the properties of being cannot be really distinct from being. Therefore the properties of being are not properties *in the strict sense*, but rather properties *in the wide sense*.

3° Hence two conditions are required for properties of being:

a) they presuppose being and result from it, and so are proper to every being as such, i. e., in as much as it is being;

b) they are not really distinct from being, but distinct from it only by a distinction of reason.

4° Properties of being are explained by the fact that being is virtually multiple and superabundant, and therefore cannot be attained completely by a single concept of the intellect. But, given the concept of being, we can have other concepts of being under different aspects. These concepts presuppose the concept of being and are deduced from it, and therefore are said to express the properties of being.

But since every perfection, i.e., nature, is essentially being, properly speaking, additions cannot be made to being in the manner in which differentia is added to genus, or accident is added to substance.

Nevertheless, less properly speaking, certain additions can be made to being, in as much as certain modes of being are expressed which are not expressed by the term being.

This can happen in two ways:

a) the mode expressed is a special mode of being which does not universally result from every being; and thus we have the ten predicaments, viz., substance, quantity, quality, etc.

b) the mode expressed is a general mode of being which results from every being; and thus we have the property of being, for we have something which universally results from being, and yet is not really distinct from it.

6° The properties of being are called transcendentals.

Therefore a transcendental is defined: *that which is predicated of every being,* i. e., *that which results from being in as much as it is being.*

The transcendentals are five in number: *thing, unity otherness, truth,* and *goodness* (*res, unum, aliquid, verum, bonum*).

Some scholastics claim there are only four transcendentals: unity, otherness, truth, and goodness; and others claim that there are only three: unity, truth, and goodness. They maintain that thing, though it is one of the transcendentals, is synonymous with being, and therefore is not a property of being. Others hold the same opinion in regard to otherness. But we reply that all the transcendentals express a general mode of being which the term being does not express, and therefore they are properties of being. Hence, just as the transcendentals are five in number, so too are the properties of being five in number.

509. Statement of the thesis.

THESIS.—THE PROPERTIES OF BEING ARE FIVE IN NUMBER.

There are as many properties of being as there are general modes of being. But the general modes of being are five in number. Therefore the properties of being are five in number.

Major.—The number of the properties of being is determined by the number of the general modes of being, because the general modes of being result from being as being and can be deduced from it, and are distinct from being only by a distinction of reason.

Minor.—A general mode of being can result from being in itself, or from being in relation to another.

1° If it results from being in itself,

a) either it expresses something in being *in an affirmative manner*, and in this case we have *thing*, which expresses the essence, i.e., the quiddity of being, or, in other words, being as having its own essence, being as something ratified and firm in nature (¹);

b) or it expresses something *in a negative manner*, that is to say, the negation of division, and in this case we have *the one*, or *unity*, which is undivided being.

---

(1) Respondeo dicendum, quod, secundum Avicennam, hoc nomen « ens » et « res » differunt secundum quod est duo considerare in re, scilicet quidditatem et rationem ejus, et esse ipsius; et a quidditate sumitur hoc nomen « res ». Et quia quidditas potest habere esse, et in singulari quod est extra animam et in anima, secundum quod est apprehensa ab intellectu; ideo nomen rei ad utrumque se habet; et ad id quod est in anima, prout « res » dicitur a « reor reris », et ad id quod est extra animam, prout res dicitur aliquid ratum et firmum in natura. — *In I Sent.*, dist. XXV, q. 1, a. 4, c.

Similiter autem et nomen « rei » dupliciter sumitur. Simpliciter enim dicitur res quod habet esse ratum et firmum in natura; et dicitur res hoc modo, accepto nomine « rei » secundum quod habet quidditatem vel essentiam quamdam; ens vero, secundum quod habet esse, ut dicit Avicenna, *Metaph.*, tract. I, Cap. VI, distinguens entis et rei significationem. Sed quia res per essentiam suam cognoscibilis est, transumptum est nomen « rei » ad omne quod in cognitione vel intellectus cadere potest, secundum quod res a « reor reris » dicitur; et per hunc modum dicuntur res rationis quae in natura ratum esse non habent, secundum quem modum etiam negationes et privationes res dici possunt, sicut et entia rationis dicuntur. — *In II Sent.*, dist. XXXII, q. , a. 1, c.

2° If it results from being in its relation to another,

a) either it expresses division of one being from another, and in this case we have *other*, i.e., *otherness*, which signifies some other thing;

b) or it expresses the conformity of one thing with another, and this other can only be the soul, which knows all things by the intellect, and desires all things by the appetite, i.e., by the will.

If the general mode expresses conformity of being with the intellect, we have *the true*, i.e., *truth*.

If the general mode expresses conformity of being with the appetite, we have *the good*, i.e., *goodness*, which is defined: *that to which all things tend*.

Therefore the general modes of being are five in number: *thing, unity, otherness, truth, goodness*.

510. Formal constituent of property of being. — 1° A property of being, a transcendental, adds some general mode to being, i. e., some aspect of being which is not really distinct from being. Therefore this general mode is fictitious being, i.e., being of reason, in as much as it is conceived as distinct from being itself; v.g., the indivision of being, as the negation of division, is a being of reason.

2° Hence arises the question of the formal constituent of a property of being. If the formal constituent of a property of being is that which is added to being, its formal constituent is a being of reason, and therefore a property of being is only a fictitious being, i.e., a being of reason. In this case, being would not be really good and true, but good and true in a fictitious manner.

3° To solve the problem, we must distinguish three things in the property of being:

a) what the property of being is materially;

b) what the property adds to being;

c) what the property of being signifies, i.e., that in which it essentially consists.

4° *a*) A property of being considered materially, i.e., as regards its subject, is merely being, in as much as in reality the property of being is identified with being.

b) The addition which a property of being makes to being is a being of reason, that is to say, either a negation or a relation.

c) That in which a property of being essentially consists, i.e., what a property of being signifies, is not being considered materially, nor what the property adds to being, but is being itself as it is the foundation of and connotes what the property adds to being (1); v.g., unity does not consist formally in indivision, but in being as it is undivided. In like manner, truth does not consist essentially in the relation of being to the intellect, but in being as it has conformity with the intellect.

In other words, the property of being does not essentially signify being without that which is added to being, because in this case the concept of being and the concept of property of being would not be distinct; the property of being does not essentially signify that which is added to being, because in this case it would signify only something fictitious; the property of being essentially and formally signifies being as it connotes and is the foundation of what is added to being, that is to say, being with some aspect which the concept of being does not signify.

511. Distinction between the properties of being. —
1° Since the properties of being result from being as being, i.e., from every being, they are not really distinct from each other, nor from being, because outside of being there can be only non-being, i.e., nothing. Hence there is only a distinction of reason between the properties of being and being, and between the properties of being themselves.

2° The distinction of reason is not a distinction of reason reasoning, but a distinction of reason reasoned (nn. 121-122), for we have all the requisites of a distinction of reason reasoned.

a) We have material identity on the part of the thing signified, because being and its properties designate the same subject, namely, being itself.

----

(1) JOANNES A SANCTO THOMA, *Cursus Theol.*, t. I, pp. 518-519 (Sol.).

b) We have the foundation on the part of the thing, because being is virtually multiple, and therefore can be attained by different concepts, in as much as it is considered under one or another aspect. In other words, we have a virtual distinction in being, on account of the eminence of being.

c) We have no formal identity between being and its properties or between one property and another property. For the definitions of being, unity, goodness, truth, etc., are not the same.

Hence the distinction that obtains between being and its properties, and between the properties themselves, is a distinction of reason reasoned.

512. Order of the properties of being. — 1° The first concept we have is the concept of being, for the properties of being are in being as in a subject, and they all add something to being.

2° Since being is a compound of essence and existence, in the second place comes thing, which expresses being as having an essence, i.e., being as having firmness in nature.

3° In the third place comes *unity*, which results from being in an absolute manner and expresses negation of its division.

4° In the fourth place is *otherness*, for once being is apprehended as undivided in itself, it is immediately apprehended as divided from every other being.

5° *Truth* holds the fifth place. Truth results from being i.e., from what is simply being; goodness results from perfect being; something is desired in virtue of some perfection by which it can attract the appetite. And being (esse simpliciter) is prior to perfect being.

6° *Goodness* holds the last place.

Hence we have the following order between being and its properties:

a) being;

b) thing;

c) unity;

d) otherness;

e) truth;

f) goodness.

POINTS FOR REVIEW

1. Distinguish between property in the strict sense and property in the wide sense.

2. *a*) What is a transcendental? *b*) What does the term *thing* express? *c*) What is *otherness*?

3. Explain what a property of being signifies, and state what addition it makes to being.

4. Explain how the properties of being are distinct from each other, and how they are distinct from being.

TEXTUS. — Respondeo dicendum quod sicut in demonstrabilibus oportet fieri reductionem in aliqua principia per se intellectui nota, ita investigando quid est unumquodque; alias utrobique in infinitum iretur, et sic periret omnino scientia et cognitio rerum. Illud autem quod primo intellectus concipit quasi notissimum, et in quo omnes conceptiones resolvit, est ens, ut Avicenna dicit in principio Metaphysicae suae (lib. I, c. IX). Unde oportet quod omnes aliae conceptiones intellectus accipiantur ex additione ad ens. Sed enti non potest addi aliquid quasi extranea natura, per modum quo differentia additur generi, vel accidens subjecto, quia quaelibet natura essentialiter est ens; unde etiam probat Philosophus in III Metaphys. (com. 1), quod ens non potest esse genus, sed secundum hoc aliqua dicuntur addere supra ens, in quantum exprimunt ipsius modum qui nomine ipsius entis non exprimitur. Quod dupliciter contingit: uno modo ut modus expressus sit aliquis specialis modus entis, sunt enim diversi gradus entitatis, secundum quos accipiuntur diversi modi essendi, et juxta hos modos accipiuntur diversa rerum genera; substantia enim non addit supra ens aliquam differentiam, quae significet aliquam naturam superadditam enti, sed nomine substantiae exprimitur quidam specialis modus essendi, scilicet per se ens; et ita est in aliis generibus. Alio modo ita quod modus expressus sit modus generaliter consequens omne ens; et hic modus dupliciter accipi potest: uno modo secundum quod consequitur omne ens in se; alio modo secundum quod consequitur unumquodque ens in ordine ad aliud. Si primo modo, hoc dicitur, quia exprimit in ente aliquid affirmative vel negative. Non autem invenitur aliquid affirmative dictum absolute quod possit accipi in omni ente, nisi essentia ejus, secundum quam esse dicitur; et sic imponitur hoc nomen *res*, quod in hoc differt ab *ente*, secundum Avicennam in principio Metaphys., quod *ens* sumitur ab actu essendi, sed nomen *rei* exprimit quidditatem sive essentiam entis. Negatio autem, quae est consequens omne ens absolute, est indivisio; et hanc exprimit hoc nomen *unum*: nihil enim est aliud *unum* quam ens indivisum. Si autem modus entis accipiatur secundo modo, scilicet secundum ordinem unius ad alterum, hoc potest esse dupliciter. Uno modo secundum divisionem unius ab altero, et hoc exprimit hoc nomen *aliquid*, dicitur enim aliquid quasi aliud quid, unde sicut ens dicitur unum, in quantum est indivisum in se, ita dicitur aliquid, in quantum est ab aliis divisum. Alio modo secundum convenientiam unius entis ad aliud; et hoc quidem non potest esse nisi accipiatur aliquid quod natum sit convenire cum omni ente. Hoc autem est anima, quae quodammodo est omnia, sicut dicitur in III de Anima (text. 37). In anima autem est vis cognitiva et appetitiva. Convenientiam ergo entis ad appetitum exprimit hoc nomen *bonum*, ut in principio Ethic, dicitur: *Bonum est quod omnia appetunt.* Convenientiam vero entis ad intellectum exprimit hoc nomen *verum.* — *De Veritate*, q. 1, a. 1.

UNITY

513. Comprehension of unity. — 1° All conceive unity as the opposite of division. Unity results from the destruction of division. Hence the one, i.e., unity, is that which is undivided in itself.

2° Avicenna, thinking of that unity which is the principle of number and which adds something, namely, quantity, to the substance of being, believed that unity which is convertible with being adds something to being, just as whiteness adds something to man. But this is entirely false: a thing is one by its being. If a thing were one by anything else than its being, this other would be one; and, since this other would be one by something other than its being, regress into infinity would result (¹). Hence we must conclude that unity which is convertible with being does not add anything to being, but is only the negation of division.

3° Hence the concept of unity is formed in this manner:

a) first, we conceive being;

b) secondly, we conceive division;

c) thirdly, we conceive the negation of division (²).

---

(1) I, q. 11, a. 1, c.
(2) Ad quartum dicendum, quod unum privative opponitur multis, inquantum in ratione multorum est quod sint divisa. Unde oportet quod divisio sit prius unitate non simpliciter, sed secundum rationem nostrae apprehensionis. Apprehendimus enim simplicia per composita. Unde definimus punctum, *cujus pars non est;* vel, *principium lineae.* Sed multitudo etiam secundum rationem consequenter se habet ad unum; quia divisa non intelligimus habere rationem multitudinis, nisi per hoc quod utrique divisorum attribuimus unitatem. Unde unum ponitur in definitione multitudinis, non autem multitudo in definitione unius. Sed divisio cadit in intellectu ex ipsa negatione entis. Ita quod primo cadit in intellectu ens. Secundo, quod hoc ens non est illud ens; et sic secundo apprehendimus divisionem; tertio, unum; quarto, multitudinem. — I, q. 11, a. 2, ad 4.

The division which negates unity is not the division in nature from which multitude derives, because multitude results from unity; but it is the division between being and non-being (1). Hence unity negates that being is at the same time being and non-being.

4° Unity includes two things, viz., being and the negation of division, just as the blind includes man and the privation of sight. But, whereas blindness formally consists in the privation of sight, unity does not consist in the negation of division, because in that case unity would not be a property of being, but its negation.

Hence there are three things to be considered in unity:

a) the subject, i.e., unity materially considered, which is being absolutely understood, just as the blind, as regards subject, i.e., materially understood, is man;

b) what unity adds to being, namely, the negation of division;

---

(1) ... Ambae siquidem propositiones sunt verae: et quod *divisio est prior unitate simpliciter*, idest secundum se, *in esse intelligibili* tamen (eo quod, divisio negatio est, quae ens rationis est): et quod *divisio est posterior unitate simpliciter*, idest *secundum esse simpliciter*, quod est esse in rerum natura; esse enim intelligibile est secundum quid tantum.

Prima propositio probatur ex dictis. Non enim est intelligibile quod affirmatio non sit prior negatione. Esse autem unum est *esse hoc et non esse non hoc:* ubi patet quod in ratione unius clauditur negatio alterius extremi contradictionis. Extrema igitur contradictionis, quorum est ipsa divisio, praecedunt naturaliter unitatem. Primo enim est *homo*, et in eodem priori est *non homo*, in esse intelligibili, et sic est divisio. Deinde *homo est homo et non est non homo*, quod est esse unum, idest indivisum. Non enim est divisum in se, ita ut sit *homo et non homo*. Penes privationem enim hujusmodi divisionis, unumquodque est et dicitur unum: si *unum* privativum nomen est, ut supponimus. Nullum autem inconveniens est negationem divisionis esse priorem negatione unitatis: quamvis impossibile sit positionem divisionis in re esse ante positionem unitatis.

Secunda autem propositio patet ex se. Non enim oportet, ad hoc quod homo sit et intelligatur unus, ut negatio hominis sit in aliqua natura, puta bovina aut coelesti. Si enim solus homo esset, unus nihilominus esset: sicut, ante mundi creationem, Deus erat unus, et *non Deus* in nulla erat re; creatis autem aliis, posita est divisio Dei a *non Deo* in rerum natura. De qua divisione dicit littera quod non est prior simpliciter, ut patet ex calce responsionis, ubi dicitur: *secundo apprehendimus quod hoc ens non est illud ens, et sic apprehendimus divisionem.* Quid clarius? *Hoc ens non illud ens* dicendo, divisionem in rerum natura expressit. Et propter eamdem divisionem dixit quod simplicia ex compositis definimus. Divisionem ergo tam realem quam positivam posposuit unitati formaliter: non autem contradictoriam in esse intelligibili. — CAJETANUS, *Comm.,* in I, q. 11, a. 2. — N. VI.

c) that in which unity formally consists, and this is being as it is the foundation of and connotes the negation of the division of being itself, in as much as being does not intrinsically include being and non-being.

Hence the one, i.e., unity, is formally defined: *being as undivided.*

514. Extension of unity.—1 ° In its comprehension, unity makes an addition to being, that is to say, it adds the negation of division to it. But, in its extension, it is convertible with being, i.e., it results from being as being, so that every unity is being, and every being is a unity.

2° Proof. — 1° *Every unity is being.* If every unity were not being, a unit sometimes could be nothing, because what is not being is nothing.

2° *Every being is a unity.* Everything undivided is a unity. But every being is undivided. Therefore every being is a unity (¹).

The *major* is evident from the notion of unity, i.e., of the one.

Minor. Being is simple or composite. If it is simple, it is undivided, as is evident; if it is composite, it remains being only as long as its parts are not divided. Hence every being is undivided.

515. Division of unity. – 1° Unity is transcendental or non-transcendental. *Transcendental* unity is the indivision of being as such; *non-transcendental* unity is the indivision of being of a particular kind.

2° Transcendental unity is either unity *of simplicity*, in as much as it is the unity of a being which lacks parts; or unity *of composition*, in as much as it is the unity of a being which is composed of parts.

---

(1) I, q. 11, a. 1, c.

3° Unity of composition is either unity *of being of itself* (entis per se), i.e., of being which has only one existence, or unity *of accidental being*, i.e., of being which has not one existence, but which is composed of several complete essences and several existences, which are accidentally united to each other either *extrinsically* by juxtaposition (unity of aggregation), or by final and efficient extrinsic causality (by mutual action and passion) by tending to a common end (unity of the state); or *intrinsically* by intrinsic actuation, as accident is united to substance, or one accident is united to another accident.

4° Non-transcendental unity is either unity *of reason*, or *real* unity.

Unity of reason is the unity of being, as it is a particular kind of being by abstraction. This kind of unity is either specific or generic.

Real unity is the unity of being, as it is a particular kind of real being.

5° Real unity is either *formal* or *material.*

Formal unity is the unity of being in as much as it is formally or quidditatively a particular kind of being; and this unity is either specific or generic.

Material unity is the unity of being as it is individually, i.e., materially, a particular kind of being.

6° Material, i.e., numerical, unity is either *substantial* (numerical unity of substance), or accidental (numerical unity of accident).

7° Accidental unity is the unity of accidents as individuated by substance, and the unity of quantity as quantity is individual by itself. The latter is the predicamental unity which appertains to quantity. It signifies undivided being as *quantitative*, i.e., as *having extension.*

516. Notion of multitude.—In unity, there is indivision, i.e., the negation of division; in multitude, there is division. Yet division constitutes multitude only in as much as unity is given to each of the members of the multitude. Hence multitude presupposes division, which directly and of itself destroys unity, and superadds to division unity in each of its members.

Therefore multitude is defined: *that which is composed of units, one of which is not the other;* or, in other words, it is a plurality of units which are distinct from each other.

a) Composed of units: of beings each of which has unity.

b) One of which is not the other: one is divided and distinct from the other.

517. Transcendental multitude, predicamental multitude. – Transcendental multitude is *multitude of beings as such;* v.g., a multitude of angels.

Two elements are contained in the concepts of multitude:

a) units, i.e., undivided beings;

b) the division of each being from all other beings in the multitude.

Predicamental multitude is *multitude measured by a unit.*

Three elements are contained in the concept of predicamental multitude:

a) units, i.e., undivided beings;

b) the division of one being from the other beings of the multitude;

c) the formality of measure.

Since measure is that by which the quantity of a thing is known, predicamental multitude, i.e., number, is proper only to things which have quantity.

On account of the imperfection of our knowledge, we conceive transcendental multitude as quantitative number.

518. Opposition between unity and multitude. — 1° Unity materially considered is not opposed to multitude, because under this aspect unity designates entity. Entity is not opposed to multitude, because a multitude is composed of several entities, and nothing is composed of its opposites.

2° But unity is opposed to multitude in as much as division is found in multitude, and the privation of division in unity. This opposition is privative opposition, as is evident because it is the opposition between division and its privation.

3° Unity is also opposed to multitude *relatively* under another aspect, that is to say, not in as much as division and indivision alone are considered, but in as much as unity and its plurality are considered.

Multitude contains not only division, but the unity of the individual divided members, from which multitude derives. Under this aspect, unity is the principle of multitude, and is related to it, just as a principle is related to what proceeds and is derived from it. Hence relative opposition obtains between unity and multitude, just as between father and son.

4° Unity and multitude have another relative opposition in the genus of quantity, which is the opposition between the measure and the measured, for predicamental multitude is defined: *multitude measured by a unit.*

POINTS FOR REVIEW

1. State and prove the falsity of Avicenna's teaching in regard to unity

2. Explain how the concept of unity is formed, what unity as subject is, what addition it makes to being, and in what it essentially consists; and prove that every being is one.

3. Define: transcendental unity, formal unity, material unity, and multitude.

4. Distinguish between transcendental multitude and predicamental multitude.

5. Under what aspect is there *a)* privative opposition, *b)* relative opposition between unity and multitude?

TRUTH

519. Notion and division of truth. — Truth, according to all, is that which has a relation to the intellect. Philosophers teach that this relation is a certain conformity. Hence they define truth: *the conformity between a thing and an intellect.*

Again, according to common sense, truth is of two kinds: truth which is predicated of things and does not admit of the fictitious; v.g., gold can be either true gold, or fictitious gold, as chrysorin; and truth which is predicated of knowledge and does not admit of falsity; v.g., the proposition: *man is a brute,* though true, i.e., not fictitious, as a proposition, is false in as much as it expresses false knowledge of the intellect.

Truth which is attributed to reality, i.e., to things, is *fundamental* truth, *transcendental* truth, *ontological* truth, and is defined: *the conformity of a thing to an intellect,* in as much as the thing has being conformed or conformable to the intellect (¹).

The ostensive part of general Metaphysics deals with transcendental truth.

Truth which is predicated of knowledge of the intellect is formal truth, and is defined: *the conformity of an intellect to a thing, as known by the intellect.*(²)

The defensive part of general Metaphysics deals with formal truth.

520. Transcendental truth does not consist in extrinsic denomination. — 1° Extrinsic denomination obtains when something derives its name from something extrinsic as from a form. Thus medicine is called healthful from the

---

(1) I, q. 16, a. 5.
(2) *De Veritate*, q. 1, a. 1, et a. 4. — *Contra Gentes*, l. I, c. 60.

health which is in the animal, and of which it is the cause.   In like manner, color is called healthy from the health which is in the animal, in as much as it is the effect of this health.

2° Created things are effects of the truth which is in the divine intellect; and things are the cause of the formal truth which is in the created intellect.

3° Vasquez holds that the transcendental truth of a thing consists only in its extrinsic denomination from the formal truth of the intellect.

Hence this opinion implicity contains the following conclusions:

a) the truth of a thing does not derive from something intrinsic to itself, i.e., things are not intrinsically true;

b) truth is primarily in the intellect;

c) truth is attributed to a thing, only because the thing is the cause of formal truth in the intellect, just as health is attributed to medicine, not because medicine is intrinsically healthful, but because medicine is the cause of the health which is in the animal.

4° We do not deny that a thing can be true by extrinsic denomination from the truth which is in the intellect [1]; but we affirm that the transcendental truth of a thing does not consist in such extrinsic denomination.

The transcendental truth of a thing consists in that by which the thing is distinguished from the fictitious; v.g., gold is true in as much as it is distinct from fictitious or false gold. But a thing is distinct from the fictitious or false by something intrinsic to itself, and not merely because it is the cause of truth in the intellect.   Hence the transcendental truth of a thing does not consist in extrinsic denomination.

_____

(1) Ad tertium dicendum, quod licet veritas intellectus nostri a re causetur, non tamen oportet quod in re per prius inveniatur ratio veritatis; sicut neque in medicina per prius invenitur ratio sanitatis quam in animali. Virtus enim medicinae, non sanitas ejus, causat sanitatem; cum non sit agens univocum.   Et similiter esse rei, non veritas ejus, causat veritatem intellectus. Unde Philosophus dicit quod opinio et oratio vera est ex eo quod res est, non ex eo quod res vera est. — I, q. 16, a. 1, ad 3.

521. Derivation of the transcendental truth of things. — 1° The true is distinguished from the fictitious or false by its transcendental truth. But this distinction between the true and the false depends on some rule, i.e., on some measure. Hence there must be some rule from which the transcendental truth of a thing is derived.

2° There are three rules, i.e., measures, which enable us to discern the truth of a thing:

  a) the proper and original causes of the thing;

  b) the essential predicates, i.e., the definition of the thing;

  c) the effects and proper accidents of the thing.

We can discern, for example, that a man is noble, because he was engendered by noble parents; and we say that he is a true man, because the definition of man is applicable to him, or because he possesses the special accidents proper to man.

3° Although properties and effects are means of our discerning the truth of a thing, they are not the real measure which establishes the transcendental truth of a thing. Indeed, properties and effects result from the essence of a thing, and therefore presuppose the truth of the essence. Thus the properties of gold result from true gold.

The truth of a thing can be discerned also by its essential predicates. Nevertheless, essential predicates are not the real measure which establishes the truth of a thing, because essential predicates are not really distinct from the thing of which they are predicated, but are identified with it. The thing defined and its definition are not distinct in reality.

Therefore we come to the conclusion that the real measure of transcendental truth is the proper and original cause from which every specific determination of reality and essence derives. This first and original cause is the divine ideas, i.e., the divine intellect.

Hence the transcendental truth of things is derived from the divine intellect. Therefore transcendental truth is defined: *being as conformed to the divine intellect.*

522. Formal constituent of the transcendental truth of God. — God is the first truth, as He is the measure of all the truth of being derived from Him. Hence the transcendental truth of God does not derive from another, but it is God's very act of intellection. In other words, God's transcendental truth is the conformity of the divine essence with the divine intellect, not in as much as the divine essence is measured by the divine intellect, but in as much as the divine essence is identified with the divine intellect and the divine act of intellection (¹).

523. Formal constituent of the transcendental truth of finite being. — The transcendental truth of finite being is constituted by the actual conformity of created being to the divine intellect, by which finite being is measured. In other words, the transcendental truth of finite being is the relation of created being, as measurable, to the divine intellect as to its measure.

Hence finite being, as transcendentally true, has a real relation to the divine intellect as to its exemplar cause. This relation is a transcendental relation to which a predicamental relation is added.

This relation is a transcendental relation, because finite being is referred, as to the whole of its entity, to the divine intellect, i.e., to the divine idea, as to its exemplar cause.

To this transcendental relation is added a predicamental relation, for we have all the requisites for the existence of a predicamental relation:

a) a real term;

b) a real subject;

c) a real foundation.

---

(1) Respondeo dicendum quod, sicut dictum est (art. 1), veritas invenitur in intellectu, secundum quod apprehendit rem ut est; et in re, secundum quod habet esse conformabile intellectui. Hoc autem maxime invenitur in Deo. Nam esse suum non solum est conforme suo intellectui, sed etiam est ipsum suum intelligere; et suum intelligere est mensura et causa omnis alterius esse et omnis alterius intellectus; et ipse est suum esse et intelligere. Unde sequiter quod non solum in ipso sit veritas, sed quod ipse sit ipsa summa et prima veritas. — I, q. 16, a. 5, c.

The real term is the divine intellect; the real subject is the entity of finite being; and the real foundation is the real dependence of finite being on the divine intellect. Therefore, just as there is a predicamental relation between son and father, so too there is a predicamental relation between finite being, as transcendentally true, and the divine intellect. This predicamental relation is in finite being. In the divine intellect there is no real relation to finite being, but only a relation of reason.

524. Transcendental truth as a property of being. —

1° Three elements are found in a property of being, as we have already pointed out:

a) the subject, which is being itself;

b) the addition which the property makes to being, and this is a being of reason;

c) the formal constituent of the property, which is being as connoting a being of reason.

2° Being as conformed to the divine intellect does not include the relation of reason which is added to being. Infinite being is in conformity to the divine intellect by sovereign identity; finite being is conformity to the divine intellect in as much as it has a twofold real relation to it:

a) the transcendental relation by which the transcendental truth of finite being is constituted;

b) the predicamental relation which is added to the transcendental relation.

Hence the transcendental truth of being, although constituted by its conformity to the divine intellect, is not a property of being, if truth is considered under the aspect of this conformity. Transcendental truth, under this aspect, does not add a relation of reason to being, but is the very entity of being, as this entity is conceived as identified with the divine act of intellection, in the case of infinite being; and, in the case of finite being, it is the very entity of being, as this entity is conceived as having a real relation to the divine intellect.

3° Therefore we conclude that the transcendental truth of being, as it is a property of being, is the truth of being, as being has a relation to the intellect which it moves ([1]).   This relation whichbeing has to the intellect which it moves is a relation of reason, not a real relation.

4° Hence there are four elements in transcendental truth as a property of being:

a) being absolutely considered;

b) being as considered in conformity to the divine intellect; by this conformity transcendental truth is constituted not a property of being, but as an entity, for it is nothing other than an entity relatively conceived, i.e., conceived as in conformity to its exemplar cause;

c) the relation of reason which transcendental truth adds to being, in as much as it implies a relation of reason to the intellect which being moves;

d) being itself as it connotes that relation of reason.

Transcendental truth, as a property of being, is formally constituted by being, in as much as being connotes a relation of reason to the intellect which it moves.

525. Extension of transcendental truth. — 1° Transcendental truth has the same extension as being: it is convertible with being, and hence being is transcendentally true in as much as it is being.

2° Proof. — 1° *Everything which is true, i.e., every truth, is being:* because otherwise truth would be nothing.

_____

(1) Et sic ipsum ens, ut in se habens esse et praedicata constitutiva, pertinet ad conceptum essentiae; ut autem incipit exprimere connotationem aliquam extra se, v.g., comparationem ad intellectum vel ad voluntatem, sic ipsum ens, ut comparative, se habet ut propria passio suimet, ut absolute. Nec tamen ut exprimit habitudinem realem praecise importat passionem, quia prout sic adhuc intra limites ipsius entitatis continetur ut entitas est: et sic non explicat neque connotat aliquid ultra ipsam, quo se habeat ut passio, sed adhuc ipsam entitatem solum explicat. Potius ergo dicitur veritas superaddere respectum rationis ad conceptum entis, licet prius includat habitudinem illam priorem ad intellectum divinum cui conformatur: quia per hanc priorem habitudinem, quae entitativa est, adhuc entitas ipsa consideratur, non connotatio superaddita, quae rationis solum esse potest, si superadditur ad ens. — JOANNES A SANCTO THOMA, *Cursus Theol.*, t. II, p. 598 (Sol.).

2° *Every being is true:* everything intelligible is true, because the intelligible is being as it is related to an intellect. But every being is intelligible, for being is the formal object of the intellect. Therefore every being as being is true ([1]).

526. Truth of artificial things. — An artificial thing, as every being, is true by its relation to the divine intellect as to its first exemplar cause. But an artificial thing is dependent too on the intellect of an artificer, because it is constituted dependently on the mind of an artificer.

527. Truth of speech. — *a)* Speech may be considered as a sign of the judgment of the intellect, and, under this aspect, it is true or false in as much as it expresses the formal truth or falsity of the intellect.

b) Speech may be considered as *a certain thing*, and under this aspect, its truth, just as the truth of any artifact, is dependent on the idea of the speaker ([2]).

528. Falsity in things. — 1° Falsity is not opposed to ontological truth which is convertible with being; for, under this aspect, the false could only be nothing.

2° Falsity is opposed to formal truth and hence, properly speaking, can only be in the intellect.

Falsity is defined *the non-conformity of the intellect with reality, which the intellect regards as a conformity.*

3° Nevertheless, falsity is attributed to things by extrinsic denomination as a result of the falsity of the created intellect; and thus it is predicated of things in many ways: *a)* in as much as the created intellect makes a false judgment on something; v.g., in the case of an intellect which would make the judgment: Peter is a brute, Peter, in this case, may be called a false brute; *b)* or in as much as a thing is the cause of falsity in the intellect. Thus a thing which is similar in external acci-

---

(1) I, q. 16, a. 3.
(2) I, q. 16, a. 6.

3

dents to other things can cause falsity in the human intellect, since human knowledge derives, by means of external accidents, from the senses; v.g., tin may be called false silver, because it is similar to silver in color, etc. ([1]).

POINTS FOR REVIEW

1. Distinguish between transcendental truth and formal truth.

2. State what is meant by the truth of a thing by extrinsic denomination, and explain why transcendental truth does not consist in this kind of truth.

3. Explain why the transcendental truth of being derives neither from the properties of thing, nor from essential predicates.

4. Compare the transcendental truth of God and the transcendental truth of finite being as regards their formal constituent.

5. What is transcendental truth as a property of being?

6. Prove that every being is transcendentally true.

7. Explain how falsity can be found in things.

---

(1) I, q. 17, a. 1.

GOODNESS

529. Comprehension of goodness. — 1° Goodness is used here as signifying not moral goodness, but transcendental goodness, as goodness is property of being.

There are three distinct elements in every property of being:

a) the subject, which is being;

b) the addition which the property makes to being, namely, a being or reason;

c) the formal constituent of the property of being.

Hence we must consider these three elements of goodness as it is a property of being.

2° All are agreed that being is good in as much as it is perfect. Good formally excludes evil. But evil consists in the defect and privation of some proper perfection. Hence goodness formally consists in perfection.

3° Perfection, like the perfect, may be considered under two aspects:

a) in the genus of constituent formal cause;

b) in the genus of final cause which attracts, i.e., moves the appetite.

Perfection, indeed, formally constitutes and informs the perfect thing, for a thing is constituted by some actuality, and every actuality is a perfection.

Again, perfection attracts and moves as a final cause, for an end is desired as the perfection of the one desiring it; and the one desiring it tends to it as to something which perfects it. Perfection does not perfect the appetite as the constituent of the appetite, but as the term and object in which the appetite attains its perfection.

4° Perfection, as the constituent of a perfect thing, cannot be a property of being, because as such it is not conceived as added to entity, but as appertaining to essence, i.e., to constituted entity.

Perfection, under the aspect of its attracting the appetite, can be conceived as a property of being, for as such it adds a relation of reason to being. Perfection, considered under this aspect, is related to the appetite, as something giving perfection, as the desirable to the perfectible. But the relation of the desirable to the perfectible is a relation of reason, for the desirable does not depend on the perfectible for its being.

5° Hence there are three distinct elements in the comprehension of goodness:

a) a subject, which is perfect being;

b) a relation of reason which goodness adds to being; and this relation is desirability, i.e., the relation of being to the appetite, in as much as being, as final cause, can perfect the appetite;

c) the formal constituent of goodness as a property of being, which is being in as much as it connotes and is the foundation of the relation of reason to the appetite.

6° Hence goodness is defined: *that which is desirable*, or *that to which all things tend* ([1]).

It is to be observed that the verb *tend*, used in the foregoing definition, signifies not actual tending, i.e., desire, but rather the aptitude of a being to be actually desired by the innate or elicited appetite ([2]).

530. Extension of goodness. — 1° Goodness is convertible with being, and hence has the same extension as being. Not only is it true that every good is being, but every being, as being, is good. But being which as such is good is being in act.

---

(1) *Ethic.*, l. I, c. 1.
(2) I, q. 6, a. 2, ad 2.

For being is good in as much as it is perfect. But being is perfect in as much as it is in act. Being in potency is imperfect being. Hence being in as much as it is in potency is lacking in goodness, just as it is lacking in being, although being in potency, in as much as it has the formality of being, participates in the formality of goodness.

2° We shall prove that every good is being, and that every being is good.

a) *Every good is being.* Everything perfect is being; otherwise it would be nothing. But every good is perfect. Therefore every good is being.

b) *Every being, as being, is good.* A being is perfect in as much as it is being. But a thing is good in as much as it is perfect. Therefore a thing is good in as much as it is being; in other words, every being, as being, is perfect ([1]).

Major. — A thing is in act in as much as it is being: for being (existence) is the ultimate actuality of a thing. But a thing is perfect in as much as it is in act: act is perfection. Therefore a thing is perfect in as much as it is being.

The *minor* is evident from the notion of goodness. Since goodness does not admit of evil, i.e., of the privation or lack of due perfection, perfection is its formal constituent. Hence a thing is good in as much as it is perfect.

531. Goodness consists formally in mode, species, and order. — 1° A thing is good in as much as it is perfect. Moreover, a thing is perfect which lacks nothing in accordance with the mode of its perfection. But, in order that we know the mode of the perfection of a thing, we must consider its form: for a thing is what it is by its form.

2° The form presupposes determination, i.e., commensuration, of its principles, material or efficient. This commensuration is called *mode*, for measure marks the mode.

3° The form is signified by the species, because a thing is constituted in its species by its form.

---

(1) I, q. 5, a. 1.

4° Inclination to an end, or to an action, or to something of this kind results from form: for a thing, in as much as it is in act, acts and tends to what appertains to it in accordance with its form. This inclination which results from form appertains to *order*.

Hence goodness, as it consists in perfection, formally consists in *mode*, *species*, and *order* ([1]).

532. Division of goodness. — 1° Goodness is essentially divided into goodness *of utility*, goodness *of rectitude*, and goodness *of pleasure*.

Goodness of utility is *goodness which is desired as means to an end*.

Goodness of rectitude is *goodness which is desired as the last thing absolutely terminating the movement of the appetite*.

Goodness of pleasure is *goodness which terminates the movement of the appetite, as procuring the rest of the appetite which possesses it*.

2° Goodness is accidentally divided in regard to its perfection, and in regard to the appetite of which it is the object.

a) As regards its perfection, goodness is *absolute* (bonum simpliciter) or *relative* (bonum secundum quid).

Absolute goodness is *goodness which is fully perfect*. Thus a thing is *absolutely good*, when it possesses all the perfection due to it.

Relative goodness is *goodness which has not all the perfection due to it, but has some perfection, in as much as it is in act*.

Similar to this division of goodness is the division into *moral* and *physical* goodness.

Moral goodness is *the goodness of the object of the will, as this object is in conformity with the rule of morals*.

Physical goodness is *the goodness of the object of the appetite, without any reference to the rule of morals*.

---

(1) I, q. 5, a. 5.

b) In relation to the appetite, goodness is *natural* or *known.*
Natural goodness is the *goodness of the object of the natural
appetite;* and known goodness is the *goodness of the object of the
elicited appetite.*

Known goodness is *sensible*, as it is the goodness of the object of the sensitive appetite, and *intellectual*, as it is the goodness of the object of the will.

533. Absolute being and absolute goodness. — 1°
Goodness and being are identical in reality, but yet are logically
distinct, i.e., distinct by a distinction of reason. Therefore a
thing is not absolute being in the same way as it is absolutely
good.

2° Being is properly such as it is in act, and as it is distinct
from what is in potency. Hence a thing is absolute being in
virtue of that which first distinguishes it from what is in potency only. But it is a thing's substantial entity which first distinguishes it from that which is in potency. Hence a thing
is absolute being by its substantial entity; and it is relative
being by acts superadded to its primary being, that is to say,
by accidents.

3° Goodness is formally perfection, and consequently
is formally ultimate perfection. Hence a thing which has not
the ultimate perfection which it should have, but is to some extent lacking in perfection, is not perfect and absolutely good,
but relatively good. But it is not the substantial entity of a
thing, but rather the accidents due to it, which give it its ultimate perfections.

Hence absolute being is only relative goodness; and absolute goodness is relative being ([1]).

534. Axioms.— 1° *Bonum ex integra causa, malum ex
quocumque defectu* ([2]), i.e., a thing is good when good in every
respect, evil when not good in any respect. Goodness is the

---

(1) I, q. 5, a. 1, ad 1.
(2) The succinctness and verbal cadence of the Latin seem to justify
our retaining the original. — Translator's note.

formal aspect of perfection, and a thing possesses perfection when there is nothing which it lacks. Hence all the constituents of being are required for goodness: *bonum ex integra causa*. Evil is the privation of due perfection. Therefore evil results from any defect: *malum ex quocumque defectu*.

2° *Bonum est diffusivum sui* i.e., goodness is diffusive of itself.—Goodness is diffusive in as much as it communicates itself to others. It is above all as final cause that goodness diffuses itself. For good is desirable, and therefore as an end attracts the appetite, and perfects it.

Goodness diffuses itself too as efficient cause. For a thing is good in as much as it is perfect and in act. But a thing acts only in as much as it is in act. Hence good, as good, acts, and in acting communicates its being and goodness to others ([1]).

535. Evil is not a nature. — 1° *Preliminaries.* *a*) Evil, according to common sense, is the opposite of good, and therefore signifies the absence of good, Again, according to common sense, evil is not the mere negation, but the privation of a due perfection; v.g., the privation of health in an animal is an evil. But no one would say that the negation of health in a stone is an evil.

b) Certain early philosophers, as the Manicheans, held that there was a supreme principle of evil, just as there is a supreme principle of good. Of course, this opinion is untenable.

2° *Proof.*— No privation is a nature. But evil is a privation. Therefore evil is not a nature.

Major.— A privation is the remotion of a perfection or nature.

536. Subject of evil is a good. — The privation of a perfection requires a subject which is deprived of this perfection. But evil is the privation of a perfection due to a thing, i.e., to a subject. Therefore evil requires a subject which is deprived of

_____

(1) *Contra Gentes*, l. I, c. 37.

a perfection due to it. But a subject which is deprived of a perfection which is due to it is a being, and consequently a good. Therefore the subject of evil is a good.

537. Good is the cause of evil. — Every cause, even the cause of a privation, is a being. But every being is a good. Therefore good is the cause of evil.

538. Evil is caused by good only accidentally. — What is not desired of itself is caused only accidentally. But evil is not desired of itself. Therefore evil is caused only accidentally.

Minor. — A thing which is not desirable is not desired of itself. But evil, as the privation of a good, i.e., of what is desirable, is not desirable. Therefore.

539. Evil accidentally derives from good in two ways. 1° It can derive from an efficent cause, in as much as this efficient cause is defective, i.e., of limited power.

2° It can derive from an effect, and this in two ways: *a*) because of the indisposition of the subject, i.e., of the matter, from which the defect in the perfection, i.e., in the form received, derives; *b*) because of the form produced, in as much the production of one form excludes another form.

POINTS FOR REVIEW

1. Explain why goodness formally consists in perfection.

2. Under what aspects can perfection be considered?

3. Define goodness; name the distinct elements found in its comprehension; and prove that it formally consists in mode, species, and order.

4. Distinguish between goodness of utility, goodness of rectitude, and goodness of pleasure.

5. Explain why absolute being is not absolute goodness.

6. Why does evil result from any defect?

BEAUTY

540. Definition of the beautiful. — The beautiful is defined: *that which pleases when seen*, i.e., known; or *that whose apprehension pleases.*

Therefore two elements are found in the beautiful: *knowledge* and *complacence.*

a) The knowledge found in the definition of beauty is above all intellectual knowledge. Sense knowledge can be included in the apprehension of beauty, only in so far as the senses subserve the intellect.

b) The complacence which results from the apprehension of beauty is not the pleasure of the appetive faculty, but the complacence of the cognitive faculty itself. This complacence consists in a vital proportion between the cognitive faculty, as knowing, and its object as actually known.

Pleasure in the appetive faculty results from this complacence in the cognitive faculty. Therefore beauty is a *species of goodness* in a certain special sense. Beauty has a relation to the appetite, in as much as it is first pleasing to the cognitive faculty. In other words, the appetite desires beauty, in as much as beauty first is perfective of the cognitive faculty (¹).

---

(1) Ad tertium dicendum, quod pulchrum est idem bono sola ratione differens. Cum enim bonum sit quod omnia appetunt, de ratione boni est quod in eo quietetur appetitus. Sed ad rationem pulchri pertinet quod in ejus aspectu seu cognitione quietetur appetitus; unde et illi sensus praecipue respiciunt pulchrum qui maxime cognoscitivi sunt, scilicet visus et auditus rationi deservientes; dicimus enim pulchra visibilia et pulchros sonos. In sensibilibus autem aliorum sensuum non utimur nomine pulchritudinis; non enim dicimus pulchros sapores aut odores. Et sic patet quod pulchrum addit supra bonum quemdam ordinem ad vim cognoscitivam; ita quod bonum dicatur id quod simpliciter complacet appetitui, pulchrum autem dicatur id cujus apprehensio placet. — I-II, a. 27, a. 1, ad 3.

541. Formal beauty and objective beauty. — Just as we make a distinction between truth as it exists in the intellect and as it exists in reality, so too we distinguish between beauty as it exists in the intellect and as it exists in reality.

1) Beauty as it exists in the intellect, i.e., formal beauty, is the vital proportion between the intellect in act and the object actually known, i.e., the complacence of the intellect by which the intellect vitally tends to an object as known and proportionate to itself.

2) Beauty as it exists in reality, i.e., fundamental, objective beauty, requires three objective conditions: *integrity*, *due proportion* or harmony, order, and *clarity* or splendor. These conditions are required because,

a) things which are not integral are not pleasing; for a faculty does not rest in a diminished, i.e., incomplete, object;

b) things which lack orderly arrangement are not pleasing; for knowledge apprehends multiplicity objectively presented as unity, by giving parts orderly arrangement with each other in unity of apprehension. If the parts are naturally in proportion, they and the whole resulting from them are the object of knowledge, i.e., they are pleasing when seen;

c) things whose perfection and order are not clearly visible, but somewhat hidden, are not pleasing, because in this case the faculty has only imperfect perception of its object (¹).

Since integrity, order, and clarity are the foundation of the desirability by which truth is pleasing to the cognitive faculty, beauty is defined: *the splendor of order, the splendor of truth.*

Again, since integrity, order, and splendor exist in material things in virtue of substantial form, beauty may be defined: *the splendor of form*, the resplendence of form.

542. Extension of beauty. — Beauty is a *transcendental*, and is convertible with being; but it does not seem to be a property of being, because it does not add a being of reason to being, since it is formally the splendor of truth.

(1) DE WULF, *L'Oeuvre d'Art et la Beauté*, Louvain, 1920, pp. 212-214. — S. FRANÇOIS DE SALES, *Traité de l'amour de Dieu*, l. I, c. 1, pp. 24-25.

1° *Everything beautiful is a being:* for beauty is truth which is pleasing, and truth is convertible with being.

2° *Every being is beautiful:* there is perfect proportion between being as such and the intellect as such, so that the intellect of itself rests and delights in the contemplation of being.

Any being whatsoever is objectively beautiful. However, it does not follow from this that any being whatsoever is beautiful to the human intellect. The human intellect is defective, and depends objectively on the senses. Hence man's aesthetic contemplation is dependent on the condition of the senses and the splendor of order in a material thing as such; and hence something can be objectively beautiful, even if man, because of his condition, cannot find delight or pleasure in it.

543. Powers which apprehend beauty. — *a*) Only the intellect can apprehend the relation of conformity of a beautiful thing to a cognitive power: for only the intellect knows and apprehends relations ([1]).

b) For the same reason, only the intellect apprehends the relation of proportion and harmony of parts to each other, i.e. fundamental beauty.

c) Nevertheless, the senses, under the influence of reason, apprehend, in the concrete, things which are in orderly arrangement with each other and parts which are in proportion to each other, in as much as they apprehend a whole disposed in this way or that. Without the influence of reason, the senses apprehend a beautiful thing only materially, not formally, i.e., they have knowledge of parts, but do not apprehend even in the concrete the order of these parts, because they are not concerned with this order. Therefore the merely sensitive knowledge of the brute can have no part whatsoever in the enjoyment of the beautiful.

d) The senses are not all in the same way capable of perceiving beauty in the concrete. The superior senses, sight,

---

(1) J. MARITAIN, *Art et Scolastique*, Paris, 1927, pp. 35, 36, 40. — DE WULF, *op. cit.*, pp. 136 sq.

hearing, and the phantasy, which is very active and construc-
tive, cooperate with the intellect in pleasurable knowledge.
The inferior senses, taste, smell or olfactory sense, and touch,
in as much as they are concerned with their own proper objects,
cannot attain beauty. Yet, in as much as they are concerned
with a mediate sensible (sensible commune), which is common
to them and the superior senses, as quantity and figure, they
can attain beauty. Thus a blind man can attain the beautiful
form of a statue by touching the statue.

544. Opposite of beauty. — Ugliness is the opposite of
beauty. But since beauty is a transcendental and convertible
with being, metaphysical ugliness is impossible. Hence, though
there can be ugliness in a particular order, it cannot exist in the
order of being as such.

Since beauty is the splendor of order, ugliness is the lack of
order, i.e., is disorder. But disorder occurs in both the physical
order and in the moral order. Therefore physical evil as such,
error, and sin, as things which lack order, are ugly, not beautiful.

Human knowledge, on account of its deficencies, is not
beautiful in itself; but its lack of beauty, i.e., its ugliness, is not
always apparent.

CHAPTER III

DIVISION OF BEING BY POTENCY AND ACT

Prologue. — Act and potency divide being and every genus of being. In this chapter, we shall deal first with the notions of act and potency; secondly, with the division of being by potency and act; and thirdly, with the relation of act and potency. Hence there will be three articles in this chapter.

Notions of act and potency
- Origin of the notions of act and potency
- Extension of the notions of act and potency
- Description of potency
- Description of act
- Division of potency
- Division of act

Division of being by act and potency
- Statement of the question
- Thesis: Potency and act so divide being that whatsoever exists is either pure act, or is necessarily composed of potency and act, as its first intrinsic principles
- Act, because it is perfection, can be limited only by potency, which is capacity for perfection
- In an order in which act is pure, i.e., not received into potency, it is unlimited and unique

Relation of potency and act
- Act and potency are in the same genus
- Potency is specified by act
- Potency can be reduced to act only by being in act
- A thing cannot be, in the same respect, in potency and in act
- In the order of generation, potency is prior in time to act
- Act, strictly speaking is prior to potency

_____

NOTIONS OF ACT AND POTENCY

545. Origin of the notions of act and potency. — Since all knowledge begins with the senses, the notions of act and potency are derived from sensible things, and especially from motion which we observe by the senses. Thus when a piece of wood has become a statue, it is a statue *in act*. But before this piece of wood was able to become a statue, it was in potency to be a statue, and hence was a statue *in potency*.

In like manner, when we perform an operation, we are said to perform an *act*. But, to perform an operation, we must have a real power destined for that operation. Thus the brute is not capable of an *act* of intellective knowledge, because is has not the *power* (potency) of intellection. But man is capable of an *act* of intellective knowledge, because he has a real *power* (potency) of intellection.

Hence the notions of act and potency are derived from motion (¹).

546. Extension of the notions of act and potency. — The notions of act and potency are derived from motion, and therefore it is in mobile things that first we find potency and act. Nevertheless, potency and act not only are found in

_____

(1) Potentia et actus, ut plurimum dicuntur in his quae sunt in motu, quia motus est actus entis in potentia. — *In Metaph.*, l. IX, l. I, n. 1770.

Ostendit *quid sit esse in actu;* et dicit, quod hoc nomen actus, quod ponitur ad significandum endelechiam et perfectionem, scilicet formam, et alia hujusmodi, sicut sunt quaecumque operationes, veniunt maxime ex motibus quantum ad originem vocabuli. Cum enim nomina sint signa intelligibilium conceptionum, illis primo imponimus nomina, quae primo intelligimus, licet sint posteriora secundum ordinem naturalem. Inter alios autem actus, maxime est nobis notus et apparens motus, qui sensibiliter a nobis videtur. Et ideo ei primo impositum fuit nomen actus, et a motu ad alia derivatum est. — *In Metaph.*, l. IX, l. 3, n. 1805.

mobile things, but they divide being in general ([1]), and hence any being either is composed of potency and act, or is pure act.

Hence the notions of potency and act are extended from mobile being to every being, and are accepted as fundamental notions in philosophy.

547. Description of potency. — Neither act nor potency can be properly defined, for they are the first principles of being. But the first principles of being cannot be defined, since there cannot be regress into infinity in definitions.

But potency can be made manifest from examples, and can be described in relation to act.

A thing in potency is a possible thing.

A possible thing may be understood in a logical sense, and, under this aspect, it is that which is not repugnant, i.e., that whose subject and predicate are not repugnant.

A possible thing may be understood too in a real sense, as when we say: a man can walk, i.e., has power or *potency* to walk; a piece of wood can become a statue. In this sense, potency is a real principle which has relation to motion, active or passive. And since motion is act, potency may be described: *a real principle which connotes a real relation to act.*

548. Description of act. — As we have pointed out already, act cannot be properly defined. Moreover, act cannot be described as fully as potency. For, *first*, we know potency by means of act, but we do not know act by means of potency. Thus we know that a man has intellective power (potency), because he is capable of an act of intellection. Furthermore, the first

---

(1) Sed principalis intentio hujus doctrinae non est de potentia et actu secundum quod sunt in rebus mobilibus solum, sed secundum quod sequuntur ens commune. Unde et in rebus immobilibus invenitur potentia et actus, sicut in rebus intellectualibus.

Sed cum dixerimus de potentia, quae est in rebus mobilibus, et de actu ei correspondente, ostendere poterimus et de potentia et actu secundum quod sunt in rebus intelligibilibus, quae pertinent ad substantias separatas, de quibus postea agetur. Et hic est ordo conveniens, cum sensibilia quae sunt in motu sint nobis magis manifesta. Et ideo per ea devenimus ad cognitionem rerum immobilium. — *In Metaph.*, l. IX, l. 1, nn. 1770 et 1771.

thing known by the intellect is being an act; and we reach the
concept of being in potency only from the concept of being in
act.   *Secondly*, although potency can be described by its relation to act, act cannot be described by relation to potency.
Indeed, we know act with relation to potency, when we know
act from motion.   But act does not connote an essential relation to potency.   When act has relation to potency, this relation is accidental to act as such.

Hence the notion of act can be derived only from examples.
A thing is a being in act when it exercises its own existence.
Matter is in act when it is made determinate by form.   A person sees in act when he has that perfection which is vision.
Therefore act may be simply called: *perfection*.   Perfection is
act, and act is perfection.   Existence, like form or vision, is
perfection.

549. Division of potency. — 1° Potency is first divided
into objective potency and subjective potency.

Objective potency is the ideal aptitude of a non-existent
thing to exist founded in the non-repugnance of a subject and
predicate; v.g., the world was objectively possible before it was
created.

Objective potency is also called logical potency.

Subjective potency is the capacity or aptitude of an existent
thing for act, v.g., the potency by which a piece of wood can
receive the act, i.e., the form, of a statue.

Subjective potency is real potency, i.e., it is a real principle
which connotes a relation to act.

2° Subjective potency is pure or mixed.

Pure potency is potency which of itself has no act whatsoever.   First matter is pure potency (cf. n. 226).

Mixed potency is imperfect act, in as much as it is act which
is in potency to further act; v.g., the created intellect is a second
act which is added to a rational substance, but is a potency in
respect to intellection.

3° Potency is receptive or passive, and operative or active.

Receptive potency, also called *passive potency*, is the real capacity of being a patient, i.e., of being acted upon by another, that is to say, the real capacity of receiving act from another.

Operative potency, also called *active potency*, is the real capacity for acting or doing; v.g., the senses are operative powers.

4° Subjective potency is proximate or remote.

Proximate potency is potency which can be reduced immediately to act.

Remote potency is potency which can be disposed by degrees for act.

550. Division of act. — 1° Act is first divided into pure act and mixed act.

Pure act is act which admits of no potency whatsoever. Pure act is God Himself, Who is all-perfect, i.e., possesses the plenitude of all perfections.

Mixed act is act which admits of potency, i.e., it is act which is received into potency, or it is act which is in potency to act of another order.

2° Mixed act is entitative or formal.

Entitative act (act of existence, act in the order of existence) is the very being of a finite thing, i.e., it is the existence of a finite being. Entitative act is mixed act in as much as it is received into potency which limits it, not in as much as it is in potency to further act — for existence is ultimate act.

Formal act (act of essence, act in the order of essence) is the act by which a thing is determined and perfected in its species; v.g., substantial form. There are two aspects under which formal act is mixed act:

a) it is act received into potency, and at the same time is in potency to further act; thus substantial form is the act of first matter, and is in potency to further act, i.e., to existence.

b) it is act which, though not received into potency, is in potency to further act; thus the form of an angel is not act received into potency, i.e., into matter, but it is in potency to further act, i.e., to existence, from which its essence is really distinct.

3° Formal act is called first act or second act.

First act is act which does not presuppose an anterior act, but which awaits a subsequent act; v.g., substantial form.

Second act is act which presupposes an anterior act; v.g., an accident. Hence second act is accidental act.

Yet, act may be called *first* or *second* in an entirely relative sense.

Thus a faculty, as the intellect, which, in an absolute sense, is second act, may be called first act in relation to its operation.

Similarly entitative act, i.e., existence, is called second act in relation to formal act, i.e., to form.

POINTS FOR REVIEW

1. Give the derivation of the notions of potency and act.

2. Describe potency and act, and show whether or not act connotes a relation to potency.

3. What do you understand by the following terms: pure potency, mixed potency, pure act?

4. In how many ways can act be mixed? Explain.

DIVISION OF BEING BY ACT AND POTENCY

551. Statement of the question. — We find act and potency first in mobile being. Here we are concerned with the question of whether act and potency are found in being as such, i.e., in being as being.

Act, as we know, is *perfection*.

Subjective potency is a real principle which connotes a relation to act, as the determinable to its determination, as the perfectible to perfection.

2° In the thesis, we state that potency and act so divide being that whatsoever exists is either pure act, or is necessarily composed of potency and act.

Being is used to signify complete being, i.e., being which has actual existence.

Pure act is act in which there is no potency whatsoever.

Potency and act, as the constituents of a being, are not complete beings, i.e., beings which have their own existence, but the *parts* of a complete being, i.e., the intrinsic constituents of a being. In a word, potency and act are the first intrinsic principles of being, i.e., the first realities by which a finite being is intrinsically constituted.

3° When we say that act and potency divide being, we mean not that act and potency are inferiors of being, as species are inferiors of genus, but that act and potency are the principles of being, so that every being which exists is either pure act, or results from act and potency.

4° All who admit the existence of only one being, as the pantheists, or who deny the existence of motion, as Heraclitus, deny the notions of act and potency.

All Scholastics admit the existence of potency and act in mobile being. But all of them do not admit that act and potency are two distinct constituent principles of finite being. Thus Suarez ([1]) admits only a distinction of reason reasoned between act and potency, as the constituents of finite being.

Scotus ([2]) too denies that act and potency are really distinct constituents of finite being.

St. Thomas and his disciples hold that infinite being is pure act, and that finite being is composed of potency and act, as its two really distinct constituent principles.

Statement of the thesis.

> **THESIS.**—POTENCY AND ACT SO DIVIDE BEING THAT WHATSOEVER EXISTS IS EITHER PURE ACT, OR IS NECESSARILY COMPOSED OF POTENCY AND ACT, AS ITS FIRST INTRINSIC PRINCIPLES.

Infinite being is pure act; finite being is necessarily composed of potency and act, as its first intrinsic principles. But whatsoever exists is either infinite being or finite being. Therefore potency and act so divide being that whatsoever exists is either pure act, or is necessarily composed of potency and act, as its first intrinsic principles ([3]).

Major.— a) *Infinite being is pure act.*— The infinitely perfect is pure act, i.e., is perfection without imperfection. But infinite being is infinitely perfect: because being and perfection are convertible. Therefore infinite being is pure act.

b) *Finite being is necessarily composed of potency and act, as its first intrinsic principles.*— Finite being is limited, and therefore has two intrinsic constituents: the perfection of being and the limitation of this perfection. But the limitation of the perfection of being does not derive from this perfection, because it is its negation; and it cannot come from non-being, because

---

(1) *Disputationes Metaph.*, disp. XXXI, sect. XIII, nn. 9, 1 °.
(2) *In I Dist.*, 39, q. 1. — *In III Dist.*, 6, q. 1.
(3) *Thesis I* s. Thomae.

non-being is nothing. Consequently the limitation of the perfection of being must derive from some positive limiting principle which is really distinct from act, i.e., from perfection, that is to say, it must derive from potency ([1]).

Therefore finite being is necessarily composed of potency and act, as its first intrinsic principles.

Minor. — The existence of finite being is evident from internal experience: I, as distinct from other beings, am a finite being. Later, we shall prove the existence of infinite being, i.e., of God (cf. nn. 729-751). But there is no intermediate being between finite being and infinite being, because they are immediate opposites. Therefore whatsoever exists is either finite being or infinite being.

553. Act, because it is perfection, can be limited only by potency, which is capacity for perfection. — The truth of this proposition is evident from what we have already said. For limited act must have two constituents: perfection and the limitation of perfection. But the limitation of perfection cannot derive from perfection itself, or from the simple negation of perfection, which is nothing, but must come from a principle which is really distinct from act, that is to say, from potency ([2]).

554. In an order in which act is pure, i. e., not received into potency, it is unlimited and unique. — 1° *Preliminaries. a)* Order is used here to signify the consideration under which something falls; v.g., we say: in this order of ideas. Therefore acts are of different orders when they fall

---

(1) Adhuc, omnis actus alteri inhaerens terminationem recipit ex eo in quo est; quia quod est in altero est in eo per modum recipientis. Actus igitur in nullo existens, nullo terminatur: (utputa) si albedo esset per se existens, perfectio albedinis in ea non terminaretur, quominus haberet quidquid de perfectione albedinis haberi potest . . .

Item, tanto actus aliquis est perfectior, quanto minus habet potentiae permixtum. Unde omnis actus, cui permiscetur potentia, habet terminum suae perfectionis; cui autem non permiscetur aliqua potentia, est absque termino perfectionis. — *Contra Gentes*, l. I, c. 43.

(2) *Thesis II* s. Thomae.

under different considerations. Thus the act of existence and the act of essence do not belong to the same order. Again, acts of essence belong to different orders when these acts are specifically distinct.

b) Act is unlimited in an order when it possesses all its perfection. But act can be unlimited in a particular order, without its being unlimited in all orders, i.e., without its being absolutely infinite; v.g., the form, i.e., the act, by which each angel is constituted is not received into potency, because the angel is essentially a simple form. Therefore each angel possesses all the perfection of its species, but yet is a strictly finite being.

c) An act is unique in an order when it does not admit of the existence of another act of the same order; v.g., an angel does not admit of the existence of another angel in the *same species*, because the form by which an angel is constituted does not admit of material, i.e., numerical, multiplication, because it is not received into matter.

2° *Proof.*— *a*) *In an order in which act is pure, i.e., not received into potency, it is unlimited.*— The principle of the limitation of act is the potency into which it is received. Hence in an order in which act is pure, i.e., not received into potency, it is unlimited.

b) *In an order in which act is pure, i.e., not received into potency, it is unique.*— If act not received into potency could be multiplied, its multiplication would have to derive from itself. But act, in a given order, cannot be multiplied by itself: otherwise it would be distinct from itself, and would belong to an order which would be really distinct from its own order. Therefore, in an order in which act is pure, i.e., not received into potency, it is unique; and act which is finite and multiplied in a given order is in true composition with potency.

POINTS FOR REVIEW

1. State the teaching *a*) of Suarez, *b*) of St. Thomas on the composition of act and potency in finite being.

2. Explain why *a*) infinite being is pure act, *b*) finite being is a composite of act and potency, and *c*) act which is not received into potency must be unique in its own order.

RELATION OF POTENCY AND ACT

555. Act and potency are in the same genus. — 1°
We are here concerned with act to which potency is *essentially*
related as to its completing and specifying principle.

, 2° When we say that act and potency are in the same
genus, we do not mean that they are of necessity in the same
predicamental genus, so that, v.g., if an act is in the genus of
quality, the potency which is essentially related to it is also
in the genus of quality; rather potency and act are said to be
in the same genus in this sense: if the act is in the genus of
substance, the potency will be in the genus of substance; if the
act is in the genus of accident, the potency will be in the genus
of accident.

3° The axiom thus understood can be explained very
easily.

The principle which specifies and completes a substance is
a substantial complement. Now it is repugnant, of course,
that an accident be a substantial complement.

In like manner, the principle which specifies and completes
an accident is an accidental complement. It is absurd that
something which belongs to the genus of substance be an accidental complement.

Hence, if a potency is in the genus of substance, the act
which gives it its essential completion must be in the genus of
substance; if a potency is in the genus of accident, the act
which gives it its completeness must be in the genus of accident.

556. Potency is specified by act. — A thing is specified by that by which it is defined, for species and definition are convertible terms. But potency is defined by act, for potency of its very essence is a real principle which connotes a transcendental relation to act. Therefore potency is specified by act.

557. Potency can be reduced to act only by a being in act. — Being in potency is devoid of perfection ; act is perfection. But what is devoid of perfection cannot endow itself with perfection, and consequently must receive its perfection from another. But this other cannot impart perfection unless it possesses perfection, i.e., act, in itself. Therefore a being in potency can be reduced to act only by a being in act.

558. A thing cannot be, in the same respect, in potency and in act. — To be in potency is to be devoid of perfection; and to be in act is to possess perfection. But it is impossible that a thing, from the same point of view, possesses perfection and does not possess it. Hence a thing cannot be, in the same respect, in potency and act.

559. In the order of generation, potency is prior in time to act. — A thing is engendered from a being in potency. Hence, in the order of generation, i.e., in the order of material cause, potency is prior in time to act, for a thing is engendered in as much as it is reduced from potency to act.

560. Act, strictly speaking, is prior to potency. — 1° Act is prior to potency in its formal aspect, for potency is defined by act.

2° Act is prior to potency in perfection, for act is the perfection of potency.

3° Act is prior to potency in the order of efficient causality, for a being in potency can be reduced to act only by a being in act.

POINTS FOR REVIEW

1. Are act and potency in the same genus? Explain.

2. Explain why potency is specified by act, and why potency can be actuated only by a being in act.

3. Is act prior to potency from every point of view? Explain.

4. Explain why it is impossible that a thing be in potency and act in the same respect.

DEFENSIVE PART OF GENERAL METAPHYSICS

INTRODUCTION

561. Names of the tract. — Authors variously denominate this part of philosophy.

a) Some hold that this part of philosophy deals with means employed by the human intellect to know truth; and they call it *Major* or *Material Logic*. This opinion, we maintain, is entirely untenable.

b) There are various other opinions in regard to the nature of the problem with which this part of philosophy deals, and consequently various names, corresponding to these opinions, are assigned to this tract: it is a critical examination (¹) of human knowledge, and is called *Critica* (from the Greek work χρίνειν, to discern); or it is concerned with the criteria by which truth can be distinguished from falsity, and is called *Criteriology* (from χριτήριον and λόγος); or it deals with the nature and value of human knowledge, especially intellectual knowledge, in the acquisition of truth, and is called *Epistemology* (from the word ἐπίσταμαί, to be able to know, to be apt), *Noetics* (νοῦς, νοος and δίχη, justification of the intellect), *Gnosiology*, *Theory of Knowledge*, or simply *Tract on Truth*.

We do not regard these opinions as absolutely untenable. However, we maintain that the scientific study of the problem of the truth of human knowledge requires a different approach.

562. Approach to the problem of human knowledge.
The question which concerns us at present is whether the hu-

---

(1) The Latin word *Critica*, of which an accurate English translation is perhaps impossible, seems well suited to denominate such a study, and hence we are presuming to adopt it as an English philosophical term. — Translator's note.

man intellect can have true and certain knowledge.   But first
we must know how to approach the problem, that it to say,
what must be the starting-point of our investigation of the
problem.

1° We could perhaps begin with the nominal definitions of
certitude and truth, and afterwards investigate whether certitude and truth are found in human knowledge.   But this method of approach to the problem presupposes that the human
intellect can know truth with certitude, and this precisely is the
problem we must solve.   For we presuppose that our intellect
can distinguish with certitude between certitude and its opposite, and can have true knowledge of truth: for, in order that
we know what truth is, the knowledge which we have of truth
must be true.   Hence we may not accept this method of approach to the problem.

2° Some authors begin their examination of the value of
human knowledge as follows: they start out with universal
doubt, either positive, or feigned, i.e., doubt regarding the aptitude of the intellect to know truth with certitude; afterwards
they investigate whether they must recant this universal doubt.
They adopt this method of approach because, as they point
out, sceptics, against whom we are arguing at present, hold
universal doubt, i.e., they doubt everything.

We can start out with universal doubt by making use of
the contradictorily opposed propositions:

The intellect is capable of certain knowledge.

The intellect is not capable of certain knowledge.

a) The intellect withholds its assent by not pronouncing
that one of the propositions, is true, and the other false.   But
this kind of doubt, called negative universal doubt, is impossible, because the intellect already presupposes something as
certain: it holds with certitude that two contradictory propositions cannot be true and false at the same time.

Moreover, this doubt presupposes the existence of knowledge, for doubt requires knowledge.

b) The intellect gives its assent to the proposition: *the intellect is not capable of certain knowledge,* and in this case we have positive universal doubt. But such assent already affirms with certitude the incapacity of the intellect for certain knowledge, and also the existence of knowledge — for negation requires knowledge.

From this it is evident that our solution of the problem of the value of human knowledge cannot be initiated by the adoption of universal doubt, feigned or positive.

3° Other authors, as Geny ([1]), affirm that Critica is concerned not with the native capacity of the intellect for knowledge, but with the value of its object. They introduce the problem by proposing two questions.

a) Can we form propositions of which we are absolutely certain in regard to the object of our knowledge? This is the question of *scepticism*.

b) What is the value of this object as regards reality? Is it a production of our own, i.e., of our mind? If it is, is it wholly our production, i.e., completely independent of any external reality; or is it only partially our production, i.e., dependent on some external reality? This is the question of *idealism*.

This method of attacking the problem is untenable.

It starts out by presupposing that an object as it exists in the intellect is not one and the same as the object which exists in reality. But such a presupposition is inadmissible, for it is the same thing which is found in reality, and which is known by the intellect. If an a priori distinction is made, as regards reality, between the thing known and the thing existing, the solution of the problem of the value of our knowledge becomes impossible: it is an implicit admission that our intellect attains things not as they are in themselves, but as they exist in the intellect. In this case, we can never prove that the thing which is in the intellect corresponds to the thing as it is in reality, because we presuppose that the human intellect cannot attain a thing as it is in itself.

---

(1) *Critica de cognitionis humanae valore inquisitio,* Romae, 1932, p. 6.

In other words, the proponents of this opinion presuppose that a proposition which is *certain* is not at the same time *true*. This contention is, of course, inadmissible, as we shall prove later.

4° Marxists, i.e., the advocates of modern communism, teach that the problem of the relation between human knowledge and reality cannot be attacked in a speculative manner, but must find its solution in the realm of the practical. They maintain that we can perceive conformity between our knowledge and external things only when we produce external things, or at least when we make use of natural things for our own purpose. ([1])

---

(1) The question whether objective truth can be attributed to human thinking is not a question of theory but is a practical question. In practice man must prove the truth, i.e., the reality and power, the « this-sidedness » of his thinking. The dispute over the reality or non-reality of thinking which is isolated from practice is a purely scholastic question. — KARL MARX, *Theses on Feuerbach*.

But the question of the relation of thinking and being has yet another side: in what relation do our thoughts about the world surrounding us stand to this world itself? Is our thinking capable of the cognition of the real world? Are we able in our ideas and notions of the real world to produce a correct reflection of reality? In philosophical language this question is called the question of the « identity of thinking and being », and the overwhelming majority of philosophers give an affirmative answer to this question. With Hegel, for example, its affirmation is self-evident; for what we perceive in the real world is precisely its thought-content — that which makes the world a gradual realisation of the absolute idea, which absolute idea has existed somewhere from eternity, independent of the world and before the world. But it is manifest without more ado that thought can know a content which is from the outset a thought-content. It is equally manifest that what is here to be proved is already tacitly contained in the presupposition. But that in no way prevents Hegel from drawing the further conclusion from his proof of the identity of thinking and being that his philosophy, because it is correct for his own thinking, is therefore the only correct one, and that the identity of thinking and being must prove its validity by mankind immediately translating his philosophy from theory into practice and transforming the whole world according to Hegelian principles. This is an illusion which he shares with well-nigh all philosophers.

In addition there is yet another set of different philosophers — those who question the possibility of any cognition (or at least of an exhaustive cognition) of the world. To them, among the moderns, belong Hume and Kant, and they have played a very important role in philosophical development. What is decisive in the refutation of this view has already been said by Hegel — in so far as this was possible from an idealist standpoint. The materialistic additions made by Feuerbach are more ingenious than profound. The most telling refutation of this as of all other philosophical fancies is practice, viz., experiment and industry. If we are able to prove the correctness of our conception of a natural process by making it ourselves, bringing it into being out of its conditions and using it for our own purposes into the bargain, then there is an end of the Kantian incomprehensible « thing-in-itself ». — ENGLES, F., *Ludwig Feuerbach*, N. Y., 1934, p. 31.

This opinion is inadmissible, because, if we do not know in a speculative way whether our knowledge attains reality, we do not know whether practice is a reality.   Therefore practice cannot give us certitude that there exists a relation between human knowledge and external things.

5° The problem of human knowledge, from the point of view of our present study of it, may be stated in the question: does truth exist?   In other words, universal doubt must be our starting-point (¹).

But this universal doubt must not be either positive or feigned, for, as we have already said, both are impossible.

We are going to begin with universal doubt merely as a problem for which we must find a solution.   In other words, we initiate the problem by posing the proposition: *perhaps truth does not exist;* and we do so simply in order that we may examine it, to find out whether it is true, or whether it is false and the doubt it expresses is untenable.

There are two reasons why we must study this problem: *a)* certain philosophers deny the existence of any truth; *b)* it is the function of Metaphysics to establish the existence of truth in general (²).

563. Solution of the problem of human knowledge.

1° Since all knowledge begins with the senses, some might think that an exposition of the truth of human knowledge should begin with an examination of the problem of whether or not the senses can attain external things; and, having established that the senses are capable of attaining external things, should proceed to show that the human intellect, which is objec-

---

(1) ... Aliae scientiae considerant particulariter de veritate: unde et particulariter ad eas pertinet circa singulas veritates dubitare: sed ista scientia, sicut habet universalem considerationem de veritate, its etiam ad eam pertinet universalis dubitatio de veritate; et ideo non particulariter, sed simul universalem dubitationem prosequitur. — *In Metaph.*, l. III, l. 1, n. 343 (Cathala).

(2) ... Dicit ergo primo, quod ad hanc scientiam, quam quaerimus de primis principiis, et universali veritate rerum, necesse est ut primum aggrediamur ea de quibus oportet dubitare, antequam veritas determinetur. Sunt autem humusmodi dubitabilia propter duas rationes. Vel quia antiqui philosophi aliter susceperunt opinionem de eis quam rei veritas habeat, vel quia omnino praetermiserunt de his considerare. — *Ibidem*, n. 338.

tively dependent on the senses, is capable of the attainment of external things.

But this method of attacking the problem is inadmissible. Since the external senses cannot reflect by a distinct act (in actu signato — cf. n. 363), they cannot have knowledge of their conformity to external things. Only the intellect can have knowledge of this conformity. Hence, to establish that the external senses are capable of attaining external reality, we must first know that the intellect is capable of knowledge of truth.

2° Therefore the first step towards the solution of the problem of human knowledge must consist in an investigation of whether the human intellect is capable of knowledge of truth.

But the intellect derives its knowledge of truth from first principles which are certain and true; and, if the first principles are certain and true, the intellect can deduce conclusions that are certain and true ([1]).

Hence we must now find out if there is some certain and true first principle which is presupposed in all intellective knowledge.

If there exists such a first principle, we may conclude that the human intellect is capable of attaining truth.

If no such first principle exists, we must conclude that the human intellect is not capable of the attainment of truth.

3° Hence the part of philosophy which deals with the problem of human knowledge, i.e., with the value of human knowledge, is the defensive part of Metaphysics.

It is a part of Metaphysics, because it is first and essentially concerned with the first principle, which pertains to being as being. Being is the formal object of Metaphysics.

---

(1) In unoquoque genere ille est maxime cognoscitivus, qui certissima cognoscit principia; quia certitudo cognitionis ex certitudine principiorum dependet. Sed primus philosophus est maxime cognoscitivus et certissimus in sua cognitione: haec enim erat una de conditionibus sapientis, ut in proemio hujus libri patuit, scilicet quod esset certissimus cognitor causarum; ergo philosphus debet considerare certissima et firmissima principia circa entia, de quibus ipse considerat sicut de genere proprie sibi subjecto. — *In Metaph.*, l. IV, l. 6, n. 596 (Cathala).

It is the defensive part of Metaphysics, because it reflects on first principles, not for the purpose of demonstrating them, but in order to set them forth and defend them.

In the light of the foregoing remarks, the part of philosophy which sets forth the value of human knowledge may be called Critica, provided that by Critica we mean the material part of Metaphysics.

564. Division of the defensive part of Metaphysics. —
In the defensive part of Metaphysics, we shall first consider the first principle of intellective knowledge, and, secondly, truth itself.   Hence there will be two books in this part of our work.

Book I: The first principle.

Book II: Truth.

POINTS FOR REVIEW

1. What is the etymological significance of the following names: Critica, Criteriology, Epistemology, and Noetics?

2. What is meant by the terms: positive universal doubt, feigned universal doubt?

3. Describe how the problem of human knowledge is attacked by such authors as Geny, how the Marxists deal with it, and how, in our solution of it, we must begin from universal doubt.

4. Explain why the problem of human knowledge must be solved by a study of the first principle, and why the study of it belongs to Metaphysics.

BOOK I

The first principle

THE ONLY CHAPTER

Prologue. — The first book contains only one chapter, in which we are primarily concerned with the study of the first principle of intellective knowledge. When we have completed our study of the first principle, we shall deal with the problems of scepticism and idealism, both of which will be shown to be untenable. Although scepticism and idealism are not essentially distinct, but two aspects of one and the same error, we deal with them separately, in order to facilitate our exposition of them. Hence there will be three articles in this chapter.

The first principle
⎧ Statement of the question
⎨ Proposition: The first principle is the principle of contradiction
⎪ Significance of the principle of contradiction
⎩ Principle of identity

Universal scepticism
⎧ Statement of the question
⎨ Thesis: Universal scepticism is impossible
⎩ Difficulty

Idealism
⎧ Statement of the question
⎪ History of idealism
⎨ Thesis: Idealism is untenable
⎩ Difficulties

THE FIRST PRINCIPLE

565. Statement of the question. — 1° The first principle is characterized by three conditions ([1]).

a) The first principle must be *most certain*, i.e., the *best known* and *most fixed* of all principles, so that no one can err concerning it, or deny it.

Some may perhaps entertain doubt concerning it, or may express verbal denial of it, as Heraclitus did. But it is one thing to give oral expression to something, and quite another thing to really think it, i.e., to be convinced of the truth of it.

b) The first principle must not be a *postulate*, i.e., an *hypothesis*.

A postulate is a hypothetical enunciation which does not contain an absolute truth, but which signifies something true from supposition ([2]); in other words, it is a principle which is commonly accepted, not because of immediate evidence, but because of the consequences of its negation.

Thus the first principle would be a postulate if it were held as true on the supposition that the knowledge of the human intellect is true.

But the first principle must not be held as true on the supposition that the knowledge of the human intellect is true, but must be known by all who have knowledge of anything other than the first principle.

c) The first principle must be *indemonstrable:* it must be, as it were, naturally known, i.e., immediately evident.

In other words, the first principle must be the most general

---

(1) *Metaph.*, l. IV, c. 3, 1005b, 10. — L. 6 s. THOMAE.
(2) *In Periherm.*, l. I, l. 1, n. 8 (Leonina).

of propositions, which can be immediately known from a knowledge of its terms.

The first principle is said to be naturally known. By this we mean not that it is innate in the intellect, but that the intellect, in virtue of the influence of its very nature, immediately knows the first principle from the knowledge of its terms, which it has from experience.

Hence the first principle must be most certain; it must not be postulated, but must be naturally known.

2° According to Descartes, the principle: *I think, therefore I am* (I exist), is the first principle.

According to Aristotle, the first principle is the principle of contradiction, whose logical enunciation is as follows : *it is impossible that a thing be and not be at the same time and in the same respect.* In other words, being and non-being are contradictorily opposed; v.g., man cannot at the same time and under the aspect be man and not be man.

566. Exposition of Aristotle's opinion.

PROPOSITION.— THE FIRST PRINCIPLE IS THE PRINCIPLE OF CONTRADICTION.

The first principle must be most certain; moreover, it must not be a postulate, i.e., a hypothetical proposition, but must be naturally known, i.e., indemonstrable. But the principle of contradiction fulfills these three conditions. Therefore the first principle is the principle of contradiction.

The *major* is evident from the statement of the question.

Minor.— a) *The principle of contradiction is most certain, so that no one can either err concerning it, or deny it.*— A person who denies the principle of contradiction holds two contrary opinions at the same time; v.g., if he holds the opinion: *Peter is a man*, he must at the same time support the opinion: *Peter is not a man*. But, even though a person can give oral expression to contrary opinions, it is impossible for him to hold contrary opinions at the same time. For, if a person denies the principle of contradiction and maintains that he holds contrary opinions, he at the same time admits that he does not hold contrary opinions, for contrary opinions at the same time would not be contrary.

Hence all argumentation and all propositions presuppose that the principle of contradiction is most certain; for, if this were not so, argumentation and the formation of propositions would be impossible.

b) The principle of contradiction is not a postulate, i.e., a hypothetical enunciation.— The principle of contradiction is a principle which is presupposed in every demonstration as well as in every proposition. Hence it is not admitted on the supposition of some truth, but is accepted as true in an absolute way, i.e., independently of any other truth.

c) The principle of contradiction is naturally known, i.e., indemonstrable.— From the fact that the principle of contradiction is presupposed in every other proposition and in every demonstration, it cannot be known from demonstration or from any kind of inquiry or investigation, but must be immediately and naturally known, i.e., indemonstrable.

2° *From the refutation of Descartes.*— A principle which presupposes the principle of contradiction is not the first principle. But the principle: *I think, therefore I am*, presupposes the principle of contradiction. Therefore the principle: *I think, therefore I am*, is not the first principle, but the first principle is the principle of contradiction.

The *major* is evident.

Minor.— Unless the principle of contradiction is first admitted, *I think* has the same signification as *I do not think*, *I am* has the same signification as *I am not*, and therefore the principle: *I think, therefore I am*, has no determinate signification.

567. Significance of the principle of contradiction. — The principle of contradiction manifests, in a very evident and indivisible manner, two things to us.

1° The principle of contradiction shows us that being, i.e., that which has relation to existence, is intelligible.   For the intellect knows that it is impossible for a thing to be and not to be at the same time and in the same respect, and by this very fact it can know beings, and can distinguish them from non-beings.

In other words, the principle of contradiction, because it is dependent on the knowledge of being (¹), shows us that being is intelligible, i.e., is transcendentally true.

2° The principle of contradiction manifests that the intellect is made to conform to being, i.e., to that which is, that is to say, it shows the truth of intellective knowledge.

In other words, the principle of contradiction shows itself to be the supreme law of all being and of all reality, and also the supreme law of intellective knowledge.   Briefly, the principle of contradiction shows that intellective knowledge is certain in as much as it is true, i.e., in as much as it attains being, because the principle of contradiction manifests itself in an indivisible manner to be both certain and true.

If we understand this, we have the solution of the problem of human knowledge.

568. Principle of identity.— Certain scholastic philosophers, especially of modern times, hold that the principle of identity: *being is being*, is the first principle.

We should like to make the following observations in regard to this opinion.

---

(1) Ad hujus autem evidentiam sciendum est, quod, cum duplex sit operatio intellectus: una, quae cognoscit quod quid est, quae vocatur indivisibilium intelligentia: alia, qua componit et dividit: in utroque est aliquod primum: in prima quidem operatione est aliquod primum, quod cadit in conceptione intellectus, scilicet hoc quod dico ens; nec aliquid hac operatione potest mente concipi, nisi intelligatur ens.   Et quia hoc principium, impossibile est esse et non esse simul, dependet ex intellectu entis, sicut hoc principium, omne totum est majus sua parte, ex intellectu totius et partis: ideo hoc etiam principium est naturaliter primum in secunda operatione intellectus, scilicet componentis et dividentis.   Nec aliquis potest secundum hanc operationem intellectus aliquid intelligere, nisi hoc principio intellecto.   Sicut enim totum et partes non intelliguntur nisi intellecto ente, ita nec hoc principium omne totum est majus sua parte, nisi intellecto praedicto firmissimo principio. — *In Metaph.*, l. 1V, l. 6, n. 605 (Cathala).

a) When we say: *being is being*, being, as it is predicate, is understood as excluding non-being.   Thus in saying: *being is being*, we mean that being in itself does not include being and non-being, or, in other words, *being is undivided*, i.e., *is one*.   For being is one in as much as it excludes non-being (n. 513).   Hence, if the principle of identity is understood in this way, it presupposes the principle of contradiction, which is the first principle.

b) Our adversaries raise the objection that the principle of contradiction is a modal proposition, and therefore that it pre-supposes an absolute proposition, the kind of proposit;on used for the enunciation of the principle of identity.

We reply that, in the case of the principle of contradiction, the mode expresses the opposition between truth and falsity, between affirmation and negation, as it immediately results from the very nature of being.   Therefore the principle of contradiction, which is immediately dependent on a knowledge of being, must be a modal proposition.

c) Some maintain that every negation presupposes an affirmation, and therefore that the principle of contradiction, which is negative, presupposes an affirmative proposition, i.e., the principle of identity.

We reply: every negative proposition does not necessarily presuppose an affirmative proposition; but both negation and privation presuppose something positive.   The principle of contradiction, because it results from a knowledge of being, pre-supposes something positive, namely, being as known by the intellect.

POINTS FOR REVIEW

1. Enunciate the principle of contradiction, and show why no one may deny it.

2. State what is meant by a postulate, and show that the principle of contradiction is not this type of principle, but is naturally known.

3. Prove that Descartes' principle, *I think, therefore I am*, is not the first principle of intellective knowledge.

4. Explain the significance of the principle of contradiction as the key to the solution of the problem of Critica.

5. Why does the principle of identity presuppose the principle of contradiction? Explain briefly.

6. Answer the following objections: the principle of contradiction cannot be the first principle, because *a*) as a modal proposition, it presupposes an absolute proposition; *b*) as a negative proposition, it presupposes an affirmative proposition.

7. Explain whether or not the principle of contradiction presupposes anything positive.

UNIVERSAL SCEPTICISM

569. Statement of the question. — 1° Scepticism means doubt. Hence universal scepticism signifies doubt concerning everything.

2° According to some philosophers (¹), there never have been sceptics who called everything into question; and of those sceptics who have existed, some doubted the value of some kinds of knowledge, v.g., knowledge of the senses, whereas others held that we cannot know things as they are in themselves.

But to deny that we can know things as they are in themselves is tantamount to the denial of the possibility of our acquiring certitude of any truth.

Moreover, sceptics tend, as a result of the arguments they use, to universal doubt of all knowledge.

a) They argue *from the fact of error:* our cognitive faculties, both sensitive and intellectual, often deceive us, without our knowing it. Therefore, conclude the sceptics, perhaps they always deceive us.

b) They have recourse to the *diallelus:* the value of the intellect can be judged only by the intellect; but the value of this judgment is dependent on the value of the intellect (²), so that we find ourselves in a vicious circle.

3° *a)* Though scepticism has its roots in an earlier day than that of Pyrrho, (365-275 B. C.), yet it was he who inaugurated universal scepticism as a philosophical doctrine. Pyr-

---

(1) V.g., V. BROCHARD, *Les Sceptiques grecs*, Paris, 1887.
(2) « Nous ne pouvons rien démontrer qu'avec notre intelligence; or, notre intelligence ne peut être reçue à démontrer la véracité de notre intelligence. » — JOUFFROY, *Mélanges philosophiques*, Paris, 1833, p. 167. — « Nous voilà au rouet », dit Montaigne.

rho and his disciples (Timon, Aenesidemus, and others), known as Pyrrhonians or *Sceptics*, taught that we cannot have certain knowledge of anything, and hence must withhold our assent — *nil comprehensi posse, assensumque retinendum* ([1]).

Later, the Academics also taught scepticism. Arcesilaus (318-245 B.C.) ([2]), Carneades (219-129 B.C.), and Sextus Empiricus (about 300 A.D.) held that being is not intelligible, and therefore that nothing is certain. They differed from the Pyrrhonians in as much as they admitted that some things are more probable than others.

b) In the modern period, some have expressed a certain diffidence in regard to the capacity of human reason for truth and certitude. Representative of this attitude in the nineteenth century are Jouffroy ([3]) and Ad. Levi. The Moralists, as Montaigne (1533-1592), Pierre Charron (1541-1603), Sanchez (1562-1632), and Pierre Bayle (1647-1706), deny the possibility of knowledge of moral good.

Others, as Rougier ([4]), Goblot ([5]), and many others regard first principles as practical conventions, and hence are not far removed from scepticism.

570. Statement of the thesis.—Universal scepticism cannot be refuted directly, because it refuses to acknowledge the principle of contradiction, in which every demonstration has its foundation; but it can be refuted from the admissions of the sceptic, for, no matter whether he admits or denies that his words have a determinate signification, he must make implicit acknowledgment of the value of the principle of contradiction.

THESIS.—UNIVERSAL SCEPTICISM IS IMPOSSIBLE.

---

(1) *Diogenes Laert.*, 11, c. 2.
(2) « Arcesilas negabat esse quidquam, quod sciri posset, ne illud quidem ipsum quod Socrates sibi reliquisset; sic omnia latere in occulto neque esse quidquam quod carni aut intelligi posset. » — CICERO, *Academia posteriora*, l. 1, c. XIII.
(3) « Nous regardons le scepticisme comme le dernier mot de la raison sur elle-même. » — *Op. cit.*, p. 167.
(4) *Les Paralogismes du Rationalisme*, Paris, 1919.
(5) *Traité de Logique*, Paris, 1918.

Universal scepticism is impossible if the sceptic implicity admits that the principle of contradiction is certain, and therefore admits that all knowledge is conformed to a determinate object, i.e., has a determinate object. But the sceptic implicity admits that the principle of contradiction is certain, and therefore admits that all knowledge has a determinate object. Therefore universal scepticism is impossible.

Minor.— a) *The sceptic implicity admits that the principle of contradiction is certain.—* When the sceptic speaks of something, v.g., of doubt, he makes a distinction between doubt and non-doubt, and therefore implicity admits the principle of contradiction.

b) *And therefore he admits that all knowledge has a determinate object.—* The admission of the value of the principle of contradiction is tantamount to admitting that all knowledge has an object: for the sceptic thinks something which is not its opposite.

571. Difficulty. — We can judge the value of our intellect only by our intellect. But this judgment in turn depends on the value of the intellect. Therefore the value of the intellect cannot be demonstrated, i.e., universal scepticism is legitimate.

Major. — By some intellectual knowledge, *I concede;* by previous knowledge of the value of the intellect, *I deny.*

Minor. — On foreknowledge of the value of the intellect, *I deny;* on knowledge of the value of the intellect that is acquired at the same time as knowledge of the first principle, *I concede.*

The refutation of scepticism does not start out with the value of the intellect as its first principle, but rather it begins with the principle of contradiction. But the admission of the principle of contradiction is equivalent to admitting at the same time that the intellect is concerned with being as its object, since the principle of contradiction concerns being. Thus the intellect acquires knowledge of its own value when it admits the principle of contradiction as certain and true.

POINTS FOR REVIEW

1. Explain what is meant by universal scepticism, and show how sceptics try to defend their position by recourse to the dialellus.

2. State the teaching of the Pyrrhonians, and show how it differs from the teaching of the Academics.

3. Show how the sceptic implicitly admits the principle of contradiction.

4. Do we judge the value of the intellect by means of the intellect? Explain.

ARTICLE III

IDEALISM

572. Statement of the question. — Idealism is the doctrine of those who teach that man cannot know an object as it exists in itself, i.e., in its nature, but can know only his own knowledge, or better his own «thought». Perhaps idealism is more accurately denominated *immanentism* or *subjectivism* ([1]), because it locks up the knowing subject in itself ([2]). In other words, it denies that we can know anything outside our knowledge, such as it is in itself.

Idealism is the opposite of realism, i.e., of objectivism, which teaches that man can know things as they are in themselves.

573. History of idealism. — In ancient times, Protagoras and many other philosophers taught that truth (the true) is anything which appears. Descartes is commonly regarded as the father of modern idealism. He claimed that the first principle of intellective knowledge is the principle: *I think, therefore I am.* But since *I*, according to Descartes, is the *soul*, and the soul is *thought*, he concluded that the thinking subject can immediately attain only its own thought ([3]); and this, indeed, is the foundation of idealism.

---

(1) E. Toccafondi, *Il problema della realta et l'inizio della metafisica critica.* — In periodo *Angelicum*, jul.-sept., 1934, p. 277 et ss.

(2) L'immanentisme est un système qui nie ou néglige toute réalité transcendante, qui aboutit à enfermer le sujet en lui-même. — Jos. de Tonquédec, *Immanence*, 3e édit., p. 8, Beauchesne, Paris, 1933.

(3) Et remarquant que cette vérité: je pense, donc je suis, était si ferme et si assurée que toutes les plus extravagantes suppositions des sceptiques n'étaient pas capables de l'ébranler, je jugeai que je pouvais la recevoir sans scrupule, pour le premier principe de la philosophie que je cherchais.

Puis examinant avec attention ce que j'étais, et voyant que je pouvais feindre que je n'avais aucun corps, et qu'il n'y avait aucun monde, ni aucun

Nevertheless, a priori and unlawfully Descartes gave a proof for the existence of God which was based on the idea of perfect being. Moreover, he claimed that our knowledge, or rather *our ideas*, represent real being, because God cannot deceive us. And it must be added that, from this point of view, Descartes safeguarded the transcendence of human knowledge.

Berkeley (1685-1753), an Anglican bishop, applied the principle of Cartesian idealism to our knowledge of bodies, and taught that bodies do not exist, but are sensations impressed by God on the souls of men. He proposed the theory of acosmic idealism. He enunciated the principle of idealism thus: *esse est percipi*, i.e., being consists in being perceived.

Hume (1711-1776) went a step farther, and, by calling into doubt the substantial nature of minds and the objectivity of principles, ended in pure phenomenalism.

Kant (1724-1804), subjecting all knowledge to critical examination, taught that being in itself which really exists cannot be known by us as it is in itself, but only as it appears to us, conditioned by the laws and forms of the thinking subject. His philosophical system is called transcendental idealism.

The followers of Kant, Fichte (1762-1814), Schelling (1775-1854), Hegel (1770-1831), thinking that being in itself is superfluous, taught that only the representations of the thinking subject exist. Therefore they fashioned absolute idealism.

Some of the later disciples of Kant, as Renouvier and Hamelin, admit the existence of many thinking subjects (pluralistic idealism); but others, as Lachelier, Gentile, etc., admit only one thinking subject (monistic idealism).

---

lieu où je fusse; mais que je ne pouvais pas feindre pour cela que je n'étais point; et qu'au contraire, de cela même que je pensais à douter de la vérité des autres choses, il suivait très évidemment et très certainement que j'étais; au lieu que si j'eusse seulement cessé de penser, encore que tout le reste de ce que j'avais jamais imaginé eût été vrai, je n'avais aucune raison de croire que j'eusse été: je connus de là que j'étais une substance dont toute l'essence ou la nature n'est que de penser, et qui pour être n'a besoin d'aucun lieu, ni ne dépend d'aucune chose matérielle. En sorte que *ce moi*, c'est-à-dire l'*âme* par laquelle je suis ce que je suis, est entièrement distincte du corps . . . — RENÉ DESCARTES, *Discours de la méthode*, texte et commentaire par Étienne GILSON, 2e édit., pp. 32-33, Paris, Vrin, 1930.

A great many modern philosophers accept idealism as a dogma based on the principle of immanence, which they regard as evident and incontestable. This principle is enunciated as follows: « To know an object as existing outside our knowledge is not to know it, for this would require that something be known and at the same time be placed outside of knowledge, and hence not be known» (Schuppe). Only accidentally different from this is the statement of the principle of immanence as formulated by LeRoy (¹), Blondel, Fonsegrive (²), Spaventa (³), Gentile, and others.

574. Statement of the thesis.

THESIS.—IDEALISM IS UNTENABLE.

1° Any philosophical theory which leads to the denial of the principle of contradiction and to universal scepticism is untenable. But idealism is a philosophical theory which leads to the denial of the principle of contradiction and to universal scepticism. Therefore idealism is untenable.

The *major* is evident from what we have already said.

Minor.— a) *Idealism leads to a denial of the principle of contradiction.*— Idealists teach that to be is to be perceived (esse est percipi), or being is thought. But if to be were to be perceived, and if being were thought, being would not be itself, but something other than itself, i.e., being would not be being. Therefore.

---

(1) Dès lors que l'on pose le réel comme un au-delà de la pensée, aucun moyen de saisie ne subsiste pour l'atteindre. Comment s'assurerait-on d'un accord entre la représentation et l'objet ? Cela supposerait une comparaison exigeant que l'on puisse appréhender l'objet autrement que par la pensée. — LE ROY, *Bulletin de la société française de philosophie*, 25 février, 1904, p. 154.

(2) Si le concept d'une chose en soi peut offrir un sens, si même on peut concevoir un sujet en soi, le concept d'un objet qui serait en même temps en soi et objet de la connaissance est nettement contradictoire, de même que le concept d'un sujet de la connaissance qui serait en même temps connu comme en soi. Car dire: objet de la connaissance, c'est dire: connu; et dire: sujet de la connaissance, c'est dire: connaissant. Or il est de toute évidence que le connu, en tant que connu, n'est pas en soi, puisqu'il est en tant que connu; et il est tout aussi évident que le connaissant, en tant que connaissant, n'est pas en soi, puisqu'il est en tant que connaissant. — FONSEGRIVE, *Essais sur la connaissance*, p. 186.

(3) Un au-delà de la pensée est impensable... Il faut que l'objet de l'affirmation coïncide avec l'affirmation même.

b) Idealism leads to universal scepticism.— According to
idealism, the knowing subject passes judgment not on being,
but on what appears to it, i.e., on the appearances of being.
Therefore it follows that, if two men express contrary opinions, v.g., if one expresses the opinion that man is an *animal*,
and the other expresses the opinion that *man is not an animal*,
both statements are true, because each of the two men passes
judgment on what appears to him; and at the same time their
statements are false, because the contrary of each of the opinions
is true (¹). And the obvious result of this is universal scepticism.

2° Idealism teaches that the intellect can attain only its
own conceptions, and hence cannot attain external things.
But the intellect, in attaining its own conceptions, knows external things.(²) Therefore idealism is untenable.

The *major* is evident from the principles of idealism.

Minor.— A conception of the intellect is either a definition
or an enunciation. But the definition and the enunciation are
the instruments which the intellect forms for itself, in order that
it may pass judgment on external things, i.e., on things outside
itself. In other words, the definition and the enunciation give
the intellect an objective representation of the external thing,
so that the movement of the intellect to the definition and the
enunciation and its movement to the external thing are one and
the same movement. Therefore the intellect, in attaining its
own conceptions, attains external things.

3° *From its false consequences.*— If we admit idealism, it
follows that all scientific knowledge is set at naught: for, according to idealism, sciences deal not with things which are outside
the soul, but only with the intelligible species which are in the
soul, i.e., with ideas (³). Therefore idealism is untenable.

575. Difficulties. — 1° A thing in itself is distinct from the thing
known, i.e., the thing as the object of knowledge. But the intellect can

---

(1) ARIST., *Met.*, lib. IV.— *Ibid.*, lect. 9, s. Thomae.— I, q. 85, a. 2.
(2) I, q. 85, a. 2, ad 3. — CAJETANUS, *Commentaria* supra illum articulum,
nn. IX, X, XI.
(3) I, q. 85, a. 2, c.

attain a thing only as known.   Therefore the intellect cannot attain a thing in itself, i.e., a thing as it exists outside the intellect.

Major. — A thing in itself is really distinct from the thing as known, *I deny;* a thing in itself is distinct from the thing as known only by a distinction of reason, *I concede.*

Minor. — The thing known is the thing in itself, *I concede;* the thing known is not the thing in itself, *I deny.*

The distinction between a thing in itself, i.e., an external thing, and the thing as known is not a real distinction, for it is the same thing which exists in itself and which is in the intellect, and hence the intellect knows the thing in itself.

There is only a distinction of reason by extrinsic denomination between the thing in itself and the thing known.   A thing is said to be known because of the knowledge we have of it.[3]

2° An object which is attained by an immanent operation of the knowing subject cannot exist outside the knowing subject.   But known being is attained by an immanent operation of the knowing subject.   Therefore known being cannot exist outside the knowing subject.

Major. — An object which is attained by an immanent operation as a term produced by this operation cannot exist outside the knowing subject, *I concede;* an object which is attained as a *term known* by the operation cannot exist outside the knowing subject, *I deny.*

Minor. — Known being is attained as a term produced by an immanent operation, *I deny;* as a term known by an immanent operation, *I concede.*

Knowledge, as an immanent operation, is wholly completed in the knowing subject; since it is an intentional operation, i.e., directed to an object which can exist outside the knowing subject, it attains this object as a term known.

3° An object which is attained by the consciousness of the knowing subject cannot exist outside the knowing subject.   But an object which is attained by knowledge as a known term is attained by the consciousness of the knowing subject.   Therefore an object which is attained by knowledge as a known term cannot exist outside the knowing subject.

Major. — An object which is directly attained by the consciousness of the knowing subject, *I concede;* indirectly, *I deny.*

Minor. — Is directly attained by the consciousness of the knowing subject, *I deny;* indirectly, *I concede.*

This argument is based on the identification of consciousness and any kind of knowledge.   But consciousness is only knowledge which directly attains *internal facts,* i.e., knowledge whose only direct object is an internal fact.   Nevertheless, there is no reason why consciousness cannot accompany knowledge of an external object, and indirectly attain the external object; v.g., when I know that I know some external object.

4° Every idea is in the knowing subject.   But everything known is an idea.   Therefore everything known is in the knowing subject (American neo-realists).

---

(3) *Ex eadem autem ratione constat,* quod relatio inter conceptum objectivum, et rem ipsam in se, non est realis: quia non est distinctio inter ista extrema, sed est eadem res ut cognita, vel ut in seipsa: inter quae solum est distinctio mediante apprehensione seu esse cognito, super quod non potest fundari realis relatio. — JOANNES A SANCTO THOMA, *Cursus Theol.,* t. II, p. 615a (Sol.).

Major. — Every idea subjectively understood (subjective concept), *I concede;* objectively understood (objective concept), *I deny.*

Minor. — Is an idea in the subjective sense, *I deny;* in the objective sense, *I concede.*

The term idea is used in one sense in the major, and in another sense in the minor, and hence four terms are used.

POINTS FOR REVIEW

1. Give the meaning of the following terms: idealism, acosmic idealism, realism.

2. Why is Descartes commonly regarded as the father of modern idealism?

3. Give an enunciation of the principle of immanence.

4. Show how idealism leads to universal scepticism.

5. Explain why the intellect, in attaining its own conceptions, knows external things.

BOOK II

Truth

Prologue. — We have learned that human knowledge is capable of the attainment of truth. Now we shall turn our attention to the study of truth as it is found in knowledge. First, we shall study truth as found in judgment; secondly, as found in simple apprehension and in reasoning; and thirdly, as found in the senses. Hence there will be three chapters in this book.

―――

TRUTH IN JUDGMENT

Prologue. — In the first chapter of this book, we shall deal first with truth in judgment, i.e., formal truth; secondly, with the states of the mind in regard to formal truth; thirdly, with ultimate criterion of formal truth; and, fourthly, with error. Therefore there will be four articles in this chapter.

Formal truth

- Statement of the question
- Thesis: Formal truth is found only in judgment; only ontological truth is found in simple apprehension
- Difficulty
- Formal truth formally consists in the adequate conformity of the formal concept with the object in reality
- Formal truth adds a predicamental relation to the act, i.e., to the judgment, of the intellect
- Comparison of formal truth and transcendental truth
- Formal falsity
- Relativism
- Corollaries

States of the mind in regard to formal truth

- Many states of the mind in regard to formal truth
- Probability
- Notion of certitude
- Division of formal certitude

Ultimate criterion of formal truth

- Statement of the question
- Thesis: The ultimate and infallible criterion of properly known truth is the evidence of truth
- Faith
- Common sense
- Historical testimony

Error

Statement of the question

Thesis: The proximate cause of error is the extension of assent beyond what was apprehended; and its remote cause is always some influence of the free will

Ultimate root and occasion of error

FORMAL TRUTH

576. Statement of the question. — 1° Truth has been already defined: *the adequation*, i.e., *conformity, of a thing and an intellect.* But truth has different meanings, as we know from common sense. When one of the senses has knowledge of an object, there is a certain conformity between a thing and the knowing faculty, but the sense is not said to know truth; v.g., when a dog sees a color, it may be said to know a *true* color, but not to know *truth.*

Similarly, if we make use of the sign, *man*, this sign is not said to signify truth or falsity. But, if we make use of a proposition, v.g., *man is an animal, snow is white*, this proposition, according to all, is said to signify a truth. Moreover, since the proposition signifies that which the intellect knows, the proposition is said to signify a truth of a kind all its own, that is to say, *a truth as known by the intellect.*

Truth as known by the intellect is called *formal truth;* but some give it the less accurate name of *logical truth.* Formal truth is distinct from *ontological truth*, i.e., *transcendental truth.*

2° We shall now define these two kinds of truth.

Trascendental or *ontological truth* is the conformity of a thing to an intellect, i.e., it is the thing itself as it is conformed to the divine intellect, and is capable of being conformed to the created intellect.

Formal truth, which is known truth, is the conformity of the intellect with the thing, this conformity being known by the intellect.

3° Truth, as it is in the intellect, is called *formal truth* for two reasons: *first*, because the term truth is first applied to a truth as it is in the intellect.   This is so because truth is first manifested to us, in as much as truth is known by the intellect;

secondly, because truth is formally manifested to us, in as much as it is known by the intellect.   Therefore such a truth is called formal, according to the formality of its manifestation and certitude.

4° Authors disagree as regards the act of the intellect in which formal truth is found.

a) Ferrariensis, Arriago, Pesch, and others hold that formal truth exists perfectly in judgment, and imperfectly in simple apprehension.

b) Suarez, John of St. Thomas, and others maintain that formal truth is found only in judgment, and that only ontological truth is found in simple apprehension.

577. Statement of the thesis.

THESIS.—FORMAL TRUTH IS FOUND ONLY IN JUDGMENT; ONLY ONTOLOGICAL TRUTH IS FOUND IN SIMPLE APPREHENSION.

First part.— *Formal truth is found only in judgment.*— Formal truth is found only in that act of the intellect in which the intellect knows its own conformity with the thing.   But only in judgment does the intellect know its own conformity with the thing.   Therefore formal truth is found only in judgment.

The *major* is evident from the statement of the question.

Minor.— In simple apprehension, the intellect knows only the thing, but in judgment, in affirming or denying a predicate of a subject, it identifies or does not identify the form which it apprehends with a subject in the same being, i.e., in the same thing.   Therefore it sees that that which it knows is in conformity with the thing. (¹).

---

(1) 1, q. 16, a. 2, c. — *De Veritate*, q. 1, a. 3.

Second part.— *Only ontological truth is found in simple apprehension.*— Only ontological truth is found in an act of the intellect in which the intellect in merely constituted in its proper nature as a faculty which knows. But in simple apprehension the intellect is merely constituted in its proper nature as a knowing faculty. Therefore only ontological truth is found in simple apprehension.

Major.— A thing, as it is constituted in its proper nature, has being comformed to the divine intellect, and capable of being conformed to the human intellect. It is in this that ontological truth consists.

Minor.— In simple apprehension, the intellect attains a being as its object. But the intellect, as it attains a being as its object, is merely constituted in its proper nature as a knowing faculty, since the intellect as a knowing faculty of its very essence has being as its object, as is certain from the principle of contradiction.

578. Difficulty. — Formal truth is found only in that act of the intellect in which the intellect reflects on its own knowledge: for formal truth is the conformity between knowledge and the thing, as this conformity is *known*. But the intellect does not reflect upon its own knowledge in judgment. Therefore formal truth is not found in judgment.

Major. — By reflection either by a special act, distinct from its judgment (in actu signato), or in a concomitant manner in its act of judgment (in actu exercito), *I concede;* only by a special act, distinct from its judgment, *I deny.*

Minor. — The intellect does not reflect on its own knowledge by a special act distinct from its judgment, *I concede;* in a concomitant manner in its act of judgment, *I deny* (1).

It is evident that the intellect, in making a judgment, does not make a special act, distinct from its judgment, in order to discover whether its knowledge is conformed to the thing known. But, in affirming that the form conceived, signified by the predicate, is identified with the thing signified by the subject, it knows by that very fact that its conception is conformed to the thing known.

579. Formal truth formally consists in the adequate conformity of the formal concept with the object in reality. — 1° There is a distinction to be made between objective concept and formal concept.

---

(1) CAJETANUS, *In I*, q. 16, a. 2.

An objective concept is *what the intellect knows of a thing*, i.e., the thing as conceived and attained by knowledge.

A formal concept is the *representation expressed by the intellect when it conceives and attains a thing.*

In judgment, the formal concept is the mental enunciation.

2° Durandus and Vasquez affirm that formal truth consists in the conformity between the objective concept and the thing in itself, i.e., between the thing as known and the thing in itself, that is to say, the thing as it is in reality.

This opinion tends to idealism, because it destroys to too great an extent the identity between the thing known and the thing in itself.

A thing known, which is an objective concept, may be considered under two aspects: either in as much as it is a certain thing, or in as much as it is extrinsically denominated by knowledge.

In as much as it is a certain thing, it is not distinct from the thing as it is in itself, but is the very thing which exists in reality.

In as much as it is extrinsically denominated by knowledge, the thing known is distinguished only by a distinction of reason from the thing in itself, in virtue of its state, i.e., its extrinsic denomination. For the thing known is the thing in itself which presupposes the knowledge by which it is denominated.

Hence, if we make a distinction of reason between the thing known, i.e., the objective concept, and the thing in itself, and later admit conformity between the thing known and the thing in itself, we must presuppose that there is conformity between our knowledge, i.e., the formal concept, and the object in reality. For there is conformity between the thing known and the thing in itself only because there is conformity between our knowledge, i.e., the formal concept, and the object as it exists in reality ([1]). In other words, we must know beforehand that

---

(1) *Confirmatur:* quia conceptus objectivus est ipsum objectum ut conceptum seu cognitum, ita quod ly *cognitum* est denominatio extrinseca ex cognitione proveniens: non enim potest intelligi conceptus objectivus, seu

formal truth is the conformity of the formal concept with the object in reality.

3° We shall now prove that *formal truth consists in the adequate conformity of the formal concept with the object in reality.*

Formal truth is found in the intellect in as much as the intellect knows truth. But the intellect knows truth in as much as the formal concept is conformed to the object in reality. Therefore formal truth consists in the adequate conformity of the formal concept with the object in reality.

The *major* is evident from our foregoing remarks.

Minor.— The intellect knows truth in as much as it knows that a thing exists. But the intellect knows that a thing exists not by an objective concept, which is the thing known, but by a formal concept, which represents the thing as it is in itself to the intellect, i.e., by a formal concept in as much as it is conformed to the object in reality. Therefore.

objectum conceptum, nisi ratione conceptus et cognitionis concipientis ipsum. Vel ergo adaequatio et conformitas inter conceptum objectivum et rem in se (in qua dicitur consistere veritas formalis) est inter conceptum in quantum est res quaedam, vel in quantum denominatur objective talis a cognitione, denominatione extrinseca. — Primo modo esse non potest: quia res illa, quae est conceptus objectivus, non est alia res ab ea quae in re invenitur: eadem enim res, quae est in se, est etiam cognita et objecta intellectui; et sic inter ipsam in statu objectivo, et in re, non datur conformitas seu adaequatio, sed identitas et unitas in ratione rei; unde non esset capax falsitatis et inadaequationis, quia semper est identitas et unitas quantum ad entitatem et rem talis conceptus cum re et entitate quae est a parte rei; ergo numquam inter ipsos potest esse falsitas et inadaequatio. At conceptus qui in nobis habet veritatem formalem, est talis quod potest habere inadaequationem et falsitatem; ergo non potest esse conceptus objectivus, sed formalis. — Si autem ista conformitas sumatur inter conceptum objectivum et rem in se, non ratione entitatis quae una et eadem est, sed ratione status et denominationis qua dicitur objective esse conceptum et attactum, talis denominatio cogniti et objecti supponit ipsam cognitionem et conceptum formalem, a quo fit illa denominatio objectivi in ratione objectivi; ergo supponit etiam adaequationem ipsius conceptus formalis cum re quae est objectum: quia si cognitio ipsa, seu conceptus formalis, non esset adaequatus rei, nec etiam objectivus (qui in quantum talis a formali denominatur) adaequatus esset prout talis. Prius ergo est conceptum formalem esse adaequatum rei in se, quam conceptum objectivum sub denominatione objectivi; ergo si inter objectivum et rem in se ponitur adaequatio veritatis formalis, a fortiori debet poni inter ipsum conceptum formalem et rem in se; et principalius in ipso, cum sit forma intrinsece reddens intelligentem, et extrinsece denominans rem objectam et cognitam, quae est conceptus objectivus in ratione objectivi. — JOANNES A SANCTO THOMA, *Cursus Theol.*, t. II, p. 606 (Sol.).

580. Formal truth adds a predicamental relation to the act, i. e., to the judgment, of the intellect. — 1°
It is certain that the judgment of intellect, in which alone formal truth is found, has a relation to the thing.   For a judgment is true in as much as it knows a thing as it is in itself.

Now the question arises: is the relation which formal truth adds to the act, i.e., to the judgment, of the intellect a transcendental relation, a relation of reason, or a predicamental relation?   Let us see.

2° Suarez affirms that the only addition which formal truth makes to the act of the intellect is a transcendental relation to the object as it exists in reality.   Hence, according to Suarez, formal truth is the act of knowledge transcendentally related to the object and connoting it as it exists in reality.

This affirmation is inadmissible.   A thing is transcendentally related to an extrinsic term in as much as it is related to this extrinsic term by its absolute entity.   Hence the transcendental relation remains, even when the extrinsic term is changed; v.g., the soul has a transcendental relation to the body; and, even when the body corrupts, the soul retains its transcendental relation to the body.   But, if the object is changed, formal truth no longer exists, but is changed into falsity; v.g., the enunciation, *Socrates is seated*, is true as long as Socrates is seated; but, if Socrates ceases to be seated, the enunciation becomes false.

Hence formal truth adds something more than a transcendental relation to the act of the intellect; it adds either a relation of reason or a predicamental relation (cf. n. 151, 2) to the act of the intellect.   Therefore we are now confronted with the question: is this addition a relation of reason or a predicamental relation?

3° A distinction must be made between speculative truth and practical truth.

Truth is pratical in as much as the intellect is factive of the things which it measures.   Under this aspect, the intellect has only a relation of reason to things, for the relation of the measure to the measurable is a relation of reason, because the measure has no real dependence on the measurable.

Truth is speculative in as much as the intellect is measured by the thing. Formal truth, as speculative, adds to knowledge, i.e., to the act of the intellect, a real, i.e., predicamental, relation to the thing, if the thing exists either in itself, or in its cause, or in its effect. We have in this case everything required for the existence of a predicamental relation:

a) a real subject;

b) a real term;

c) a real foundation;

4° a) The real subject is the act of knowledge, i.e., the formal concept, the intellect as knowing.

b) The real term is the thing in which the knowledge of the intellect is terminated.

c) The real foundation is the real dependence of the act of knowledge on the external thing, because the act of the knowledge is really measured by the thing as it is in itself.

581. Comparison of formal truth and transcendental truth. — 1° Truth, in general, is defined: *the conformity of an intellect and a thing.* Truth, considered only under the aspect of its being a conformity, appertains equally to the intellect and to things: a thing is true in as much as it is conformed to its examplar, i.e., to its idea; and the intellect is true in as much as it is conformed to things.

2° But, if we consider the conditions of truth, we find that truth does not appertain equally to the intellect and to things: under some aspects, truth is found chiefly in things; and, under other aspects, it is found chiefly in the intellect.

Truth may be considered under the following aspects:

a) as immutable and firm;

b) as a property of being, which distinguishes true being from fictitous being;

c) as the object of the intellect;

d) as manifested;

e) as a measure, or as a thing measured;

f) as named, i.e., according to the derivation of its name.

3° *a*) Truth, considered from the point of view of immutability and firmess, is found chiefly in the divine intellect, from whose ideas truth in creatures derives. Hence truth, under this aspect, is in creatures only by participation. Yet, truth as participated by creatures is found chiefly in things rather than in the created intellect, because the created intellect wholly derives its foundation of firmess and certitude from things.

b) Truth, as a property of being and as the object of the intellect, is found essentially and chiefly in things.

c) As manifested, truth is found essentially and chiefly in the intellect, because the manifestation and apprehension of truth are in the intellect only. Truth as manifested is called formal truth, from the formality of its manifestation, and, as we pointed out earlier (n. 520), is found in things only by extrinsic denomination.

d) As a measure, truth is found principally in the divine intellect, because the divine intellect is the principle and measure of all things.

In things, truth is found as measured by its conformity and relation to the divine intellect; and as measuring, by its relation to the created intellect. Indeed, the created intellect derives its truth from its conformity to things.

In the created intellect, truth is found, as regards the speculative intellect, as something measured, because the speculative intellect is dependent on its object, as on its measure and mover. As regards the practical intellect, truth is found in the created intellect as a measure, because the practical intellect regulates and determines the things which it makes.

e) From the point of view of the derivation of its name, truth is found first in the intellect, i.e., truth first derives its name from formal truth. Indeed, truth receives its name from the kind of truth which is the better known and the more manifest to us; and this is truth as found in the intellect.

4° Absolutely speaking, we must state that *in creatures* transcendental truth is more perfect than formal truth, for divine truth immediately descends to things, and from things is communicated to the knowledge possessed by the intellect ([1]).

582. Formal falsity. — Just as the conformity of knowledge with reality is truth, so the non-conformity of knowledge with reality is falsity.

The non-conformity of knowledge with things is of two kinds: negative and positive.

a) The *non-conformity* of knowledge with a thing is *negative* when knowledge does not represent everything which is in the thing; v.g., when we say: man is a living being.

This non-conformity renders the knowledge not false, but incomplete. Thus, for example, no one would say that a statue of Mercury which does not represent everything found in Mercury is a false statue of that Roman god.

b) The *non-conformity* of knowledge with a thing is *positive* when the knowing subject attributes something to a thing which does not belong to it, or when it excludes from a thing something which belongs to it. It is in this that falsity formally consists, for to say that a thing is what it is not, or to deny that it is what it is, is to say what is false.

Hence formal falsity is defined: *the positive non-conformity*, i.e., the positing of non-conformity, *between knowledge and a thing.*

583. Relativism. — 1° *Preliminaries. a*) Philosophical relativism (*logical relativism, logical evolutionism*) is the teaching of those who contend that any judgment we make concerning a thing may be changed and yet always be a true judgment, even though the thing concerning which the judgment is made remains entirely unchanged. Furthermore, the advocates of relativism maintain that all true propositions *must change* with the evolution of the mind, in order that they may remain true of a determinate object.

---

(1) JOANNES A SANCTO THOMA, *Cursus Theol.*, t. II, p. 618 (Sol.).

b) The root of relativism is *idealism*, which teaches that our knowledge does not attain things as they are in themselves, but attains only their modifications in us, and conceives truth as the conformity of our judgments with these modifications.

c) Philosophical relativism has been condemned by the Church ([1]).

2° The proposition which follows is a statement of the truth which relativism denies.

PROPOSITION.—IF A THING REMAINS UNCHANGED, EVERY TRUE PROPOSITION CONCERNING IT MUST REMAIN UNCHANGED.

If a thing remains unchanged, whatever is predicated of it must always pertain to it or not pertain to it.   But a true proposition is a proposition in which something is predicated of a subject as pertaining or not pertaining to it.   Therefore.

Major.—If this were not so, the principle of contradiction would be set at naught: a thing could be and not be at the same time and in the same respect.

584. Corollaries. — 1° Therefore a true proposition concerning eternal, necessary, and immutable objects is eternal, necessary, and immutable.

2° If a thing is changed, a true proposition concerning it, considered before the change, must remain unchanged; but, in order that the proposition remain true concerning the thing when *changed*, it too must be changed.   This can be illustrated by a consideration of the proposition: *Peter is seated.*   If later Peter is not seated, the proposition remains true in as much as Peter was seated *at the former moment.*   But, if we consider Peter as having undergone a change, i.e., as not seated, the proposition must be changed, in order that it remain true. And this is the reason why in Cosmology we did not condemn Ein-

---

(1) DENZINGER-BANNWART, n. 2058.

stein's physical principle of relativity. Quantity considered according to various circumstances, i.e., according to various systems of reference, changes, and therefore its definition must be changed.

POINTS FOR REVIEW

1. Define: truth in general, formal truth, logical relativism.

2. Give two reasons why truth, as it is known by the intellect, is called formal truth.

3. How does the intellect reflect on its own knowledge in judgment?

4. Explain why the following statements are true, or are false: a) a thing as known is distinct from the thing in itself; b) formal truth consists in the conformity between the objective concept and the thing in itself; c) formal truth adds only a transcendental relation to the act of the intellect.

5. State what relation to the thing formal truth adds to the act a) of the practical intellect, b) of the speculative intellect.

6. Explain how truth is found in things and also in the created intellect as a measure and as the measured.

7. Why, strictly speaking, is transcendental truth more perfect than formal truth in creatures?

8. What is the root of logical relativism?   Explain.

STATES OF THE MIND IN REGARD TO FORMAL TRUTH

585. Many states of the mind in regard to formal truth. — Formal truth, we recall, is the conformity of intellective knowledge with reality.   On account of the imperfection of the human intellect, this conformity cannot be equally perspicuous in all judgments, and therefore there must be various states of the human mind in regard to truth.   These states are the followings: *nescience, ignorance, error, doubt, opinion,* and *certitude.*

a) Nescience is the simple negation of undue knowledge; v.g., the negation of jurisprudence in a medical doctor as such.

b) Ignorance is the lack of due knowledge; v.g., the lack of jurisprudence in a judge.

c) Error is a judgment which is not in conformity with reality i.e., it is a state of the intellect in which the intellect assents to something as true which is false; v.g., man is a donkey.

d) Doubt is a state of the mind in which the mind adheres to neither of two contradictory propositions on account of the fear of erring.   In doubt there is no judgment, but rather the suspension of judgment.

Doubt is *negative* if there is suspension of judgment because there is not sufficient reason for adherence to one of the two contradictory propositions rather than to the other.

Doubt is *positive* if there is suspension of judgment because the reasons for each of the two contradictory propositions seem to be of equal value.

e) *Opinion* is a state of the mind in which adherence is given to one of two contradictory propositions, but with fear of the opposite.

Suspicion is not essentially distinct from opinion. Suspicion is defined: the assent of the intellect given to one of two contradictory propositions for a light reason.

Opinion formally consists in the weak assent of the intellect. This weakness of assent causes fear in the appetite, for fear is not properly an act of the intellect, but rather is an act of the appetite in regard to evil.

f) *Certitude* is the determination of the intellect to a given object (ad unum).

586. Probability. — 1° Probability is the opposite of certitude. And, since certitude is the determination of the intellect to a given object, i.e., a total determination, probability is a partial or incomplete determination of the intellect.

2° Probability is found both *in reality* and *in the intellect*.

Probability in reality obtains when a future effect is not completely determined in its causes; v.g., we say that a future event which results from a defectible cause is probable.

Probability in the intellect is a determination of the assent of the intellect which is not complete, but only partial; v.g., in opinion.

Probability in the intellect can result either from probability in reality, or from a deficiency of knowledge which is not completely measured by a thing which can be certain in itself; v.g., if a judge has knowledge of the perpetration of a crime only from witnesses, or from signs which do not completely manifest the perpetration of the crime.

3° Probability admits of degrees, and therefore opinion can be probable, more probable, or most probable.

The probability of one opinion is not always and necessarily lessened by the probability of the opposite opinion, because there can be disparate motives for each opinion; but, if the reasons are from the same source, the probability of one opinion lessens the probability of the opposite opinion, as is self-evident.

Similarly, the greater probability of one opinion does not destroy the probability of the opposite opinion, because the probability of an opinion can be destroyed only by the complete evidence of the opposite opinion.

587. Notion of certitude.—1° Certitude is the *determination of the intellect to a given object* (ad unum) ([1]), or it is the *firm adherence of the intellect to its knowable object* ([2]).

2° Certitude may be considered either as it is found in the intellect, i.e., as *formal certitude*, or as it is a cause which produces firmness of assent of the intellect, i.e., as *certitude as a cause*.

Formal certitude is the *certitude which is found in the act of the intellect*.

Certitude as a cause is *certitude considered in the cause which produces formal certitude*.

3° But the cause which determines the assent of the intellect is either an object, or it is the will.   Hence certitude as a cause is either *objective* or *subjective*.

Objective certitude is *the certitude of the object which manifests itself to the intellect and obtains its assent*.

Subjective certitude is *the certitude of the will which makes the intellect adhere to a truth*.

588. Division of formal certitude. − 1° Formal certitude, considered in reference to the speculative intellect and the practical intellect, is *speculative* and *practical*.

Speculative certitude is *the certitude of the intellect, as the intellect is measured by things*, i.e., the certitude of a judgment

---

(1) *In III Sent.*, dist. 23, q. 2, a. 2, q. 3, c.
(2) *In III Sent.*, dist. 26, q. 2, a. 4, c.

whose object is a speculative truth; v.g., the certitude of the principle of contradiction.

Practical certitude is the certitude *of the prudent*, i.e., *prudential certitude*, as the intellect directs human acts in conformity with the rules of human life, or it is the certitude *of the artificer*, i.e., *of art*, as art is governed by its own proper rules. In other words, practical certitude is the certitude of a judgment whose object is a practical truth; v.g., the certitude of judgment proper to an artist.

2° Formal certitude, considered in relation to the truth of things, is *intrinsic* or *extrinsic*.

Intrinsic certitude is *the certitude of the intellect when it assents to a truth known in itself*, i.e., *in its evidence*. In other words, it is the certitude of a judgment which attains a truth in itself. This takes place when the intellect, in the light of evidence, perceives the conformity of its knowledge to the thing known.

Extrinsic certitude is *the certitude of the intellect when it assents to a truth not because it attains it in itself, but because it has knowledge of its evident credibility or probability;* v.g., the certitude of a person who never saw Rome, but who knows Rome exists (certitude of credibility); the certitude of a physical law known by a sufficient induction (certitude of probability).

3° Intrinsic certitude may be *physical* or *metaphysical.*

Physical certitude is *certitude which is founded on experimental and intuitive knowledge;* v.g., Peter exists.

Metaphysical certitude is *the certitude which obtains when a truth is known, immediately or mediately, from the notion of its terms;* v.g., the whole is greater than any of its parts.

4° Extrinsic certitude may be certitude *without objective incertitude*, or *probable* certitude.

Extrinsic certitude without objective incertitude is *certitude which results from divine faith;* for divine testimony is infallible, so that a person who assents to a truth on account of divine testimony can have no fear of erring in regard to the object he believes, even though he does not attain this object in itself.

Probable certitude (1) is *certitude which results either from human faith, or from evidently probable motives.*

This kind of certitude is called probable, because it is the determination of the intellect in regard to things which are true in the majority of cases; v.g., a judge who bases his condemnation of malefactors on the testimony of men gives a correct judgment in the majority of cases.

It is to be observed that probable certitude is concerned with truth manifested by evidently probable testimony or motives, not with the testimony itself or with the probable motives, of which it is possible to have intrinsic certitude.

5° From the point of view of reflexion, certitude is either *vulgar* or *scientific.*

Vulgar certitude is *certitude which is not based on explicit and reflex knowledge of motives;* v.g., the knowledge of natural reason.

Scientific certitude is *certitude which is based on explicit and rflex knowledge of motives;* v.g., the philosophical knowledge of God's existence.

6° From the point of view of the influence of the will, certitude is either *necessary* or *free.*

Necessary certitude is *certitude concerning truths in which the assent of the intellect is forced by evidence, so that the will can give its approval of it by following it, but cannot, as long as the evidence remains, seriously withold or revoke that approval;* v.g., certitude concerning first principles.

Free certitude is *certitude concerning truths in which the assent is not forced by evidence, but is only reasonably necessary.* In this case, the will can and ought to command the intellect to give its assent, but it can also prevent the intellect from giving its assent.

_____

(1) II-II, q. 70, a. 2, c.

POINTS FOR REVIEW

1. Define: error, positive doubt, negative doubt, probability in general, certitude as a cause, objective certitude, subjective certitude, formal certitude, prudential certitude, and probable certitude.

2. Distinguish between: ignorance and nescience; doubt and opinion; probability in the intellect and probability in reality; speculative certitude and practical certitude.

3. Is certitude of faith intrinsic certitude? Explain.

———

ULTIMATE CRITERION OF FORMAL TRUTH

589. Statement of the question. — 1° A criterion (χριτήριον), in general, is a means used to judge a thing. Therefore a criterion of truth is a means by which a truth is recognized, and is distinguished from falsity. It is defined: *a means which manifests truth.*

2° The means which manifests formal truth in the human mind is either subjective, — the intellect and the other cognitive powers, — or objective. Therefore we make a distinction between a *subjective* criterion and an *objective* criterion.

Since the human intellect and the other cognitive powers are measured by things and are dependent on them, these faculties cannot be the ultimate criterion of truth.

3° The objective criterion can be understood: *a)* as *particular*, i.e., in a certain determinate order; v.g., the supreme criterion of all *demonstrable* truth is the principle of contradiction; *b)* as *ultimate* and *universal*, i.e., in as much as it is valid for all truth and certitude (of the natural order).

4° We state in the thesis that the criterion of all properly known truth, i.e., truth known in itself, is the evidence of truth.

a) A properly known truth, i.e., a truth known in itself, is a truth to which the intellect gives its assent, because it perceives the connexion between the subject and predicate, either from experience, v.g., Paul is sick, or immediately from the notion of the terms, as in first principles, or from reasoning, as in a conclusion. Known truth, i.e., truth known in itself, is distinct from believed truth, of which we shall speak later.

b) The evidence of truth, which the philosophers of old described as *the brillance of truth which ravishes the assent of the mind* (fulgor veritatis assensum mentis rapiens), is defined: the *transcendental truth of being which actually causes formal truth*, i.e., *a true judgment.*

5° The evidence of truth is an infallible criterion because it admits of no error or falsity in the intellect.

6° *a*) The Traditionalists teach that the utimate criterion of all truth is either the authority of the human race, as was the opinion of Lamennais (1782-1854); or, as Huet (1630-1721) thought, divine authority, i.e., divine revelation as proposed in the teaching of the Church.

b) Thomas Reid (1710-1796) and the Scottish School, called the school of common sense, maintained that the criterion of all truth is a blind instinct of nature which compels us to firmly admit certain things. Gratry (1805-1872) claimed that it is a certain interior and divine sense or sentiment.

c) The Pragmatists, as William James (1842-1910), hold that this criterion is utility for public or private life: anything that contributes to public or private happiness is true. In other words, success in life is the measure of truth.

d) Descartes taught that a clear and distinct idea is the ultimate criterion of all truth.

590. Statement of the thesis.

> **THESIS.**—THE ULTIMATE AND INFALLIBLE CRITE-
> RION OF PROPERLY KNOWN TRUTH IS THE
> EVIDENCE OF TRUTH.

First part.— *The ultimate criterion of properly known truth is the evidence of truth.*— The ultimate criterion of properly known truth is the means by which the intellect ultimately perceives that the form, i.e., the nature, signified by a predicate is identified or not identified with its subject. But the means by which the intellect ultimately perceives that a form, i.e., a nature, signified by a predicate is identified or not identified with its subject is the evidence of truth. Therefore the ultimate criterion of properly known truth is the evidence of truth.

Major.— Since the intellect perceives the connexion between the subject and predicate in any properly known truth, the means by which it ultimately perceives this connexion is the ultimate means which manifests truth, i.e., is the ultimate criterion of truth.

Minor.— The intellect ultimately perceives that the form signified by the predicate is identified or not identified with its subject in as much as the being to which the predicate is attributed is manifested to it as actually known, i.e., as evident.

Second part.— *The evidence of truth is an infallible criterion.* The means by which the intellect perceives that the form signified by a predicate is identified or not identified with its subject is an infallible criterion. But it is by means of the evidence of truth that the intellect perceives that the form signified by a predicate is identified or not identified with its subject. Therefore the evidence of truth is an infallible criterion.

Major.— If the intellect perceives that the form signified by a predicate is identified or not identified with its subject, there can be no question of falsity or of error, for otherwise the intellect would perceive and not perceive.

591.— Faith.— Faith is *thought with assent on account of the authority of a witness,* i.e., *the assent given to a truth on account of the knowledge and truthfulness of a witness.* It is obvious that the authority of a witness derives from his knowledge and truthfulness.

If we assent to a truth on the authority of God, we have *divine faith;* if the witness of the truth to which we give our assent is a creature, we have *created faith.*

2° Believed truth is not known: when the intellect gives its assent to a truth on the authority of a witness, its certitude is not intrinsic, because the intellect does not attain the truth in itself; its certitude is extrinsic. In other words, the intellect does not assent to a truth, because it is moved to do so by the evidence of an object, but rather because it is moved by the will, which regards the assent to the truth as a good.

3° We shall now explain briefly the process of an act of faith.

First, the intellect makes a speculative judgment of credibility, in as much as it judges that the truth proposed for its belief is not contradictory or absurd, and that the testimony of the witness is worthy of belief.

Secondly, given the act of simple complacence of the will, i.e., the act of simple volition in regard to the truth proposed and the testimony of the witness, the intellect makes a practical judgment by which it perceives that it would be a good to assent to the truth proposed, and to accept the testimony of the witness.

Thirdly, the will accepts this practical judgment of the intellect, and approves of the acceptance of the testimony of the witness and of the assent to the truth proposed.

Fourthly, the intellect, moved by the will, accepts the testimony of the witness, and assents to the truth proposed.

4° Therefore there are four cases of certitude in an act of faith:

a) the speculative certitude of the intellect, which passes judgment on the credibility of the truth proposed, i.e., which judges that the truth proposed is not absurd, and that the testimony of the one proposing the truth is worthy of belief;

b) the practical certitude of the intellect, which judges that assent to the truth proposed is a good;

c) the certitude of the will, i.e., *subjective certitude*, by which the will accepts the good proposed by the intellect. This certitude is a participation of the practical certitude which the intellect already possesses, and it is the cause of the subsequent assent of the intellect to the truth proposed.

d) the certitude of the intellect, in as much as it assents to the truth proposed. This certitude is not caused by the evidence of the truth proposed, but by the subjective certitude of the will. In other words, this certitude is not intrinsic, but rather is extrinsic.

592. Universal consent.— The consent of mankind is universal when all men, or at least the majority of men, admit the same truth .

Universal consent is the testimony of the human race; hence it does not make known a truth in itself, i.e., it does not produce knowledge of a truth, but rather it engenders an act of created faith in the person who accepts this testimony.

2° The universal consent of mankind, as an argument from authority, is of value when it is concerned with internal facts of which we have immediate consciousness, as, for example, with the existence of liberty, or with truths which are immediately known or almost immediately known, as, for example, with the precepts of the natural law; with the existence of the Supreme Author of the finality of the world. .

Furthermore, the universal consent of mankind in regard to truths such as these is not only an argument from authority, but is also an indication that the intellect has knowledge of these truths by the force of natural inclination. For the force of the natural inclination of the intellect explains the unanimous consent of mankind in regard to one and the same truth, provided that there is nothing which can explain its common error; v.g., for a long time all men believed that sun revolved around the earth, because they studied only the appearance of the movements of the sun and the earth.

593. Historical testimony. — Testimony, in general, is the manifestation by which a person makes known something he knows to another.

Testimony is divine or human, according as its author is God or a man. It is historical, if it is concerned with facts; dogmatic, if concerned with doctrine. Testimony may be oral, written, or handed down by monuments, etc.

2° To judge the value of historical testimony, there are three things which we must know:

a) whether the testimony is certain;

b) whether the witness has knowledge of what he reports i.e., whether the witness is not deceived;

c) whether the witness is truthful, i.e., whether the witness is not a deceiver.

3° In dealing with living witnesses who report facts of which they have immediate knowledge, we must examine the nature of the facts, the intellectual and moral qualities of the witnesses, the circumstances of the testimony, etc.

4° In the case of facts of the past, testimony can be oral, written, or monumental, i.e., transmitted by monuments.

a) If testimony is oral, we have oral tradition. In this case, an examination of its authenticity must be made. If it is found to be authentic, then the knowledge and truthfulness of the witnesses must be investigated.

b) If the testimony is written, the authenticity of the book must be investigated, i.e., we must find out whether it is the work of the author to whom it is ascribed, i.e., whether it contains, without interpolation or omission, the text of its author, and how it must be interpreted. Moreover, we must always investigate the question of the truthfulness of the author and of the sources of his information.

c) If the testimony is transmitted by means of monuments, v.g., by paintings, works of architecture, articles of clothing, implements of war, coins, seals, instruments of manual operation, etc., it must be examined in the light of internal and external signs, and according to the special rules employed in the study of the history of art, of numismatics, etc.

POINTS FOR REVIEW

1. Explain what you understand by each of the following terms: criterion (in general), criterion of truth, subjective criterion of truth, ultimate criterion of truth, evidence of truth.

2. Is there more than one kind of certitude found in an act of faith? Explain.

ERROR

594. Statement of the question. — 1° Error is illegitimate assent to what is false, i.e., it is a false judgment of the intellect: the intellect affirms that a thing is such as it is not, or denies that it is such as it is; in other words, the intellect makes an affirmation or denial opposed to objective reality. Error is *illegitimate* assent: for sometimes assent to what is false may be *legitimate* when, v.g., naturally or morally certain assent is given to something false, simply because physical or moral laws are not observed.

2° Error presents the following difficulty: since judgment presupposes simple apprehension, how is error possible? Error, it would seem, presupposes the apprehension of something which is not an object of knowledge. But what is not an object of knowledge cannot be apprehended. This difficulty, which Plato had raised in ancient times, led Spinoza and Cousin to affirm that error properly so-called does not exist, but only inadequate knowledge. But yet it is an evident and undeniable fact that error, in the proper sense of the term, does exist.

3° This same difficulty in regard to error led Descartes to the opinion that an erroneous judgment is not an act of the intellect, but an act of the will. Of course, this opinion is entirely untenable, for the simple reason that every judgment is formally an act of the intellect.

4° According to the teaching of Scholastics, an erroneous judgment derives formally and proximately from the intellect.

It s proximate cause is the extension of assent beyond what was apprehended. This extension results from the fact that in the assent some addition is made to what was apprehended of the subject; v.g., there is affirmed of a subject a predicate other than the predicate which was apprehended in it; or the intellect denies that a predicate is in a subject, because it apprehends the subject without its predicate. Hence error does not presuppose the apprehension of what does not exist, for there is always the apprehension of some predicate which is falsely affirmed or denied of a subject, but results from the fact that a person expresses a false opinion concerning things of which he has no knowledge ([1]).

The remote cause of error is the influence of the free will, in as much as the free will, desiring the assent of the intellect to a proposition whose evidence does not necessarily determine the intellect, efficiently moves the intellect to assent to it. The free will desires the assent of the intellect on account of *passion* or *prejudices*, or simply because of *precipitation, hastiness in acting*, etc.

595. Statement of the question.

THESIS.— THE PROXIMATE CAUSE OF ERROR IS THE EXTENSION OF ASSENT BEYOND WHAT WAS APPREHENDED, AND ITS REMOTE CAUSE IS ALWAYS SOME INFLUENCE OF THE FREE WILL.

First part.— *The proximate cause of error is the extension of assent beyond what was apprehended.* — The proximate cause of error is either the apprehension of what is not an object of knowledge or the extension of assent beyond what was apprehended. But the apprehension of what is not an object of knowledge is intrinsically repugnant. Therefore the proximate cause of error is the extension of assent beyond what was apprehended.

Minor.— Apprehension of its very nature is the apprehension of some object, and therefore the apprehension of what is non-existent is intrinsically repugnant.

_____

(1) *De Malo*, q. 3, a. 7.

Second part. — *The remote cause of error is always some influence of the free will.* — The remote cause of the assent of an intellect which is not necessarily determined by its object is always some influence of the free will ([1]).   But error is the assent of an intellect which is not necessarily determined by its object.   Therefore the remote cause of error is always some influence of the free will.

Minor. — In the case of error, the intellect cannot be determined by its object to give its assent, for the object is not presented to it as evident, i.e., as necessarily true.

596. Ultimate root and occasion of error. — *a)* The ultimate root of error, i.e., the reason why *we can err*, is the weakness of our nature: since human nature is the lowest of natures endowed with intellectuality and is immersed in matter, it depends objectively on the senses, and acquires knowledge by a slow step-by-step process, by the transition from confused knowledge to distinct knowledge.   *b)* The occasion of error is either the *falsity of the senses;* or the nature of certain things which, because of their *immateriality*, are too remote from the senses, and therefore remain quite obscure to us; or the innumerable *mutual relations* of resemblance, of occurrence in space and time, etc., of material things, which easily lead to the danger of confusion.

POINTS FOR REVIEW

1. Explain why error is illegitimate assent to what is false.

2. Why did Spinoza affirm that error properly so-called does not exist?

3. Did Descartes hold that error is an act of the intellect?   Explain whether or not his opinion is tenable.

4. What is the proximate cause, the remote cause, the ultimate root, and the occasion of error?   Give reasons for your answers.

---

(2) II-II, q. 1, a. 4. — *In III Sent.*, dist. 23, q. 2, a. 2, q. 1.

CHAPTER II

TRUTH IN SIMPLE APPREHENSION
AND IN REASONING

Prologue.— We turn now from the study of truth in judgment to the study of truth in simple apprehension and in deductive reasoning. Since simple apprehension attains universals, we must devote some time to the study of universals. Hence there will be three articles in this chapter.

Truth in simple apprehension
{
Statement of the question
Thesis: Simple apprehension is essentially always true; accidentally it can be false
The intellect cannot be deceived concerning self-evident principles
}

Universals
{
  I. Statement of the problem
  II. Moderate realism
      Statement of the question
      Thesis: The direct universal-as-regards-the-thing-conceived exists in singulars as identified with them; the direct universal - in - its - state - of - abstraction and the reflex universal exist only in the intellect
  III. Nominalism
      Statement of the question
      Thesis: Nominalism is untenable
  IV. Conceptualism
      Statement of the question
      Thesis: Universals are not mere concepts
  V. Exaggerated realism
      Statement of the question
      Thesis: The universal does not exist apart from singulars, nor does it exist numerically the same in the singulars of which is predicated, nor formally as a universal in each singular thing
}

Truth in deductive reasoning

- Statement of the question
- Adversaries
- Thesis: Deductive reasoning is a source of new and true knowledge

TRUTH IN SIMPLE APPREHENSION

597. Statement of the question. — 1° Simple apprehension is defined: *the operation by which the intellect perceives a quiddity, without affirming or denying anything of it.*

2° We have already pointed out that only ontological truth is found in simple apprehension. Hence formal falsity cannot be found in it, but only falsity as in a false thing, in as much as the intellect, as a result of its act of simple apprehension, is led to make a false judgment on a thing.

3° St. Thomas teaches ([1]) that simple apprehension is *essentially* always true, and only accidentally can be false.

a) Simple apprehension is essentially true because it cannot, in virtue of the proper form by which the intellect is constituted in an act of simple apprehension, be deficient in truth, just as, for example, it is impossible for a man, in virtue of the form which is the rational soul, not to be a man.

b) Simple apprehension can be accidentally false in as much as it can be deficient in truth in virtue of something which is a consequence of its form, or which is accidental to its form, just as, for example, a man can fail to have two feet, because to be bipedal is a consequence of man's nature.

598. Statement of the thesis.

THESIS.— SIMPLE APPREHENSION IS ESSENTIALLY
ALWAYS TRUE; ACCIDENTALLY IT CAN
BE FALSE.

---

(1) I, q. 16, a. 3, et q. 17, a. 3. — *De Veritate*, q. 1, a. 3 et a. 12.

First part.— *Simple apprehension essentially is always true.*— Simple apprehension is essentially always true, if the intellect is constituted in its act of simple apprehension in as much as it has the form of another as of another, i.e., if it receives and possesses the form of another in such manner that this form still remains the form of the other as object. But the intellect is constituted in its act of simple apprehension in as much as it has the form of another as of another. Therefore simple apprehension is essentially always true.

Major.— If the intellect is constituted in its act of simple apprehension in as much as it has the form of another as of another, it is not able not to know the form, i.e., the quiddity, of the other.

Minor.—This is made manifest in judgment, especially in the principle of contradiction, in which the intellect perceives that the form signified by the subject and the form signified by the predicate belong to another, because it identifies or does not identify them in the same thing.

Second part.— *Simple apprehension can be accidentally false.*— Simple apprehension can be accidentally false, if it can be false because of judgment, i.e., because of the process of inquiry that precedes it. But simple apprehension can be false because of judgment, i.e., because of the process of inquiry that precedes it. Therefore simple apprehension can be accidentally false.

Major.— Simple apprehension can be false in two ways because of the process of inquiry that precedes it: a) by the attribution by the intellect of the definition of one thing to another; v.g., if a person, because of the false judgment he forms of what his senses tell him of a donkey, were to define a donkey *a rational animal;* b) or by the intellect's combining concepts which are incompatible in a definition; v.g., if a person were to define man: *an insentient rational animal.*

599. The intellect cannot be deceived concerning self-evident principles. — Self-evident principles are principles which are immediately known from their very terms. Hence there is no antecedent process of inquiry in regard to them, and therefore there can be no possibility of falsity, i.e., the intellect cannot be deceived in regard to them.

POINTS FOR REVIEW

1. Is it correct to say that simple apprehension is essentially true? Explain.

2. Show how simple apprehension can be accidentally false.

UNIVERSALS

I

STATEMENT OF THE PROBLEM

Everything we see existing about us is an individual, i.e., a singular thing, as Peter, this dog, that picture. On the other hand, we attribute universal predicates to these existing things: we say, for example, Peter is a man, is an animal, is a living being, etc. Hence arises the problem: what is the relation of universal predicates to the individual things of which they are predicates? Have these predicates any objective reality?

Such is the great problem of universals, a problem which has always commanded the attention of philosophers.

The earliest philosophers dealt with the problem. In the Middle Ages, it was more explicitly set forth; and, indeed, the controversies that arose concerning it occasioned the spilling of human blood in the streets of Paris.

In our own times, the problem is still of greatest importance, for on its solution depend the various systems concerned with the validity of human knowledge.

The principal opinions offered by philosophers as a solution of the problem of universals are the following: Moderate Realism, Nominalism, Conceptualism, and Exaggerated Realism.

We shall give a brief analysis of each of these opinions.

II

MODERATE REALISM

600. Statement of the question. — 1° Moderate realism was proposed by Aristotle, and received its determination from St. Thomas.

2° To understand this doctrine, we must first consider the meaning of a universal.

Etymologically, a universal signifies something one and multiple. Therefore it may be considered under two aspects: as one and as multiple. And thus we have the direct universal and the reflex universal.

3° The direct universal (metaphysical universal, universal of first intention) is one quiddity, one nature, abstracted from its individuation, i.e., *one nature as stripped of its singularity;* v.g., man.

The direct universal may be considered under two aspects: *a)* as regards what is conceived, and thus we have the *universal-as-regards-the-things-conceived* (quoad rem conceptam) ; *b)* as regards its state of abstraction from singularity, as it exists in the intellect, i.e., as regards the mode in which the thing is conceived (quoad modum concipiendi), and thus we have the *universal-in-its-state-of-abstraction.*

4° The reflex universal (formal universal, logical universal, universal of second intention) is nature abstracted from singularity, considered by the intellect in its relation to its inferiors, i.e., as capable of existing in them and of being predicated of them .

Hence a reflex universal presupposes a direct universal, i.e., an abstracted nature, and it adds to it the relation of this abstracted nature to inferiors, i.e., to singulars. This relation is constituted by the intellect by its comparing the direct universal with its inferiors. Thus, when I conceive man, a direct universal is produced; when I conceive man as capable of existing in many individuals, and as predicable of them, a reflex universal is produced.

5° According to moderate realism, the direct universal-as-regards-the-thing-conceived exists in singular things as identified with them; and the direct universal-in-its-state-of-abstraction and the reflex universal exist only in the intellect.

601. Statement of the thesis.

THESIS.—THE DIRECT UNIVERSAL-AS-REGARDS-THE-THING-CONCEIVED EXISTS IN SINGULARS AS IDENTIFIED WITH THEM; THE DIRECT UNIVERSAL-IN-ITS-STATE-OF-ABSTRACTION AND THE REFLEX UNIVERSAL EXIST ONLY IN THE INTELLECT.

First part.— *The direct universal-as-regards-the-thing-conceived exists in singular things as identified with them.*— A predicate which is attributed to singular subjects exists in them as identified with them. But the direct universal-as-regards-the-thing-conceived is attributed to singulars. Therefore the direct universal-as-regards-the-thing-conceived exists in singulars as identified with them.

Major.— In predication a subject and a predicate are identified in the same being.

Minor.— When we say: Peter is a man, we affirm that Peter is the same being as the being which is conceived as man.

Second part.— *The direct universal-in-its-state-of-abstraction exists only in the intellect.*— The direct universal-in-its-state-of-abstraction is nature conceived as stripped of its singularity. But nature stripped of its singularity exists only in the intellect. Therefore.

Minor.— Nature as it exists in reality is singular, and it

an only be stripped of its singularity in as much as the intel-
ect considers it without considering its individuation.

Third part.— *The reflex universal exists only in the intel-
ect.*— A being of reason exists only in the intellect.   But the
reflex universal is a being of reason.   Therefore the reflex universal exists only in the intellect.

Minor.—A reflex universal is an abstracted nature considered in its relation to singulars.   But this relation is constituted by the intellect by comparing the direct universal with
singulars, and therefore it is a being of reason.   Therefore.

III

NOMINALISM

602. Statement of the question. – Nominalists claim
that universals are mere *names*, not concepts.   In ancient times,
certain philosophers, as Heraclitus, who taught that all things
are in perpetual flux and who admitted only sensible knowledge,
professed nominalism, and, indeed, scepticism.

In the Middle Ages, Roscelin (d.1121) was the chief representative of nominalism.   He taught that a universal name
immediately designates a group of representations and of singular things.

After the seventeenth century, nominalism became wide-
spread under the form of *empirism*, in as much as empirism admits only sensible knowledge.

Modern nominalists commonly teach that a universal name
corresponds only to a concrete sensible image, which is common,
in as much as it is very imperfect.   Thus a statue can represent
some indeterminate man or other.

Representative of modern nominalists are such men as

Hobbes (¹), Berkeley (²), Hume (³), Condillac (⁴), Mill (⁵),
Taine (⁶), Ribbot, Wundt, etc.

603. Statement of the thesis.

THESIS.— Nominalism is untenable.

Nominalism is untenable, if a universal name signifies neither a singular, nor a group of singulars, nor a common image.
But a universal name does not signify a singular, or a group of
singulars, or a common image.   Therefore nominalism is untenable.

Major.— Nominalists teach that a universal signifies a singular, or a group of singulars, or is a common image.

Minor.— *a)* Not a singular, for in this case the name would
not be universal; *b)* nor a group of singulars; for when we say:
Peter is a man, the meaning would be: Peter is a group of men,
which, of course, is inadmissible; *c)* nor a common image. For
the common image, according to the admission of our adversaries, is something that is entirely fluid, mobile, quite confused,
which, only on account of its mutability, can successively represent several singulars.   But a universal name signifies something which always remains the same, and is most determinate;
v.g., color, as predicated of red, white, black, etc., is something
which always remains the same and is most determinate.
Therefore.

---

(1) *Leviathan.*
(2) *A Treatise concerning the Principles of Human Knowledge*, 1710.
(3) *A Treatise of Human Nature.*
(4) *Essai sur l'origine des connaissances humaines*, sect. 5, 6, 7, Oeuvres,
Paris, 1798, pp. 214-218.
(5) *An Examination of Sir Hamilton's Philosophy.*
(6) « Ce que nous appelons une idée générale, une vue d'ensemble, n'est
qu'un nom, non pas le simple son qui vibre dans l'air et ébranle notre oreille,
ou l'assemblage de lettres qui noircissent le papier et frappent nos yeux, non
pas même des lettres aperçues mentalement, ou ce son mentalement prononcé,
mais ce son ou ces lettres doués, lorsque nous les apercevons ou imaginons,
d'une propriété double, la propriété d'éveiller en nous les images des individus
qui appartiennent à une certaine classe et de ces individus seulement, et la
propriété de renaître toutes les fois qu'un individu de cette même classe et
seulement quand un individu de cette même classe se présente à notre mémoire
ou à notre expérience. » — *De l'Intelligence*, t. I, l. 1, c. 2, IV, 7e édit., Paris,
1895, pp. 42-43.

IV

CONCEPTUALISM

604. Statement of the question. — Conceptualists differ from Nominalists in as much as they admit that we can have truly universal concepts. But they claim that there is nothing whatsoever in reality which corresponds to these concepts.

In *antiquity*, certain Stoics (third century, B.C.) are cited who, though not denying the validity of sensible knowledge, held that conceptions or .ideas could be formed by the mind which are of use to us, but which represent nothing in reality.

In the *Middle Ages*, the chief representative of conceptualism was William of Ockam (d. 1347). He denied that a universal represented anything found in a singular thing. A universal exists only in the soul, and it is a sign which can, because of its symbolism, designate different things. Thus when we say: Peter is a man, the meaning of the proposition is: Peter is one of these things whose symbol can be *man*.

Locke (1632-1704) contended that universal ideas are not derived from reality, but are made by the mind for its own use. (1).

A most rigid form of conceptualism was taught by Kant. On the one hand, he affirmed the universality of our concepts, and, on the other, he denied that we can know the essences of things.

The most recent form of conceptualism is *present-day pragmatism*. According to pragmatism, the one and only reality is a vital process (élan vital) which is essentially dynamic and continually evolving. By universal concepts the mind renders this fluid reality immobile, and divides it into fixed,

---

(1) To return to general words, it is plain by what has been said that general and universal belong not to the real existence of things; but are the inventions and creatures of the understanding, made by it for its own use and concern only signs, whether words or ideas. — *Essay Concerning Human Understanding*, Book III.

rigid units, for the purpose of adapting the reality to the exigencies of action, — hence the name pragmatism, — but not for the purpose of knowing it.   We have knowledge of reality by a prelogical intuition, which is an intellectual sympathy by which the mind, abandoning its fixed concepts, makes its own the fluid life of the reality.

Representatives of this teaching are H. Bergson, (1859-1941), W. James (d.1910), Peirce (d.1914), J. Dewey, A. Sidgwick.

605. Statement of the thesis.

THESIS.—Universals are not mere concepts.

1° *From judgment.*— In judgment, a universal is predicated of a singular; v.g., we say: Peter is a living being.   But, if universals were mere concepts, a universal could not be predicated of a singular thing.   Therefore universals are not mere concepts.

Minor.— The intellect predicates a universal of a singular thing because it sees that the notes of the universal predicate are attributable to the singular thing, and are found in it.   But, if the intellect sees that the notes of the universal predicate are attributable to the singular thing, a universal cannot possibly be merely a concept which does not express the nature of a singular thing: otherwise the intellect would see something and not see it.

2° *From the danger of scepticism.*— If universals were mere concepts, scepticism would be tenable.   But scepticism is untenable.   Therefore.

Major.— If universals were mere concepts, we would have no knowledge of reality when we predicate a universal of a singular, and therefore scepticism would be admissible.

V

EXAGGERATED REALISM

606. Statement of the question. — Exaggerated realsm teaches that universals exist not only in name and in the mind, but also formally in reality, i.e., universals as such exist in ·eality.

a) Platonic realism.— Plato taught that universals exist formally as universal entities in an intelligible and immutable world, a world which the soul contemplated before its union with the body.   The sensible world is constituted by a participation of the intelligible world; and, when it is perceived by the senses, it recalls the intelligible world to the soul's memory.   Thus, besides the men whom we see, there exists in the intelligible world the existing idea of man, i.e., subsisting Man. All men are constituted by a participation of subsisting Man. And this is the reason why the universal concept which signifies subsisting man is predicated of singular men.   And so it is with all things, with the wolf, color, quantity, etc.

b) Medieval exaggerated realism.— 1) William of Champeaux (d.1120) at first taught that a universal is numerically same in all singular things of which it is predicated; v.g., the human nature of Peter and Paul is numerically the same, and is only accidentally modified in them.

2) Later, he rejected his earlier opinion, and taught that a universal is multipied in the indivliduals to which it is attributed, but that it remains a universal in each of them, as distinct from their singularity.   More briefly, he taught that a universal formally exists in each singular thing.

Closely allied to this opinion is the opinion of Scotus, who affirms that specific nature is individuated by its *thisness*, which is formally distinct from it before the consideration of the intellect.

607. Statement of the thesis.

THESIS.— THE UNIVERSAL DOES NOT EXIST APART
FROM SINGULARS. NOR DOES IT EXIST
NUMERICALLY THE SAME IN THE SIN-
GULARS OF WHICH IT IS PREDICATED,
NOR FORMALLY AS A UNIVERSAL IN
EACH SINGULAR THING.

First part.—*The universal does not exist apart from singulars.*— 1° If a universal existed apart from singulars, it could not be predicated of singulars: But a universal is predicated of singulars. Therefore a universal does not exist apart from singulars.

Major.—Universals are predicated of singulars in as much as the intellect sees that they are identified with singulars. But, if universals existed apart from individuals, they could not be identified with singulars, and would be things entirely distinct from them. Therefore.

2° If universals exist apart from singulars, they exist in themselves. But universals cannot exist in themselves. Therefore.

Minor.— Man can exist only in as much as he has these bones and this flesh, i.e., only in as much as he is an individual, i.e., a singular being. Similarly, an accident exists only in as much as it is received into a singular subject.

Second part.— Against the earlier opinion of William of Champeaux.— *The universal does not exist as numerically the same in the individuals of which it is predicated.*— 1° The earlier opinion of William of Champeaux is opposed to the testimony of conscience, by which every man perceives that he is a substance distinct from every other substance.

2° It leads to pantheism, for just as it admits of only one man, so it would have to admit of only one animal, one living being, one substance, and *one being.*

Third part.—Against the later opinion of William of Champeaux.— *The universal does not exist formally as a universal in each singular thing.*

1° If a universal existed formally as such in each singular thing, it would be singular and universal at one and the same time. But it is repugnant that a thing be at the same time singular and universal. Therefore a universal does not exist formally as such in each singular thing.

Major.— If a universal is formally in a singular thing, the generic and specific nature of every singular thing is universal in reality. But whatever is predicated of a generic and specific nature in reality is predicated of the singular thing; v.g., if man is rational, Peter is rational. Therefore, if a universal existed formally in every singular being, a being would be at the same time singular and universal; v.g., Peter, who is a singular being, would be at the same time universal man [1].

2° This opinion is opposed to true judgment in which a universal is identified with a singular thing, when v.g., we say: Peter is a man.

3° Moreover, this opinion is opposed to all predication. For, if a universal existed in a singular thing, it would be a part of this singular thing. But no part is predicated of the whole; v. g., we do not say: Peter is his head. Therefore.

POINTS FOR REVIEW

1. Briefly explain the aspects under which a direct universal may be considered.

2. Explain what is meant by the reflex universal, and show how it is distinct from the metaphysical universal.

3. Name and briefly outline the principal philosophical opinions concerned with the solution of the problem of universals.

---

[1] Enarratio Cajetani supra *De Ente et Essentia*, c. 4, 2. 8.

TRUTH IN DEDUCTIVE REASONING

608. Statement of the question. — 1° Reasoning in general is defined: *the operation by which the mind acquires knowledge of a truth from the knowledge of other truths which it already possesses.*

2° Deductive reasoning is reasoning by which the mind proceeds either immediately (categorical syllogism) or mediately (hypothetical syllogism), in virtue of the connexion of terms, from universal premises to a conclusion that is less general or particular.

3° In the thesis, we state that deductive reasoning is a source of new knowledge in as much as the conclusion caused by the premises expresses a truth not known before. Reasoning is also a source of true knowledge when it proceeds from true premises.

609. Adversaries. — Certain philosophers, especially since the time of the Renaissance, have denied the efficacy of a syllogism which is the expression of deductive reasoning. They argue from an example, v.g., from the following syllogism:

> *All men are mortal.*
> *But Socrates is a man.*
> *Therefore Socrates is mortal.*

A person who posits the *major*, they say, either already knows that the conclusion is true, or he does not know this; if he knows it is true, the deductive process is *useless*; if he does not know that it is true, he posits the major *unlawfully*: for if a person does not know that Socrates is mortal, he cannot lawfully affirm that all men are mortal.   Therefore either the syllogism gives no new knowledge, or it fails to produce true and certain knowledge.   Such in general is the reasoning of Luther, Bacon, Descartes, Hobbes, Hume, Compte, Stuart Mill, and, in more recent times, L. Brunschwicg.

610. Statement of the thesis.

THESIS.— DEDUCTIVE REASONING IS A SOURCE OF NEW AND TRUE KNOWLEDGE.

First part.—*Deductive reasoning is a source of new knowledge.* — Reasoning by which a virtually known truth is made actually known is a source of new knowledge.   But a virtually known truth is made actually known by deductive reasoning. Therefore deductive reasoning is a source of new knowledge.

The *major* is certain, for a truth which is only virtually known is not actually known, but only its cause is actually known; hence, if it becomes actually known, it is new knowledge.

The *minor* is proved by a syllogism of the first figure.   For the subject of a universal proposition which serves the function of major premise is not the sum of singular things, but is a universal whose connexion with the predicate is known not from an enumeration of singular things, but from the notion of them. In the minor, the universal subject is extended to an inferior. And therefore the premises cause the conclusion, which is virtually contained in them as an effect.

This is illustrated by the syllogism which follows:

> *Every animal is sentient.*
> *But Peter is an animal.*
> *Therefore Peter is sentient.*

The major is known from the mere notion of the subject and predicate, and therefore it is known without the conclusion's being known.   But, from the extension of *animal* to Peter, we know not only that Peter is sentient, but we know too the reason why he is sentient.

Second part.— *Deductive reasoning is a source of true knowledge.*— A conclusion which has a necessary connexion with true premises is true. But the conclusion of a deductive syllogism has a necessary connexion with true premises. Therefore the conclusion of a deductive syllogism is true, i.e., deductive reasoning is a source of true knowledge.

Major.— A syllogism, — perfect and demonstrative, — proceeds from true premises, and leads to a conclusion which, if the rules of Logic are observed, is necessarily connected with the premises.

CHAPTER III

TRUTH IN THE SENSES

Prologue.—We have already discovered the mode in which truth exists in the intellect; and now there remains for our consideration truth as it exists in the senses. We shall consider first how truth, and, secondly, how falsity can be in the senses. Hence there will be two articles in this chapter.

Truth in the senses
  { Statement of the question
    Thesis: Formal truth is not found in the external senses, but ontological truth is found in them

Falsity in the senses
  { Formal falsity cannot exist in the external senses
    Falsity of the senses in relation to the intellect
    Deception of the external senses as regards their object
    Idealism and critical realism
    Interpretationism or theory of interpretation

TRUTH IN THE SENSES

611. Statement of the question. — 1° The external sense is defined: *an organic cognitive faculty which attains its object without the mediation of other senses.* In this article, an external sense signifies not a faculty in first act, but a faculty in second act, i.e., as actually attaining its object.

2° Formal truth is truth as known, i.e., it is the conformity between the cognitive faculty and the thing, in as much as this conformity is known by the faculty.

Ontological truth is the truth of the thing, i.e., it is the nature of the thing as it has being conformed to the Divine Intellect and conformable to the human intellect.

612. Statement of the thesis.

THESIS. — FORMAL TRUTH IS NOT FOUND IN THE EXTERNAL SENSES, BUT ONTOLOGICAL TRUTH IS FOUND IN THEM.

First part.— *Formal truth is not found in the external senses.*— Formal truth is not found in a cognitive faculty which has no knowledge of its proportion, i. e., conformity, to things. But the external senses have no knowledge of their conformity to things. Therefore formal truth is not found in the external senses [1].

Major.— Formal truth consists essentially in the knowledge of the conformity of the cognitive faculty to the thing.

---

(1) I, q. 16, a. 2, and q. 17, a 2. — *De Veritate*, q. 1, a. 9.

Minor.— A cognitive faculty which has no knowledge either of its own nature, or of the nature of its act, cannot have knowledge of its proportion to the thing. But an external sense has no knowledge either of its own nature, or of the nature of its own act; because, as a material faculty, it cannot make a complete reflection upon itself, so as to have knowledge of its own nature. Therefore.

Second part.— *Ontological truth is found in the external senses.*— Ontological truth is found in cognitive faculties which have knowledge of things. But the external senses have knowledge of things. Therefore ontological truth is found in the external senses.

Major.— A cognitive faculty, in as much as it has knowledge of things, is constituted in its proper nature as knowing, and thus it is ontologically true, just as any other thing which has its own proper nature.

613. Truth in the internal senses. — An internal sense is an organic cognitive faculty whose knowledge presupposes the knowledge of the external senses. An internal sense has knowledge of intentions as brought together into a certain comparison. Hence there is found in the internal senses a certain judgment concerning singular things, and consequently a certain participation of formal truth and falsity. Thus, from the fact that several sensations have already been united, the phantasy sometimes judges that they are again united, when in reality they are not united; v.g., a person who touches an object which usually is hot judges by his phantasy that it is hot, when in reality it is not hot; a person who reads defective orthography judges that it is correct, etc. It is for this reason that Aristotle calls the phantasy the mistress of falsity (¹).

POINTS FOR REVIEW

1. Explain whether or not formal truth is found in both the external and the internal senses.

2. Is ontological truth found in the external senses? Prove your answer.

3. Is there any justification for calling the phantasy the mistress of falsity? Explain.

---

(1) *Metaph.*, l. IV, c. 4. — *De Veritate*, q. 1, a. 11.

FALSITY IN THE SENSES

614. Formal falsity cannot exist in the external senses. — Formal falsity is the opposite of formal truth ; and it is found in cognitive faculties when they judge that something exists which does not exist, and vice versa. But the external senses are incapable of the act of judgment, for they cannot reflect on their own knowledge and perceive the conformity of this knowledge to the thing known; they are capable of apprehension only, and therefore formal falsity cannot exist in them.

615. Falsity of the senses in relation to the intellect. — The external senses can be the cause of falsity in the intellect, because they can be the cause of a false judgment in the intellect, i.e., they can lead the intellect into making a false judgment.

It is to be observed that the senses can present an object to the intellect, and that this object may be either of the following: *a)* the sensation of the sense; *b)* the thing known by the sense.

In the presentation of its own sensation to the intellect, a sense can never be the cause of falsity in the intellect, i.e., can never deceive the intellect, In other words, a man cannot err in regard to his perception of the existence of a sensation in himself; but he can make a mistake as regards the nature of this sensation, or as regards its localization. Thus, for example, a man who is half-asleep can fancy that he sees with his eyes, when in reality this sensation exists only in his imagination, of which it is the product; a person who has had a foot amputated can fancy that he experiences the sensation of pain in that foot, whereas in reality he suffers pain in the wound left by the surgical operation, etc.

But a sense can be the cause of falsity in the intellect in the case in which the object it presents to the intellect is a thing of which it has false knowledge.   But yet a sense, in this case, does not necessarily cause falsity in the intellect, because the intellect is capable of detecting that the knowledge of the sense is false: for just as the intellect judges things in the light of evidence, so in the same light it can pass judgment on things presented to it by the senses, and thus can discover the errors of the senses.

616. Deception of the external senses as regards their object. — 1 *Preliminaries.* — *a*) The object of external sensation, i.e., the external sensible, is divided into proper sensible (sensible per se) and accidental sensible (sensibile per accidens).

A *proper sensible* is an object which the sense really attains, in as much as its species really informs the sense.

An *accidental sensible* is a thing which of itself is not the object of the sense, but which has a connexion with it in as much as it is immediately perceived by another faculty of the sentient subject on the occasion of sensation.

The accidental sensible is such as regards all the senses, if the intellect alone has immediate knowledge of it; v.g., substance truth, being, etc.; or it is such as regards a particular sense, if it is perceived by one of the other senses; v.g., if I see a lemon pie, I can immediately perceive its taste by one of the internal senses.   In this case, the taste of the pie is an accidental sensible for the sense of sight, i.e., it is accidentally visible.

b) The proper sensible is divided into immediate sensible (sensibile proprium) and mediate sensible (sensibile commune).

An *immediate sensible* is an object which directly moves one of the senses by its own proper species; v.g., color, sound, smell, taste, etc.

A *mediate sensible* is an object which a sense indirectly attains by means of an immediate sensible.   The *mediate* sensibles are accidents which pertain to quantity.

The principal mediate sensibles are *figure, movement, rest, number*, and *magnitude*.

The mediate sensible does not inform the sense by a species which is distinct from the species of the immediate sensible, for in the species there is represented the mediate sensible, as a condition and modification of the immediate sensible.

2° In the light of the foregoing preliminary observations, we are now prepared to deal with the problem of *how the external senses can be deceived as regards their object.*

a) In the case of the immediate sensible, the external sense can never be deceived directly, i.e., it can never be deceived because of the form by which it is constituted in its act of knowledge, because this form is the likeness of its proper object, and of itself leads to the apprehension of the proper object.

But yet, in the case of the immediate sensible, the external sense can be deceived accidentally, if the immediate sensible is impeded from adequately informing it; v.g., a sweet object can taste bitter to a person suffering from a disease of the tongue.

b) In the case of the mediate sensible, the external sense can be deceived accidentally, and also directly, that is to say, because of the form, i.e., the species, by which the immediate sensible is known. The mediate sensible is known not immediately, but by means of the immediate sensible. Hence it can happen that the mediate sensible remains partially hidden to the sense, even when the immediate sensible is adequately represented to it; v.g., it is possible that a person who sees a colored object does not see its whole extension; a person looking at a piece of wood in water can be deceived as regards its position in the water and see it as if it were divided, when in reality it is not divided.

c) In the case of the accidental sensible, the external sense cannot properly be deceived, but yet can engender false knowledge in another faculty of the sentient subject; v.g., the external sense of sight can apprehend movements in an inanimate being, and in consequence lead the intellect into the error of judging that this being is living.

617. Idealism and critical realism. — Idealism, according to its general principles, holds that the external senses are incapable of knowledge of sensible objects as distinct in their real being from sensation, and capable only of knowledge of sensation. Thus the Neo-Platonists and Berkeley (1685-1753) affirm that the corporeal world does not exist, but is a mere phenomenon of consciousness.

Critical realism teaches that the external senses can have knowledge of objects as distinct from sensation, but not immediate knowledge of them. It holds that a cognitive faculty can immediately attain only its own representation. But this representation corresponds to an external object, and therefore only mediately can a sentient subject attain an external object, i.e., the external senses can have only mediate knowledge of objects.

Critical realism infers—hence the name *illationism*,—that a subjective representation corresponds to an external thing. Some of the adherents of this opinion, as Descartes and Malebranche, base their contention on the fact of God's veracity; others, including Cousin, and some Scholastics, as Cardinal Mercier, Lemaire, etc., argue from the principle of causality: a subjective representation is an effect corresponding to an external thing as to its cause.

Idealism is false because it is based on false principles.

Critical realism also is false because it is partially idealism, in as much as it affirms that a cognitive faculty can immediately attain only its own modification, but not an external object.

Moreover, both idealism and critical realism are in opposition to the testimony of the intellect, which judges, in the light of evidence, that the external senses can have immediate knowledge of external objects as distinct from sensation. This testimony of conscience, it must be remembered, is infallible, because otherwise the intellect would perceive and not perceive.

618. Interpretationism or theory of interpretation. — 1° *a)* Locke made a distinction between *primary* and *secondary* qualities of bodies. The primary qualities, in his opinion, are extension, movement and rest, number, figure, impenetrability; and the secondary qualities are color, sound, smell, taste, hardness and softness, heat and cold. He taught that only the primary qualities are objective, i.e., formally exist in things, and that the secondary qualities are subjective, and are only modifications produced by bodies in a sentient subject which has knowledge of them. Therefore he affirmed that the external senses can have sensation of secondary qualities, only because bodies by their primary qualities have the power of producing this sensation in them. In other words, secondary qualities do not formally exist in bodies, but exist only causally, i.e., fundamentally, in them.

b) The majority of modern physicists, and some modern scholastics, as Mattiussi, Frobes, Balzer, de Sinety, Necchi, Grunder, etc. are adherents of interpretationism, or, as it is also called, the theory of interpretation.

2° *Judgement on interpretationism.*

a) Interpretationism must be regarded as untenable in so far as it teaches that primary qualities (immediate sensibles) can immediately move the external senses, for in reality they can move them only mediately, i.e., by means of secondary qualities (immediate sensibles).

b) It is evident from the clear and undeniable testimony of consciousness that secondary qualities can be attained as objects of the external senses. Therefore the objectivity of secondary qualities (immediate sensibles) is undeniable. Physicists have no right to deny the objectivity of what are called secondary qualities. Physics measures things *metrically*, and therefore it does not and cannot attain qualities as such, for it is concerned only with extension.

c) Now the question arises: do immediate sensibles exist in sensible things as they are actually attained by the external senses? Our answer to this question is as follows:

First, the question cannot be solved from the experience of the external senses, because the external senses are not capable of knowledge of the conformity which exists between the thing and what they apprehend concerning it (^{1}) : there can be neither judgment nor formal truth in the external senses. Hence the external senses cannot know whether an immediate sensible exists in reality or not.

Secondary, a study of external sensation allows us to make the observations that follow.

Sensation takes place only in as much as a sense is actually a *patient* in the proper sense of the term, i.e., only in as much as a sensible thing *acts* upon the sense. Moreover, since an agent acts by means of the form which it possesses, it is possible for us to make the following distinction: an immediate sensible is attained as it exists in second act by an external sense, for action is in the patient; but an immediate sensible exists formally only in first act in a sensible thing, that is to say, as the form by which the sensible acts on the sense.

But the problem is not solved by these observations; and it still remains very obscure, and must continue to do so, because sensation, as an act of an organic faculty, is not without unintelligibility.

POINTS FOR REVIEW

1. Explain why formal falsity cannot exist in the external senses.

2. Under what aspects can the senses be considered in relation to the intellect?

3. Explain whether or not an external sense can cause falsity in the intellect when the object it presents to it is: *a*) its own sensation; *b*) a thing of which it has knowledge.

4. Show whether or not deception of the external senses is possible in regard to any of the following: immediate sensibles, mediate sensibles, accidental sensibles.

5. State the teaching of critical realism, and also of interpretationism.

---

(1) I, q. 16, a. 2.

METAPHYSICS OF FINITE BEING

INTRODUCTION

619. Division of Metaphysics of finite being. — In this part of Metaphysics, finite being is considered simply in as much as it is being. Finite being can be both a cause and an effect. Finite being, as a composite being, has both intrinsic and extrinsic causes. First, we shall study finite being in itself, and later we shall deal with causes. Hence there will be two books in this part of Metaphysics.

Book I : Finite being.

Book II : Causes.

BOOK I

Finite being

Prologue. — We shall consider finite being as regards its composition.

When we have completed our study of the composition of finite being, we shall discuss substance and accident. Hence there will be three chapters in this book.

CHAPTER I

———

COMPOSITION OF FINITE BEING

Prologue. — Finite being is composed of two really distinct principles, namely, essence and existence. Composition of substance and accidents follows as a consequence of composition of essence and existence. Hence the matter of this chapter will be studied in two distinct articles.

Distinction between essence and existence in finite being

{
Statement of the question
Opinions
Thesis: The existence of a finite being is distinguished from its essence by a positive real distinction
Corollaries
Difficulties
}

Composition of substance and accidents in finite being

{
Statement of the question
Opinions
Thesis: In every finite being, there is real composition of substance and accidents
Corollaries
}

———

ARTICLE I

———

DISTINCTION BETWEEN ESSENCE AND EXISTENCE

IN

FINITE BEING

620. Statement of the question. — 1° *a)* Essence is that by which a thing is what it is, i.e., *that by which a thing is constituted in its proper species*.

b) Existence is described: *the act by which a thing is placed outside its causes and outside the state of nothingness*.

Existence is *act*, for a thing is in act in as much as it has existence. If a thing has not existence, it is in potency, i.e., in the state of possibility.

2° Distinction is the lack of identity between several things.

a) A distinction may be either a *distinction of reason* or a *real distinction*.

A distinction of reason is the lack of identity between two or more concepts of one and the same thing; v. g., between man and rational animal.

A real distinction is the lack of identity between things, independently of the consideration of the mind: v.g., between Peter and Paul.

b) A real distinction may be either *negative* or *positive*.

A negative real distinction is the lack of identity between something positive which really exists and its negation; v.g., the distinction between light and darkness.

A positive real distinction is the lack of identity between positive things which really exist; v.g., the distinction between Peter and Paul.

3° *a*) All admit that there is a distinction of reason between essence and existence, for the concept of essence is different from the concept of existence.

b) It is obvious that there is a negative real distinction between non-existing essence, i.e., possible essence, and actual existence, i.e., existing essence.

c) At present we are concerned with the question of whether there is a positive real distinction between the actual or individual essence, as it exists in nature, and the existence of finite being. In other words, are essence and existence really identified in finite being, or are they merely united as two really distinct principles, i.e., as potency and act *by which* finite being is constituted ?

d) Finite being is used here to signify complete being, i.e., being which actually exists, whether it be substance or accident, incorporeal being, as the angel, or corporeal being.

621. Opinions. — *a*) Henry of Ghent (1217-1293), Peter d'Auriol (Aureolus) (d.1321), Durandus, William of Ockam (d.1349), Gabriel Biel (d.1495), Suarez, Vasquez, and certain philosophers of more recent times hold that the distinction between essence and existence in finite being is only a distinction of reason.

Scotus claims that the distinction between essence and existence is a formal-actual distinction from the nature of the thing.

b) The doctrine of a real distinction ([1]) is defended by the Arabian philosophers, as Alfarabi (d.950) and Avicenna (980-1037), Scholastics, as William of Auvergne, Alexander of Hales, St. Bonaventure, St. Albert the Great, St. Thomas ([2]),

(1) « Doctrina de distinctione reali inter essentiam et existentiam jam apud Aristotelem indicatur distinctione inter ens actu et ens potentia; apud s. Augustinum et Pseudo-Areopagitam et Boethium distinctione inter ens per essentiam et ens per participationem. » — GREDT, vol. II, édit. 5, p. 102.
(2) There can be no doubt that St. Thomas taught that there is a real distinction between the essence and existence of finite being. This is evident from the testimony of his adversaries, as Siger of Brabant, who attributes this opinion to him, from the teaching of his first disciples, who supported this opinion, and from texts which clearly show that this was his teaching. — Cf. I, q. 3, a. 4; III, q. 17, a. 2 — *Contra Gentes*, l. I, c. 35.

and, in more recent years, Liberatore, Sanseverino, De Maria, Pecci, Billot, Pâquet, Remer, Geny, Hugon, etc.

622. Proof of thesis.

THESIS. — THE EXISTENCE OF FINITE BEING IS DISTINGUISHED FROM ITS ESSENCE BY A POSITIVE REAL DISTINCTION.

1° Anything which is received into a thing is distinguishsed from that thing by a positive real distinction. But the existence of finite being is really received into the essence of finite being. Therefore the existence of finite being is distinguished from its essence by a positive real distinction ([1]).

The *major* is evident from its terms.

Minor.— Existence which is not really received into essence is infinite. But the existence of finite being is not infinite. Therefore the existence of finite being is really received into its essence.

Major.— Act which is not really received into potency is infinite. But existence is act. Therefore existence which is not really received into essence as into potency is infinite.

Minor.— Being which has infinite existence is absolutely infinite and pure act: for existence is the act of being as such, since being is that of which the act is existence. But finite being is not absolutely infinite, nor is it pure act, but is composed of act and potency. Therefore the existence of finite being is not infinite.

2° Finite beings are identified with each other in the fact of their having existence, but are really distinct from each other by their various essences and individual notes. But if the essence of a finite being were the same as its existence, finite beings would not be distinct from each other by their various essences. Therefore there is a positive real distinction between

---

(1) Cuncta quae ipsum esse participant, naturam habent qua esse coarctatur, ac tanquam distinctis realiter principiis, essentia et esse constant.— *Thesis III* s. Thomae.

the essence and existence of a finite being which has actual existence ([1]).

Minor.— Since finite beings are identified in as much as they have existence, they would not be distinguished from each other by their different essences if their essence were identified with their existence: for essence would not be a reality in them by which they would be distinct from each other, but rather a reality in which they would be identified with each other.

3° Anything which is really identified with another has a necessary connexion with that other, and is not predicated of it contingently.   But the existence of finite being has not a necessary connexion with the essence of finite being, and is predicated of it only contingently.   Therefore the existence of finite being is not really identified with its essence, but is distinct from it by a positive real distinction ([2]).

Major.— Anything which is really identified with another is either its constituent, v.g., man is an animal; or is its *essential* determinant by which it constitutes a third thing, just as, v.g., rational is essentially identified with animal to constitute man. In each of these two cases there is a necessary connexion between the things which are identified.

Minor.— All agree that the proposition, *this man is existing,* is a proposition in contingent matter.   And the meaning of the proposition is not: *this man as existing is existing,* for this would be tautology.   Nor does it mean: *this man as possible is existing.*   It means that existence is attributed contingently to that reality which is man.

623. Corollaries. − 1° Therefore the potency and the act by which finite being is constituted are its essence and existence.

2° Essence and existence are really distinct in finite being, i.e., in creatures; in Infinite Being, i.e., in God, Who is pure act, essence and existence are really identified.

---

(1) *De Potentia,* q. 7, a. 2, ad 9.
(2) Joannes a Sancto Thoma, *Cursus Theol.,* t. I, pp. 448-462 (Sol.).

3° In finite being, existence is neither accident (predicamental), nor properly substance. For only complete being, its
nature being considered, comes under a predicament.

Nevertheless, the existence of substance is reducible to the
predicament of substance, as its complement; and the existence
of accident is reducible to the genus of the accident of which it
is the existence.

624. Difficulties. — 1 — 1° That a reality be limited, it is sufficient
that it be produced. But the existence of finite being is produced. Therefore
the existence of finite being is limited of itself, and need not be received into
essence as act into potency.

Major. — Thus is indicated the extrinsic foundation of limitation,
I concede; the intrinsic foundation, *I deny.*

Minor. — It must be received into essence as act into potency, *I concede;*
it need not be received into essence as act into potency, *I deny.*

Every being which is produced is finite. But there ever remains the
question: how is finite being constituted intrinsically? The intrinsic constituents of finite being, we reply, are the two really distinct principles, essence
and existence.

2° But existence cannot be received into essence. Therefore the
difficulty recurs.

An act cannot be received into a potency which does not exist before it.
But essence does not exist before existence. Therefore.

Major. — Which in no way precedes, *I concede;* which does not precede
by priority of time, but yet precedes by priority of nature in the order of
material cause, *I deny.*

Minor. — Essence is not anterior to existence by priority of nature in
the order of material cause, *I deny;* is not anterior by priority of time, *I
concede.*

II — 1° It is repugnant that a thing be distinct from that by which
it is intrinsically constituted. But the real essence of finite being is intrinsically constituted as real by existence. Therefore the real essence of finite
being is not distinct from its existence.

We may disregard the *major.*

Minor. — The essence of finite being is intrinsically constituted as
really existing by existence, *I concede;* is intrinsically constituted as real,
i.e., as real potency, by existence, *I deny.*

It is a fact that essence is never found without existence, just as first
matter is never found without form. But just as first matter is not constituted as real potency in the order of essence by form, so essence is not
constituted as real potency in the order of existence by existence.

2° But the real essence of finite being is intrinsically constituted real
by existence. Therefore the difficulty recurs.

Actual essence is the same as real essence. But the actual essence of
finite being is intrinsically constituted actual by existence. Therefore the
real essence of finite being is intrinsically constituted real by existence.

Major. — Actual essence, i.e., either essence which is act in the order of existence, or essence which is actuated by existence, *I concede;* essence which is act only in the order of existence, *I deny.*

Minor. — Is intrinsically constituted act in the order of existence by existence, *I deny;* is intrinsically constituted actuated by existence, *I concede.*

There are two aspects under which a thing can be actual: either it is act, or it is informed by act.   In infinite being, i.e., in God, Who is pure act, essence is identified with existence, and therefore is act in the order of existence; in finite being, essence is distinct from existence, and therefore is not actual of itself, but only in as much as it is actuated, i.e., informed, by existence.

III — If essence and existence are the constituents of every finite being, essence and existence must be the constituents of essence, and so on into infinity.   But essence and existence are not the constituents of essence. Therefore essence and existence are not the constituents of finite being.

Major. — Of every finite being, complete and incomplete, *I concede;* of only complete finite being, *I deny.*

Minor. — Essence is complete being, *I deny;* is incomplete being, *I concede.*

IV — Distinct realities are separable.   But the real essence of finite being and its existence cannot be separated from each other.   Therefore.

Major. — Distinct realities which are not intrinsically dependent on each other, *I concede;* which are intrinsically dependent on each other, *I deny.*

Minor. — The essence and existence of finite being are naturally inseparable, *I concede;* the essence of finite being cannot be separated from its own proper existence, even by a miracle, *I deny.*

The human nature of Our Lord has not its own proper existence, but exists by the divine existence.

Real separability is the most evident sign of real distinction.   But yet separability is not a property of real distinction, and therefore is not convertible with it; v.g., figure is really distinct from quantity, but cannot be separated from it, even by divine power.

V — A positive real distinction exists only between real terms.   But the essence of finite being separated from the existence of finite being is not a real term.   Therefore.

Major. — Between real terms which are either complete or incomplete entities, *I concede;* which are complete entities, *I deny.*

Minor. — Is not a real term as an incomplete entity, *I deny;* is not a real term as a complete entity, *I concede.*

A real term can be either *that which exists,* i.e., a complete entity, or *that by which is constituted* that which exists.   Thus in finite being, essence is a real passive potency, and existence a real act which makes essence determinate; and they are the principles *by which* complete finite being is constituted.

TEXTUS. — Respondeo dicendum, quod dupliciter aliquid de aliquo praedicatur: uno modo essentialiter, alio modo per participationem; lux enim praedicatur de corpore illuminato participative; sed si esset aliqua lux separata, praedicaretur de ea essentialiter.   Secundum ergo hoc dicendum est, quod ens praedicatur de solo Deo essentialiter, eo quod esse divinum est esse subsistens et absolutum; de qualibet autem creatura praedicatur per participationem: nulla enim creatura est suum esse, sed est habens esse. Sic et Deus dicitur bonus essentialiter, quia est ipsa bonitas; creaturae autem dicuntur bonae per participationem, quia habent bonitatem; unumquodque enim, in quantum est, bonum est, secundum illud Augustini in I de Doctrina christiana, quod in quantum sumus, boni sumus. Quandocumque autem aliquid praedicatur de altero per participationem, oportet ibi aliquid esse praeter id quod participatur; et ideo in qualibet creatura est aliud ipsa creatura quae habet esse, et ipsum esse ejus; et hoc est quod Boetius dicit in lib. de Hebdomad., quod *in omni eo quod est citra primum, aliud est esse et quod est.*

Sed sciendum est, quod aliquid participatur dupliciter. Uno modo quasi existens de substantia participantis, sicut genus participatur a specie. Hoc autem modo esse non participatur a creatura; id enim est de substantia rei quod cadit in ejus definitione. Ens autem non ponitur in definitione creaturae, quia nec est genus nec differentia; unde participatur sicut aliquid non existens de essentia rei; et ideo alia quaestio est *an est* et *quid est.* Unde, cum omne quod est praeter essentiam rei, dicatur accidens; esse quod pertinet ad quaestionem *an est*, est accidens; et ideo Commentator dicit in V Metaphysic., quod ista propositio, *Socrates est*, est de accidentali praedicato, secundum quod importat entitatem rei, vel veritatem propositionis. Sed verum est quod hoc nomen *ens*, secundum quod importat rem cui competit hujusmodi esse, sic significat essentiam rei, et dividitur per decem genera; non tamen univoce, quia non eadem ratione competit omnibus esse; sed substantiae quidem per se, aliis autem aliter. Si ergo in angelo est compositio ex essentia et esse, non tamen est compositio sicut ex partibus substantiae, sed sicut ex substantia et eo quod adhaeret substantiae. — *Quodl.* 2, a. 3, c.

SUAREZ. — Dico tertio, in creaturis existentiam et essentiam distingui, aut tanquam ens in actu et in potentia, aut si utraque actu sumatur, solum distingui ratione cum aliquo fundamento in re, quae distinctio satis erit ut absolute dicamus, non esse de essentia creaturae actu existere. Ad intelligendam hanc distinctionem, et locutiones quae in illa fundantur, oportet supponere (id quod certissimum est), nullum ens praeter Deum habere ex se entitatem suam, prout vera entitas est. Quod addo, ut tollatur aequivocatio de entitate in potentia, quae revera non est entitas, sed nihil, et ex parte rei creabilis solum dicit non repugnantiam, vel potentiam logicam. Loquimur ergo de vera entitate actuali, sive sit entitas essentiae, sive existentiae; nulla enim entitas extra Deum est nisi per efficientiam Dei. Quapropter nulla res extra Deum habet ex se entitatem suam; nam illud *ex se* includit negationem habendi ab alio, id est, dicit talem naturam, quae absque alterius efficientia habeat actualem entitatem, seu potius sit actualis entitas.

Atque hinc colligitur, quo sensu verissime dicatur, actu existere esse de essentia Dei, et non de essentia creaturae. Quia, nimirum, solus Deus, ex vi suae naturae, habet existere absque alterius efficientia; creatura vero ex vi suae naturae non habet actu existere absque efficientia alterius. In hoc tamen sensu etiam non est de essentia creaturae habere actualem entitatem essentiae, quia ex sola vi suae naturae non habet talem actualitatem sine efficientia alterius; atque ita omne esse actuale, quo essentia in actu separatur ab essentia in potentia, dicetur non esse de essentia creaturae, quia non convenit creaturae ex se sola, neque ipsa sibi sufficit ut habeat hoc esse, sed provenire debet ex efficientia alterius. Ex quo manifeste fit, ut ad veritatem hujus locutionis non sit necessaria distinctio ex natura rei inter esse et rem cujus dicitur esse, sed sufficere ut illa res non habeat entitatem suam, vel potius ut non sit, neque esse possit illa entitas, nisi ab alio fiat, quia per illam locutionem non significatur distinctio unius ab alio, sed solum conditio, limitatio, et imperfectio talis entitatis, quae non habet ex se necessitatem, ut sit id quod est, sed solum id habet ex influxu alterius. Atque hinc ulterius fit, ut intellectus noster, qui potest praescindere ea quae in re non sunt separata, possit etiam creaturas concipere abstrahendo illas ab actuali existentia, quia, cum non necessario existant, non repugnat concipere earum naturas praescindendo ab efficientia, et consequenter ab actuali existentia. Dum autem sic abstrahuntur, etiam praescinduntur ab actuali entitate essentiae, tum quia neque hanc habent sine efficientia, aut ex se, aut ex necessitate, tum etiam quia non potest actualis entitas ab existentia praescindi, ut supra probatum est.   Ex hoc autem modo concipiendi nostro fit, ut in re sic concepta, praescindendo ab actuali entitate, aliquid consideretur tanquam omnino intrinsecum et necessarium, et quasi primum constitutivum illius rei, quae tali conceptioni objicitur; et hoc vocamus essentiam rei, quia sine illa nec concipi potest; et praedicata, quae inde sumuntur, dicuntur ei omnino necessario et essentialiter convenire, quia sine illis neque esse, neque concipi potest, quamvis in re non semper conveniant, sed quando res existit. Atque ex opposita ratione, ipsum actu existere, seu esse actualem entitatem, negamus esse de essentia, quia praescindi potest a praedicto conceptu, et de facto potest non convenire creaturae prout tali conceptui objicitur.   Quae omnia secus contingunt in Deo, quia, cum sit ens ex se necessarium, concipi non potest per modum entis potentialis, sed actualis tantum, et ideo actu esse, vere dicitur de essentia ejus, quia actu esse illi necessario convenit, et in re ipsa, et in omni vero conceptu objectivo divinitatis.

    ... Dicendum ergo est, eamdem rem esse essentiam et existentiam, concipi autem sub ratione essentiae, quatenus ratione ejus constituitur res sub tali genere et specie.   Est enim essentia, ut supra, disput. 2, sect. 4, declaravimus, id quo primo aliquid constituitur intra latitudinem entis realis, ut distinguitur ab ente ficto, et in unoquoque particulari ente essentia ejus dicitur id, ratione cujus in tali gradu et ordine entium constituitur.   Quomodo dixit Augustinus, 12 de Civitate, cap. 2: *Auctor essentiarum omnium, aliis dedit esse amplius, aliis minus, atque ita naturas essentiarum gradibus ordinavit.* Atque hac ratione solet essentia quidditatis nomine significari, quia illa est quae per definitionem explicatur, vel aliqua descriptione, per quam declaramus quidnam res sit, cujusve naturae.   At vero haec eadem res concipitur sub ratione existentiae, quatenus est ratio essendi in rerum natura et extra causas. Nam quia essentia creaturae non hoc necessario habet ex vi sua ut sit actualis entitas, ideo quando recipit entitatem suam, concipimus aliquid esse in ipsa, quod sit illi formalis ratio essendi extra causas; et illud sub tali ratione appellamus existentiam, quod licet in re non sit aliud ab ipsamet entitate essentiae, sub diversa tamen ratione et descriptione a nobis concipitur, quod ad distinctionem rationis sufficit.   Hujus autem distinctionis fundamentum est, quod res creatae de se non habent esse, et possunt interdum non esse.   Ex hoc enim fit ut essentiam creaturae nos concipiamus, ut indifferentem ad esse vel non esse actu, quae indifferentia non est per modum abstractionis negativae, sed praecisivae; et ideo quamvis ratio essentiae absolute concipiatur a nobis etiam in ente in potentia, tamen multo magis intelligimus reperiri in ente in actu, licet in eo praescindamus totum id, quod necessario et essentialiter ei convenit, ab ipsa actualitate essendi; et hoc modo concipimus essentiam sub ratione essentiae, ut potentiam; existentiam vero ut actum ejus. Hac ergo ratione dicimus hanc distinctionem rationis habere in re aliquod fundamentum, quod non est aliqua actualis distinctio quae in re intercedat, sed imperfectio creaturae, quae, hoc ipso quod ex se non habet esse, et aliud potest ab alio recipere, occasionem praebet huic nostrae conceptioni.

    Et hinc etiam patet ultima conclusionis pars; nam in hac locutione nomine creaturae non est intelligenda realis entitas actualis seu actu creata; nam, si cum hac reduplicatione vel compositione fiat sermo, revera creatura essentialiter petit, actu existere, ut sit creatura.   Atque in hoc sensu, sicut albedo est de essentia albi, ut album est, ita existentia est de essentia creaturae, ut res actu creata est; nam aeque vel magis formaliter illam constituit, quam albedo album.   Unde sicut est inseparabilis albedo ab albo, quin destruatur album, ita est inseparabilis existentia a creatura, quin destruatur creatura, et ideo non recte infertur, si existentia sit de essentia creaturae praedicto modo sumptae, non posse creaturam privari existentia, quia solum sequitur non posse illa privari, quin destruatur et desinat esse creatura, quod verissimum esse constat ex dictis, et ex dicendis amplius confirmabitur. Cavenda tamen est aequivocatio in illa voce, *de essentia;* nam, ut in principio hujus sectionis dicebam, interdum habere esse de essentia sua, significat habere illud ex se, et non ab alio, quomodo nulla creatura, etiamsi actu sit, habet esse de essentia sua; tamen nunc non ita loquimur, sed prout dicitur esse de essentia, id quod est primum et formale constitutivum rei; quomodo albedo est de essentia albi ut sic, quamvis non a se, sed ab alio illam habeat. Hoc ergo modo existentia vere dici potest de essentia creaturae in actu constitutae, seu creatae, ut talis est. Cum autem negatur esse de essentia creaturae actu existere, sumenda est creatura ut abstrahit seu praescindit a creatura creata et creabili, cujus essentia objective concepta abstrahit ab actuali esse aut entitate, et hoc modo negatur esse de essentia ejus actu existere, quia non clauditur in conceptu ejus essentiali sic praeciso. Ad quae omnia sufficit distinctio rationis, vel realis negativa, quae est inter essentiam potentialem et actualem. — SUAREZ, *Disputationes Metaphysicae,* disp. XXXI, sect. VII, nn. 13, 14, 15, 23, 24.

·

_____

COMPOSITION OF SUBSTANCE AND ACCIDENT
IN FINITE BEING

625. Statement of the question. — 1° Substance is a being which exists in itself. It is also called a subsisting subject, because it has its own proper existence. It is defined: *a thing*, i.e., *a quiddity, to which it appertains to exist in itself, and not in another as in its subject of inherence.*

Accident is physically described as second act, i.e., as act which gives a secondary existence to a subject which is already constituted in its primary existence. It is also called form which is secondarily added to a subsisting subject. It is defined: *a thing*, i.e., *a quiddity, to which it appertains to exist in another as in its subject of inherence.*

2° We state in the thesis that in every finite being there is composition of substance and accidents, which are distinct realities, so that accident is related to substance as act to potency.

626. Opinions. — 1° It is the common teaching of Scholastics that substance and accident exist in finite being as distinct realities.

2° Kant holds that substance is not a reality, but merely a subjective form of the mind. In like manner, Locke and Hume hold that the concept of substance is fictitious.

3° Descartes, on the contrary, taught that substance is the only reality, — extension is the body, and thought is the soul — and accidents are mere denominations which add nothing to reality. Many moderns deny the reality of substance and of accident, and their distinction from each other.

627. Statement of the thesis. — The reality of substance and of accident and the real distinction between them are affirmed by common sense. Here we are concerned with the metaphysical proof of their reality and distinction.

> **THESIS.**—IN EVERY FINITE BEING, THERE IS REAL
> COMPOSITION OF SUBSTANCE AND AC-
> CIDENTS.

1° Every finite or limited operation is a real accident added to substance. But in every finite being there is finite or limited operation. Therefore in every finite being there is real composition of substance with accidents ([1]).

Major.— Operation of itself is an act which can be limited only if it is received into a subject which it actuates and determines, i.e., only if it is received into a potency. But a subject into which operation is received as act must exist, i.e., must be constituted in its primary existence: for a thing must exist in order that it operate. Therefore limited operation must be a second act added to an existing subject, i.e., is a real accident added to substance.

Minor.— If the operation of finite being were not limited, finite being would have limited existence and unlimited operation. But this is repugant for the operation of a being is proportionate to its existence: a thing has operation in as much as it is in act, and it is in act in as much as it has existence. Therefore.

2° Finite being is really dependent on infinite being for its existence. But finite being, in as much as it is dependent on infinite being for its existence, is composed of substance and accidents. Therefore in every finite being there is real composition of substance and accidents ([2]).

Major.— Finite being is produced by infinite being.

---

(1) Est praeterea in omni creatura realis compositio subjecti subsistentis cum formis secundario addictis, sive accidentibus. — *Thesis V* s. Thomae.

(2) *De Potentia*, q. 7, a. 9.

Minor.— The real dependence of finite being on infinite being for its existence gives rise to a real relation between finite being and infinite being. But this relation is not finite being, but derives from finite being, in as much as finite being is really dependent on infinite being, in the same way as the likeness in quality of two things is not the quality itself, but a reality which results from the quality. In other words, this relation is a real accident which exists in finite being, as in substance.

628. Corollaries. — 1° The real composition of substance and accidents in finite being presupposes the real distinction between essence and existence in finite being, so that such real composition would be unintelligible if existence were not really received into essence distinct from itself ([1]). For, if essence were identified with existence, substance could not be in potency to accident, because existence is ultimate act.

2° An accident is received into a substance as into the potency which it actuates. Therefore finite substance is in potency to existence as to the first act to which it has relation, and to accident as to the secondary act to which it has relation.

---

(1) *Thesis V* s. Thomae.

CHAPTER II

SUBSTANCE

Prologue. — In this chapter, we shall first consider the nature of substance. Secondly, we shall discuss substance as terminated, i.e., supposit. And since subsistence is the formal constituent of supposit, our final consideration in the chapter will concern subsistence. Hence there will be three articles in this chapter.

Nature of substance
{
Metaphysical notion of substance
False definitions of substance
Division of substance
Derivation of the intentions of genus and differentia
}

Supposit
{
Statement of the question
Thesis: The individual nature and supposit of finite beings are really distinct
Corollaries
}

Subsistence
{
Statement of the question
Thesis: In finite beings, subsistence does not consist in a negation, nor is it substantial existence as received, but it is a substantial mode which terminates individual nature
Opinions of modern philosophers
Opinion of Suarez
What supposit adds to specific nature
Meanings of supposit
Corollary
}

NATURE OF SUBSTANCE

629. Metaphysical notion of substance. — The term substance is derived from the Latin word *substare, to stand under.* According to common sense, it is *a thing which stands under other things*, i.e., *under accidents*, and *which does not exist in another* (¹).

Substance is defined by Scholastics: *a thing*, i.e., *a quidity, to which it appertains to exist in itself, and not in another as in a subject of inherence.*

There are three elements in this definition which we may consider:

    a) the negation of existence in another;

    b) existence in itself (²);

    c) the supporting of accidents.

The last-mentioned element is expressed by the word substance, which, as we said, is derived from *sub-stare*, to stand under i.e., to support.

    a) The negation of existence in another is not the formal constituent of substance. Since essence is the first source of

---

(1) Ens per se non est definitio substantiae: ens enim non potest esse alicujus genus ... sed si substantia habere possit definitionem non obstante quod est genus generalissimum, erit ejus definitio, quod substantia est res, cujus quidditati debetur esse non in aliquo. — *De Potentia*, q. 7, a. 3, ad 4.

(2) *Esse per se* and *esse in se*, as opposed to *esse in alio*, have the same signification. Both are correct, if they are properly understood. We have adopted *esse in se, to exist in itself.*

It should be observed that *ens per se* (being by itself) has three meanings:

    a) it is opposed to accidental being, i.e., it designates one essence; in this meaning, *esse per se* belongs to each of the predicaments;

    b) it signifies *ens a se*, and thus is opposed to *ens ab alio;* in this sense, it is predicable only of God, and does not constitute the essence of substance;

    c) it signifies that which of its nature requires that it exist independently of another which supports it, i.e., of a subject of inherence. It is thus distinct from *ens in alio.* In this sense, *esse per se* is that from which the formal aspect of substance derives.

everything connected with it, its constituent cannot be a negation: for everything negative has its foundation in something
positive.

b) The supporting of accidents is not the formal constituent of substance, as certain philosophers, as Boetius, maintained: the supporting of accidents presupposes that substance
already has its nature, for, in order that it support accidents,
it must first exist as a subject.

c) Hence the formal constituent of substance is its relation
to existence in itself, i.e., substance is formally constituted substance in as much as it appertains to it to exist in itself.

NOTE.— 1° Existence in itself is not the essential constituent of substance, but is that from which the essential constituent derives, because the existence of a finite being is really
distinct from its essence.   Substance is essentially a thing, a
quiddity, which connotes a transcendental relation to existence
in itself.

2° Sometimes substance is used in a wide sense as synonymous with essence.   In this meaning, it is predicable of all the
predicaments.

3° God may be called a substance in as much as He does
not exist in another, and is not caused by another.   But, since
God is infinite being, He may not be placed in the predicament
of substance.

630. False definitions of substance. — 1° Descartes
defined substance: *a thing which so exists that it needs no other
thing in order to exist*.   This definition is ambiguous, and therefore untenable: in its obvious meaning, it is applicable only to
God, not to finite being, for it excludes *being*, as efficient cause,
by which a thing exists.

2° Spinoza defined substance: *that which exists in itself
and is conceived to exist of itself*, i.e., a thing for the formation of
whose concept the concept of no other thing is required.   This
definition, like the definition given by Descartes, is applicable
only to God.   Therefore Spinoza concludes that substance can

only be God; and thus he reaches a conclusion that is tantamount to pantheism.

3° Cousin defined substance: *a thing which contains nothing relative in its being.* This definition is pantheistic.

4° Leibniz defined substance: *a being endowed with the power of acting (action).* This definition is incomplete, because it does not touch upon the essential constituent of substance.

631. Division of substance. — 1° From the point of view of its mode of being, substance is divided into first substance and second substance.

First substance is individual, concrete substance; v.g., Peter. It is defined by Aristotle: *that which does not exist in a subject, and is not predicable of a subject.*

Second substance is universal substance according to the mode of being it has in the intellect. It is defined by Aristotle: *that which does exist in a subject, but is predicable of a subject;* v.g., man, animal.

a) It does not exist in a subject, but is identified with a subject.

b) It is predicated of a subject, as a universal is predicated of its inferior.

2° From the point of view of completeness, substance may be complete or incomplete.

Complete substance is a substance which of itself is not destined to union with another substance, in order to constitute a composite substantial essence. In other words, it is a substantial whole which can have its own act of existence; v.g., a man, a plant.

Incomplete substance is a substance which of itself is destined to union with another incomplete substance, in order to constitute a composite substantial essence; v.g., the brute soul, the human soul.

Incomplete substance can be incomplete both in the order

f species and in the order of substance, or incomplete in the
order of species only.

A substance which is *incomplete as regards both species and
substantiality* is an incomplete substance which is united to another incomplete substance to form a being of a determinate
species, and which cannot exist separated from it; v.g., the brute
soul.

A substance which is incomplete *only as regards species* is
an incomplete substance which is united to another incomplete
substance to form a being of a determinate species, but which can
exist separated from it. The *human soul* is the only incomplete substance of this kind.

3° From the point of view of physical essential composition, complete substance may be simple or composite.

Simple substance is a substance which is not composed of
incomplete substances; v.g., the human soul, the angel.

Composite substance is a substance which is composed of
incomplete substances; v.g., a man, a plant.

4° From the point of view of essence, substance is immaterial, i.e., spiritual, or material.

Immaterial substance is a substance which is intrinsically
independent of matter for its existence and its specific operation:
v.g., the human soul, the angel.

Material substance is a substance which is intrinsically dependent on matter for its existence and specific operation; v.g.,
the brute soul.

If a material substance is a connatural subject of extension.
it is called a *corporeal* substance, i.e., a body.

**632. Derivation of the intentions of genus and differ-
entia.** — Genus and differentia are concepts which are perfectly
prescinded from each other, since we can have a concept of one
without having a concept of the other; v.g., we can have a concept of animal without having a concept of rational, for otherwise every animal would be rational. Nevertheless, when a

genus and a differentia are predicated of an individual, they do
not express different things, but one and the same thing, i.e.
one and the same essence. When, for example, we say that
Peter is a rational animal, animal and rational signify one and
the same essence, i.e., the essence of Peter.

Therefore the question arises: whence are derived the intentions of genus and differentia ?

Answer: 1° When a genus expresses an essence as determinable, and a differentia expresses the same essence as determinate, the proximate foundation or source from which the intentions of genus and differentia are derived is the integral essence in as much as it is considered *by total abstraction* either as a
formality which is not yet determinate in its species, or as a
formality which is ultimately determining it in its species.

2° Since genus is *determinable* essence, it is *remotely* derived
from that which is more potential in reality; and since differentia is ultimately *determined* essence, it is *remotely* derived
from that which is more actual in reality.

Hence, *a*) in the case of corporeal substances, genus is
ultimately derived from first matter, and differentia from substantial form; *b*) in the case of created spiritual substances, as
angels, genus is ultimately derived from their immateriality
which they have in common, and differentia from the different
degrees in which they participate the perfection of being; *c*) in
the case of accidents, genus is derived from the manner in which
they affect substance; and differentia is derived from the proper
principles to which their essence is commensurate, or from their
proper effects.   Thus, for example, the differentia of a relation
is derived from the term-to-which of the relation, this term being
considered as a principle.

ARTICLE II

SUPPOSIT

633. Statement of the question. — 1° Our holy faith teaches that in Jesus Christ there are two natures, a divine nature and a singular or individual human nature, but only one person, the divine person of the Word. Therefore we may conclude that the human person of Christ is distinct from His individual human nature. But can we *prove* that they are distinct? It is with the answer to this question that this article is concerned.

2° Person is also known by the generic name supposit. Supposit is *that which exists*, for *that which exists* is properly the subject of other things, i.e., of existence, operations, and all else that pertains to it ([1]).

That which exists is that which has existence properly as its own. Therefore supposit, in its *positive* aspect, is conceived as something self-sufficient, i.e., complete, autonomous (*sui iuris*), and is subsisting ([2]). In its *negative* aspect, it is conceived as not pertaining to another, and is incommunicable.

Supposit is defined: *a subsisting, individual, complete substance* ([3]).

a) *Substance:* it does not admit of the communicability of an accident, which exists in substance as in its subject.

b) *Complete*: it does not admit of the communicability of an incomplete substance, which exists in union with another

---

(1) Et hac ratione hic homo dicitur esse suppositum, quia scilicet supponitur his quae ad hominem pertinent, eorum praedicationem recipiens. — III, q. 2, a. 3.
(2) I, q. 29, a. 2.
(3) CAJETANUS, *In I*, q. 3, a. 3. — Sometimes supposit is defined: individual substance, i.e., substance which is completely individual or entirely incommunicable.

incomplete substance; nor of the communicability of the parts of a substance, as the heart, the arms, etc., which exist in the whole.

c) Individual: it does not admit of the communicability of a universal nature, which is communicated to an individual nature by identity.

d) Subsisting: it does not admit of the communicability of an individual complete nature, which, according to the thesis, exists in the supposit as in its term, as the human nature of Christ exists in the Person of the Word as in its term.

3° Person is an intellectual supposit. Person is defined by Boethius: *an individual substance of a rational nature.* In this definition, individual substance is used in its strict sense, i.e., as completely individual and incommunicable (1). Person is a term of greater dignity than supposit, and is most fittingly used to designate an intellectual supposit, because an intellectual supposit enjoys greater dignity than a non-intellectual supposit; v.g., a person enjoys greater dignity than a brute, because an intellectual supposit has dominion over its acts in as much as it is free (2).

Person is used here in its *metaphysical meaning.* Sometimes it is used in a *psychological sense*, and, in this case, signifies a being which has consciousness of itself and of its acts (3).

Again, person has a *juridical meaning:* a man capable of presenting a case before a judge, i.e., recognized by law as the subject of rights and duties.

4° In the thesis, individual substance is used to signify the individual essence of substance. We teach that the distinction between supposit and individual nature is a real distinction, in this sense: the real distinction is not *adequate*, for supposit and individual nature are not entirely distinct from each other;

---

(1) Persona exactius a s. Thoma definitur: Distinctum subsistens in aliqua natura intellectuali. — *De Potentia*, q. 9, a. 4.

(2) *De Potentia*, q. 9, a. 1, ad 3.

(3) Dans le langage psychologique on entend généralement par « personne » l'individu qui a une conscience claire de lui-même et agit en conséquence; c'est la forme la plus haute de l'individualité. — Th. Ribot, *Les Maladies de la Personnalité*, Paris, 1884, p. 1.

rather it is *inadequate*, because supposit includes individual nature, and adds a reality to it.

5° *a*) Henry of Ghent, Durandus, Tiphanus, and others hold that there is only a distinction of reason between individual nature and supposit.

b) All Thomists and Suarez teach that there is an inadequate real distinction between the individual nature and the supposit of a finite being.

634. Statement of the thesis.

THESIS.—The individual nature and supposit of finite beings are really distinct.

Realities to which existence is attributable in different ways are really distinct. But existence is attributable in different ways to the individual nature and to the supposit of finite beings ([1]). Therefore the individual nature and supposit of finite beings are really distinct.

The *major* is evident.

Minor.— Existence is predicable in different ways of individual nature and supposit. Thus, for example, we say that Peter is a man who exists, — a principle *which*, — whereas we say that his individual nature is the principle *by which* Peter is constituted. In other words, existence is properly and truly predicated of a supposit ([2]), whereas it is predicated of an individual nature only in as much as it exists in a supposit, as in its complement ([3]). But, since finite being, and especially sensible finite being, v.g., Peter, is the object proper to the human intellect, existence is predicable of individual nature and supposit in different ways only if it is attributable to them in different ways. Therefore.

635. Corollaries. — 1° Since the principle which exists is the principle which acts, it is to the supposit that actions must

(1) III, q. 17, a. 2.
(2) *Quodl.*, 9, a. 3.
(3) III, q. 2, a. 3, ad 2.

7

be attributed: actions belong to supposits, *actiones sunt suppositorum.*

2° In God, the divine nature is communicated to the three Persons of the Blessed Trinity.   Hence the divine nature does not constitute a person distinct from the Father, the Son, and the Holy Spirit.

———

––––––

SUBSISTENCE

636. Statement of the question. — 1° Since a supposit is a subsisting substance, *subsistence* is the formal constituent of supposit. Subsistence, used in reference to person, is also called *suppositality* or *personality*. In what does subsistence formally consist? It is with the answer to this question that we are concerned in this article.

2° According to Scotus, subsistence formally consists in a twofold negation:

a) in the negation of the actual dependence of a thing on another supposit which assumes it, i.e., which draws it into its own existence;

b) in the negation of even the aptitudinal dependence of a thing on another supposit according to the order of nature, although this dependence can be supernaturally safeguarded, as happened in the case of the human nature of Christ.

3° Thomists are unanimous in teaching that subsistence formally consists in some positive perfection; but they are divided as regards what this positive perfection is.

a) Some Thomists, as Medina, Guérinois, de Aguirre Billot, Schiffini, Janssens, Remer, and others hold that subsistence is substantial individual existence as received into individual nature. Hence they maintain that subsistence is something extrinsic to nature.

b) Others follow Cajetan in teaching that subsistence is a substantial mode which terminates individual nature, just as a point terminates a line. This is the opinion followed by John of St. Thomas, the Salmanticenses, and, in more recent times, Satolli, Zigliara, Pâquet, Gredt, Lortie, etc.

Hence, according to them, subsistence belongs to the order of nature, not to the order of existence.

Subsistence is defined by Cajetan: *the pure, ultimate term of the nature of a substance.*

a) Ultimate term of the nature of a substance, i.e., that which ultimately terminates and completes the nature of a substance, so that of itself and incommunicably ([1]) it receives existence.

b) Pure term: purely a term, i.e., a purely modal and terminal principle, not a formal or material principle.

637. Statement of the thesis.

> **THESIS.**— In finite being, subsistence does not consist in a negation, nor is it substantial existence as received, but it is a substantial mode which terminates individual nature.

First part.— *Subsistence does not consist in a negation.*— 1° The opinion which holds that subsistence consists in a negation confuses subsistence with incommunicability, which is a negative property which results from subsistence.

2° That which gives individual nature a certain perfection does not consist in a negation. But subsistence gives nature a certain perfection. Therefore subsistence does not consist in a negation.

The *major* is evident.

Minor.—Subsistence constitutes an individual nature a supposit, i.e., perfectly self-supporting or sufficient for itself. But to render an individual nature perfectly self-supporting is to give it a certain perfection. Therefore.

Second part.— *Subsistence is not substantial existence as received.*— A perfection of finite beings which belongs to the order of nature is not substantial existence as received. But

---

(1) Incommunicably, i.e., without communicating with another to receive its existence.

subsistence is a perfection of finite beings which belongs to the order of nature. Therefore the subsistence of finite beings is not substantial existence as received.

Major.— In finite beings, nature, i.e., essence, and existence are really distinct, and belong to two entirely different orders (¹).

Minor.— The constituent of a special mode of being belongs to the order of nature. But subsistence constitutes a special mode of being, that is to say, a mode of being which is complete in itself and incommunicable(²). Therefore subsistence belongs to the order of nature.

Major.— Every special mode of being of finite things derives from nature: existence, of itself, merely places a thing outside of nothing and outside of its causes, and it has different modes in the measure in which it is received in different ways into essences, i.e., natures, which are really distinct from it.

Third part.— *Subsistence is a substantial mode which terminates individual nature.*— Since subsistence adds a certain perfection (first part) in the order of nature (second part) to individual nature, it must be something accidental, or a new substantial form, or a substantial mode which terminates individual nature. But subsistence is not something accidental, nor is it a new substantial form. Therefore subsistence is a substantial mode which terminates individual nature.

Major.— The enumeration is complete.

Minor.— Subsistence is not something accidental, because a supposit is a substance which is a *perfect unit in itself* (unum per se), not a being whose unity is only accidental (unum per accidens); and it is not a new substantial form, because there can be only one substantial form in a being which is essentially one, i.e., which has one nature. Therefore.

-----

(1) Essence is that by which a thing is what it is, whereas existence is that by which a thing is placed outside its causes.
(2) Persona ... significat quamdam naturam cum quodam modo existendi. Modus existendi quem importat persona est dignissimus, ut scilicet aliquid sit per se existens. — *De Potentia*, q. 9, a. 3.

638. Opinions of modern philosophers. — Descartes, Locke, Kant, and Gunther teach that personality is consciousness of self.

1° This opinion confuses metaphysical personality with psychological personality.   2° According to this opinion, one who is drunk, asleep, or distracted, etc., would not be a person, which, of course, is absurd.   3° It is very easy to disprove this opinion: actual consciousness is an operation which presupposes a principle which i.e., a person, already constituted.

639. Opinion of Suarez. — Suarez identifies the essence and existence of finite being.   He teaches that subsistence is a mode which is added to substance after existence.

The fallacy of this opinion is obvious: subsistence cannot be an accident; but it would have to be an accident if it were added to a substance after it had received its existence.

640. What supposit adds to specific nature. — 1° In material substances, supposit adds individuating principles and subsistence to individual nature.   In other words, supposit is individual nature plus individuating principles plus subsistence.

2° In simple substances, as angels, whose specific nature is of itself individual, supposit adds only subsistence to specific nature.

641. Meanings of supposit. — Subsistence has its root in nature as it is singular or individual, since it is its term. Hence supposit may be considered radically, i.e., in its root, and formally.

1° Considered in its root, supposit is the same as singular nature.

2° In its formal aspect, supposit may be considered in the abstract, or in the concrete.

a) In the abstract, it is the same as subsistence or personality.

b) In the concrete, it is singular nature as subsisting.

3° Again, supposit may be considered *adequately*. In this case, it signifies subsisting singular nature together with all that appertains to it, i.e., with existence and accidents.

642. Corollary. — Therefore we can understand how there is an individual human nature in Christ, but not a human person.

Christ's individual human nature is not terminated by its own subsistence, but by the subsistence of the Word.

CHAPTER III

ACCIDENTS

Prologue. - In this chapter, we shall deal first with accidents in general; secondly, with two particular accidents, quality and relation, the study of which belongs to Metaphysics. The study of the other accidents, as quantity, action, passion, etc., which are proper to mobile being, belongs to Philosophy of Nature.

Hence there will be three articles in this chapter.

Accidents in general
{
Metaphysical notion of accident
Division of accidents
Accident and substance
Existence of accidents without a subject
Difficulties
}

Quality
{
Notion of quality
Species of quality
Habits and dispositions
Requisites of habit
Division of habits
Subject of habits
Increase, loss, and diminution of habits
Properties of qualities
}

Relation
{
Existence of real relations
Requisites of predicamental relation
Foundation of predicamental relation
Distinction of predicamental relation from its foundation
Term of predicamental relations
Division of predicamental relation
Properties of relations
}

Appendix
{
Spiritual substance—Existence
—Nature
}

ACCIDENTS IN GENERAL

643. Metaphysical notion of accident. — An accident, in its physical aspect, is a *second act*, a *secondary form added to substance*. It may be imperfectly described as *a being which exists in another* (ens in alio).

An accident, in its metaphysical aspect, is defined: *a thing or quiddity to which it appertains to exist in another as in its subject of inherence*. We say: in its subject of inherence, i.e., in a subject already constituted in its primary existence, to which it gives a secondary existence; v.g., whiteness in Peter presupposes that Peter exists, and gives him the secondary existence of whiteness.

In accident thus defined there are three elements:

a) existence in (a subject);

b) *actual* inherence (union) of the quiddity of an accident in a subject, i.e., in a substance.

c) *aptitudinal* inherence (union) of an accident, which is the aptitude of an accident to exist in a substance, the capacity to be united to a substance.

Existence in a subject is not of the essence of an accident, because existence is not of the essence of finite being: in finite being, essence and existence are really distinct.

Actual inherence in a subject, i.e., actual union with a substance, does not constitute the essence of an accident, for such inherence or union presupposes that the essence of the accident is already constituted. Hence some philosophers hold that actual union is a mode of accidents which corresponds to subsistence in substance: just as substance becomes positively existent in itself by subsistence, so an accident becomes positively dependent on a subject by actual inherence.

Aptitudinal inherence is the formal constituent of accident, because it is the transcendental relation of an accident to exist in a subject, a relation which is really identified with the essence of the accident.   In other words, the capacity to exist in a subject is the formal constituent of an accident.

644. Division of accidents. — 1° Aristotle divides accidents into nine predicaments, i.e., supreme genera.

The secondary form added to substance, i.e., accident, can affect substance absolutely, i.e., in itself, or relatively, i.e., in relation to another subject.

1° If absolutely:

a) it renders substance distinct and determinate: *quality;*

b) or it extends substance into parts: *quantity;*

2° If relatively:

a) it relates substance to a term: *relation;*

b) or it modifies substance in relation to an external subject.

3° This extrinsic subject may be:

a) totally extrinsic,

b) or partially extrinsic.

4° If the extrinsic subject is totally extrinsic,

a) it is not a measure of substance: *habit;*

b) or it is a measure of substance.

5° If it is a measure of substance,

a) it is a measure of time: *when;*

b) or it is a measure of place, either without reference to the disposition of parts in the place: *where;* or with reference to the disposition of parts in the place: *posture.*

6° If the extrinsic subject is only partially extrinsic,

a) it is intrinsic as regards its principle: *action,* which derives its name from passion, of which it is the principle;

b) or it is intrinsic as regards its term: *passion*, which derives its name from action, of which it is the term.

This division may be presented schematically as follows:

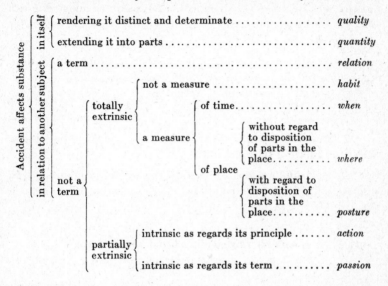

2) Accidents are also divided into absolute and modal accidents.

An *absolute* accident is an accident which immediately affects substance; v.g., quantity, color.

A *modal* accident is an accident which immediately affects an absolute accident and, by means of it, substance; v.g., the curvature of a line which immediately affects quantity.

From another point of view, certain accidents, as quantity and quality, are called absolute accidents, in as much as they are opposed to the relative accident, i.e., to predicamental relation.

645. Accident and substance.— 1° *Existence of accident and existence of substance.*— *a*) The existence of accident is not received, properly speaking, into the essence of accident, but is rather a secondary existence of substance: the subject, i.e., substance, in which an accident inheres in virtue of the essence, i.e., form, of the accident, acquires a new existence ([1]).

b) Hence, properly speaking, accidents do not exist, but a subject is modified by them. Therefore an accident is not a *being* in the strict sense, but rather is a *being of a being*, an entity of an entity, (ens entis) ([2]).

c) Nevertheless, accidental existence is not substantial existence, but is a secondary existence of substance, by which the essence of an accident is actuated, in as much as it is actually united to a substance.

2° *Causality of substance in regard to accident.*— Substance stands in relation to accidents:

1) as their final cause, because the end of accidents is the completion of their subject, i.e., the perfection of substance ([3]).

2) as their material cause, because, in as much as it is in potency, it is capable of receiving accidental forms ([4]).

3) as their efficient cause, and this in two ways:

a) it produces, by emanation, proper accidents which naturally result from it ([5]), i.e., these accidents emanate from substance; *b*) it conserves, by its continuous efflux, all accidents, even those that are contingent, in as much as it communicates to them its own secondary existence, which is at the same time the existence of accidents; v.g., not only does Peter produce his own operation, but this operation continues in existence only in as much as Peter, by his continuous efflux, i.e., causality, conserves it in its existence ([6]).

---

(1) DEL PRADO, *De Veritate Fundamentali*, l. II, c. 6, p. 136.
(2) I, q. 5, a. 5, ad 2 — I, q. 90, a. 2.
(3) I, q. 77, a. 6.
(4) *Ibid.*
(5) Accidentia non propria seu contingentia in substantia producuntur ab agente extrinseco.
(6) On dit: l'accident s'adjoint à la substance et s'y superpose. Que ces mots ne fassent pas illusion ! Les accidents, c'est la substance qui se complète et s'achève. Ils se racinent en elle, ils en sont l'épanouissement. Nés d'elle, demeurant en elle, existant pour elle, elle est la cause efficiente, leur cause finale, leur centre, en un mot... leur tout. — BRUNETEAU, *Commentaire sur le De Ente et Essentia*, p. 153.

646. Existence of accidents without a subject. — 1°
Preliminaries. 1) The question of the existence of accidents
without a subject is rather theological than philosophical.
We deal with it here because our holy faith teaches us that in
the sacrament of the Blessed Eucharist the substance of bread
and wine do not remain under the species of bread and wine,
but only the substance of the Body and Blood of Christ.   Moreover, the accidents of bread and wine do not inhere in the Body
of Christ as in their subject, for, if they did, they would not be
the accidents of bread and wine, because all accidents are individuated by the subject in which they exist.

2° Almost all scholastics teach that at least absolute accidents — thus modal accidents are excluded — can, by divine
power, i.e., by a miracle, exist without a subject.   This opinion
presupposes:

 a) that neither the actual union of accident to substance,
nor the actual existence of accident in substance constitutes the
essence of accident, for, as we have already pointed out, aptitudinal inherence is the formal constituent of accident;

 b) that God is the first efficient cause which not only produces all things, but also, as we shall prove later, actually conserves them, immediately or mediately, in their existence.
Hence God, as the first cause, conserves accidents in their
existence *by means of substance* which he uses as a second
cause.

2° Statement of the thesis.

THESIS. — ABSOLUTE ACCIDENTS CAN, BY DIVINE
POWER, EXIST WITHOUT A SUBSTANCE.

Absolute accidents can, by divine power, exist without a
subject, provided that the existence of absolute accidents without a subject is not contradictory.   But the existence of absolute accidents without a subject is not contradictory.   Therefore absolute accidents can, by divine power, exist without a
subject.

Major.— God by His omnipotence can do anything which does not imply a contradiction.

Minor.— The existence of absolute accidents without a subject would be contradictory, *a*) either because God, as the first cause, could not conserve absolute accidents without the intervention, i.e., the causality, of substance, i.e., of a second cause, *b*) or because the actual existence of accident in a subject, and the actual union of accident to a subject were of the essence of accident. But *a*) God, as the first cause, can conserve the effects of second causes without the causality of these causes (¹); *b*) neither actual existence in a subject, nor actual union of accident to substance are of the essence of accident, as we have already said. Therefore.

647. Difficulties. — 1° Accidents are more dependent on a subject than matter is on form. But matter cannot actually exist without form. Therefore accidents cannot actually exist without a subject.

Major. — Relatively speaking, *I concede;* absolutely speaking, *I deny.*

Let us disregard the minor.

Relatively speaking, accidents are more dependent on a subject than matter on form, in as much first matter is something substantial, whereas accidents are not substantial; but, absolutely speaking, matter is more dependent on form than accidents on a subject, because first matter, as pure potency, dannot be actuated by *existence* without form; but an accident, as something in act, can be actuated by existence without a subject.

2° It is repugnant that a thing whose definition contains *existence in a subject* exist without a subject. But the definition of accident contains existence in a subject. Therefore.

Major. — Actual existence in a subject, *I concede;* aptitudinal existence in a subject, *I deny.*

Minor. — Actual existence in a subject, *I deny;* aptitudinal existence in a subject, *I concede.*

3° A thing which has an exigence to exist in a subject cannot exist without a subject. But a thing whose definition contains aptitudinal existence in a subject has an exigence to exist in a subject. Therefore a thing whose definition contains existence in a subject cannot exist without a subject.

Major. — Cannot naturally exist without a subject, *I concede;* preternaturally, i.e., by a miracle, *I deny.*

Minor. — Has an absolute exigence to exist in a subject, *I deny;* has a natural exigence to exist in a subject, *I concede.*

_____

(1) Effectus enim magis dependet a causa prima quam a causa secunda. — III, q. 77, a. 1.

POINTS FOR REVIEW

1. Define: accident considered physically, accident considered meta-physically.

2. Explain the following statements: *a*) Existence in a subject is not the essential constituent of an accident. *b*) Actual inherence of an accident in a subject corresponds to the subsistence of a substance. *c*) Aptitudinal inherence in a subject is the formal constituent of an accident.

3. Is accidental existence received, properly speaking, into the essence of accidents? Explain.

4. Explain in what sense substance is the efficient cause of accidents.

5. Explain why the existence of absolute accidents without a subject is not contradictory.

———————

QUALITY

648. Notion of quality. — Quality, according to common sense, means determination.

A subject can receive determination as regards substantial entity and also as regards accidental entity.

A subject is determined as regards substantial entity by substantial specific differentia, which is called *quality* in a wide sense.

Quality, in the strict sense of the term, i.e., predicamental quality, is defined: *an accident by which the potency of a subject is made determinate as regards accidental entity* ([1]).

a) As the determinant of a subject, quality is distinct from quantity, which merely extends a subject; and also from the other accidents, which, properly speaking, do not determine, i.e., qualify, a subject, but place it in relation to a term, as *relation*, or which are derived from the relation of a subject to something extrinsic, as the accidents *where*, *when*, etc.

b) As the determinant of a subject as regards its accidental entity, quality is distinct from substantial differentia.

649. Species of quality. — There are four species of quality.

The determination of a subject as regards accidental entity can take place in the following ways:

1° in regard to the very nature of the thing; and from this determination derive *habit* and *disposition*;

---

(1) I-II, q. 47, a. 2.

2° in regard to action and passion. This determination is either in regard to the principle of action and passion, from which derives the second species of quality: *potency* and *impotency;* or it is in regard to the term of alteration and motion, from which derives the third species of quality: *passion* and *patible quality;*

3° in regard to quantity, from which derives the fourth species of quality: *form* and *figures* (¹).

Hence there are four species of quality:

Habit (habitus) and *disposition;*

Potency and *impotency;*

Passion and *patible quality;*

Form and *figure.*

Potency (power) or faculty is the proximate principle of operation; v.g., the intellect.

Impotency, in its present signification, is not the negation of potency, but rather weak potency; v.g., weak sight.

Passion is used here to signify not a special predicament opposed to action, but a quality which causes a sensible alteration, as sweetness and bitterness, or which results from a sensible alteration, as pallor and ruddiness in the face.

Patible quality is a passion which derives from a *stable and lasting,* i.e., *permanent, alteration,* as pallor in a sick person.

Figure is a quality which naturally results from the termination of quantity; in other words, it is a quality which results from the diverse disposition of quantity in natural things; v.g., the figure of a man.

Form is a quality which quantitative parts artifically have as a result of their due proportion or beauty; in other words, it is a quality which results from the diverse disposition of the parts of quantity in artificial things; v.g., the form of a house, the form of a ship.

_____

(1) *Ibidem.*

650. Habits and dispositions. — Habit, broadly speaking, is the possession of a thing.

In a stricter sense, habit is either the last of the predicaments, or it is a species of quality.

Habit, as a species of quality, is defined: *a quality whereby a subject is well or ill disposed either in itself, or in relation to something other than itself.*

a) Well or ill disposed: it is in this that a habit essentially consists.

b) In itself: a habit determines a subject in relation to the nature of the thing.

c) In relation to something other than itself: since nature is the end of generation and is directed to operation or to the product of operation as to its end, a habit, in determining a subject in relation to nature, determines it in relation to something other than itself, i.e., to an end.

When the subject is a power, the principal determination given to it by a habit is a determination in relation to operation: a power of its very nature is destined for operation.

651. Requisites of habit. — A habit implies a certain disposition for the nature of a thing, and for its operation and end, whereby a thing is well or ill disposed for its operation and end.

But there are three requisites for a thing's need of being disposed for a thing other than itself:

first, that the thing which is disposed be distinct from the thing for which it is disposed, and thus have the same relation to it as potency has to act. Hence habits are not required in God, nor can they exist in Him, for God is not a compound of potency and act: the substance of God is His operation, and God is His own end.

secondly, that the thing which is in potency to another can be determined in different ways and to different things. Hence, if a thing is in potency to another, but in such manner that it is only in potency to itself, there can be no disposition and habit in this case, because such a subject of its very nature has a due relation to this act;

thirdly, that several things concur to dispose the subject for one of the things to which it is in potency, which can be made commensurate to it in different ways, so that the subject be well or ill disposed either for a form or for an operation (¹).

Hence habits are necessary, because there are many beings for whose natures and operations several things must concur, which can be made commensurate in different ways.

652. Division of habits. — 1° From the point of view of its subject, habit may be entitative or operative.

a) An entitative habit is a habit which immediately affects a substance, and well or ill disposes its subject in itself for its existence; v.g., sickness, health, grace in the soul.

An *operative habit* is a habit which immediately affects a faculty, and well or ill disposes its subject for its operation; v.g., virtue, science.

b) An operative habit is *cognitive* or *appetitive*, as it perfects a cognitive or an appetitive faculty.

2° From the point of view of its end, habit is speculative or practical.

a) A speculative habit is a habit which disposes the intellect to *rest* in the knowledge of truth,; v.g., the science of Metaphysics.

b) A *practical habit* is a habit which disposes its subject for operation; v.g., prudence.

3° From the point of view of its origin, habit is innate, acquired, or infused.

a) An *innate habit* is a habit which a person has from the birth; v.g., some are naturally disposed for chastity.

b) An *acquired habit* is a habit which results from the repetition of acts, according to the axiom: *ex repetitis actibus fit habitus*, a habit is the result of repeated acts; v.g., science, an acquired moral virtue.

---

(1) I, q. 49, a. 4, c.

c) An *infused habit* is a habit which is produced by God in nature or in an intellectual power; v.g., grace, supernatural hope, etc.

4° From the point of view of its proper essence, habit is good, i.e., a virtue, or bad, i.e., a vice, as it well or ill disposes its subject.

Virtue is defined: *a good quality of the mind by which we live righteously and which no one ill uses* (¹), or, *a good operative habit;* and vice is defined: *a bad operative habit.*

5° From the point of view of its formal object, habit is divided into the various virtues and vices; v.g., justice, mercy, charity, etc.

653. Subject of habits.—1° The subject of the *entitative habits* is substance. Nevertheless, not every substance is the subject of habits, but only a substance which can be determined in different ways by its form.   Living substances can receive different determinations from their form; v.g., sickness and health are found in plants, animals, and men.

2° The subject of the operative habits is a power which can be determined in different ways for diverse, and even contrary, operations, that is to say, immaterial faculties, as the intellect and the will, and the sensitive powers as they operate under the command of the will (²).

3° Nevertheless, certain imitations of habits, i.e., *habits improperly so called*, are found in the sensitive powers even of animals. From repeated acts, especially under man's direction, animals can acquire a greater *aptitude* and *facility* for certain acts.

654. Increase, loss, and diminution of habits. — 1° *Increase of habits. a*) Certain habits can be increased when they are extended to objects to which they did not previously extend; v.g., the knowledge of a man who begins to have a knowledge of conclusions which before he did not possess.

---

(1) S. Aug., *De lib. arbitrio*, cc. 18 et 19.
(2) I-II, q 50, aa. 3-5-

b) Certain habits, without extending to new objects, can be increased as their subjects become more and more reduced to the acts of these habit;, and more subject to them; v.g., when knowledge becomes clearer, and virtue stronger.

2° *Loss of habits.*— Acquired habits can be lost:

a) *accidentally* (indirectly), because of the corruptible subject in which they exist;

b) and also *directly* (*of themselves*), if they have contraries, that is to say, by the exercise of contrary acts, or even by mere cessation from work, i.e., from disuse.

3° *Diminution of habits.*— The diminution of habits results from the same causes as does their loss.

655. Properties of qualities. — 1° Only qualities, but not all qualities, *have contraries*, that is to say, only those qualities have contraries which are incompatible in the same subject; v.g., virtue and vice, health and sickness.

2° Qualitie: are *the basis of accidental similarity and dissimilarity*.

3° Some qualities *admit of degrees*, as habits and dispositions.

POINTS FOR REVIEW

1. Define: quality (in the strict sense of the term), habit, entitative habit, virtue, vice.

2. Explain the derivation of the four species of quality.

3. What are the requisites of habit ?   Explain.

4. Distinguish between habit and disposition.

5. Can animals possess habits ?   Explain.

RELATION

656. Existence of real relations. — 1° *Preliminaries.* — Relation signifies an order, a respect, of one thing to another thing.

a) According to common sense, relation is logical or real.

A *logical* relation (relation *of reason*) is a relation which depends on the consideration of the intellect, in as much as the intellect establishes it either between two or more concepts; v.g., between the subject and predicate of a proposition; or between really existent things, as between a flag and a determinate country.

A *real* relation is a relation which exists in things independently of the consideration of the intellect; v.g., paternity, sonship, likeness.

b) Real relation is of two kinds: transcendental relation and predicamental relation.

A *transcendental relation* is the entity of an absolute thing related of its essence to another thing; v.g., the relation of the soul to the body, of accident to substance, of potency to act.

Hence a transcendental relation designates something *absolute* which connotes a relation to another thing. This kind of relation is called transcendental relation, because it does not constitute a genus, i.e., a special predicament of being, but transcends every genus, in as much as it is found in all genera.

A *predicamental relation* is a real accident whose whole being consists in its being a pure relation to a term; v.g., likeness, paternity. Hence there are two aspects in predicamental relation:

a) the aspect *in* (*esse in*), inherence, by which predicamental relation is an accident which has the same kind of existence as other accidents;

b) the aspect *towards* (*esse ad*), towardness, by which predicamental relation is formally constituted, and is an accident of a genus all its own, distinct from other accidents.

These two aspects of predicamental relation are not really distinct, but are two concepts under which one and the same reality is known (¹).

2° *Opinions.*— *a*) Nominalists and certain other philosophers of more recent times, as the Kantians, deny the existence of real relations.

b) The philosophers of the ante-Aristotelian age affirmed the existence of real relations, but did not admit the existence of predicamental relations.

c) Aristotle, St. Thomas, and almost all Scholastics teach that real relations in general, i.e., both transcendental and predicamental, exist; and in particular they affirm the existence of predicamental relations.

3° *Statement of the thesis.*

THESIS.— IN NATURE THERE EXIST REAL RELATIONS, SOME OF WHICH ARE PREDICAMENTAL RELATIONS.

First part.— *In nature there exist real relations.*— If real order exists in nature, real relations exist in nature. But real order exists in nature, as is evident. Therefore in nature there exist real relations.

Major.— Real order results from the real relations which exist in nature.

_____

(1) Praeter absoluta accidentia est etiam relativum, sive ad aliquid. Quamvis enim ad aliquid non significet secundum propriam rationem aliquid alicui inhaerens, saepe tamen causam in rebus habet et ideo realem entitatem distinctam a subjecto. — *Thesis VI* s. Thomae.

Second part.— *Some of the real relations which exist in nature are predicamental relations.*— If real accidents exist whose whole being consists in their being pure relations to terms, some real relations are predicamental relations. But real accidents of this kind exist in nature. Therefore some of the real relations which exist in nature are predicamental relations.

Major.— Accidents of this kind are predicamental relations.

Minor.— It is evident from examples: a likeness exists between two white objects, and yet this likeness is not a white subject, nor is it whiteness, but rather a real accident by which one white object is related to another. Similarly, paternity in Peter is not Peter, but a real accident whose whole being consists in its being a pure relation to a term, i.e., in the relation of Peter to his son. Therefore.

657. Requisites of predicamental relations. — The requisites of a predicamental relation, according to philosophers, are four in number:

1° *A really subsistent subject.*— This is immediately evident, for the subject of a real accident must be really subsistent.

2° *A real foundation.*— The relation of reference which a predicamental relation implies is real, and therefore it requires a root, a cause, a real foundation.

3° *A really existent term.* The real relation which exists in a real subject must have a real term, for a real relation to nothing is unintelligible.

4° *A real distinction between the subject and the term.*— A real relation of a thing to itself is unintelligible, for every relation is a respect, an order, of one thing to another thing, and hence requires real opposition between two things, i.e., a real distinction between a subject and a term.

658. Foundation of predicamental relation. — 1° Relation has a twofold foundation: material or remote, and formal or proximate.

The *remote foundation* is something necessarily required for relation, but from which relation does not immediately result; v.g., generative power in Peter who is a father is the remote foundation of paternity.

The *proximate foundation* is that from which relation immediately results; v.g., generative action is the proximate foundation of paternity.

2° The proximate foundation of relation is of three kinds. (¹) This is evident from the fact that a thing can be related to another in three ways:

a) the quantity of a thing can be related to another: thus we have the first foundation, which is *unity* and *number;*

b) a thing can receive something from another, or it can give something to the other: thus we have the second foundation, which is *action* and *passion;*

c) the perfection of a thing can be measured by another; thus we have the third foundation, which is *measure* and *the measurable.*

1) *First foundation:* unity and number.

The kind of unity with which we are concerned at present is not quantitative or predicamental unity only, but quasi-ontological quantity, i.e., any predicament in as much as it has the formal aspect of unity, and consequently of multitude; v.g., there is a certain unnamed relation of dissimilarity between Peter as naked and Paul as dressed on account of the negation of unity as regards the predicament of habit. Similarly, there is a certain unnamed relation as regards multiplication of the predicament *where* between Peter who is in one place and Paul who is in another place.

The principal relations which are founded on unity and number may be considered:

a) as regards substance: thus we have identity and diversity;

(1) *In Metaph.,* l. V, l. 17.

b) as regards quantity: thus we have the relations of equality and inequality;

c) as regards quality; thus we have the relations of similarity and dissimilarity.

2) *Second foundation;* action and passion.

Action and passion found relation, not only in as much as they are *actually being produced* (in *fieri*), but also in as much as they are *already produced* (in *facto esse*). In other words, action and passion are foundations of relation, because, when they are produced, they leave a subject changed; v.g., when Peter paints a picture, he has not the same relation to the picture as he had before he painted it, but rather he is related to it as artificer to artifact.

3) *Third foundation:* measure and the measurable.

From this foundation results the relation of the dependence of one thing on another, as on the measure of its being; v.g., the relation of the creature to God, the relation of the speculative intellect to an object actually known.

Predicamental relations which result from the third foundation are real on the side of one term, and unreal on the side of the other term, i.e., they are non-mutual or unilateral relations; v.g., the relation of the creature to God as Creator is real, but the relation of the God to the creature is only logical: creatures are essentially dependent on God, but God is in no way dependent on creatures.

659. Distinction of predicamental relation from its its foundations. — 1° *Preliminaries. a)* Suarez affirms that there is only a distinction of reason between a predicamental relation and its foundation.

b) Nominalists too maintain that relation makes no real addition to its subject.

c) Thomists teach that there is a real distinction between a predicamental relation and its proximate foundation.

2° *Statement of the thesis.*

THESIS.— Predicamental relation is really distinct from its foundation.

Things which are separable from each other are really distinct from each other. But predicamental relation is sometimes separable from its foundation. Therefore predicamental relation is really distinct from its foundation.

Minor.— It is evident from an example : if an animal's only offspring dies, neither the substance, nor the generative power of the animal, nor the act of generation already exercised are changed, but yet the real relation of the animal to its offspring ceases.

660. Term of predicamental relations. — 1° *Preliminaries.* Here we are concerned with the question of whether the term of a relation is something absolute or something relative. The term materially considered is certainly something absolute; v.g., Peter, the father of Paul, has a relation of paternity to Paul, who is something absolute. But we are concerned not with the material aspect of the term of predicamental relation, but rather with its formal aspect, with the formal term, with the term *by which* as such . Hence our problem is this: does predicamental relation formally attain its term as something absolute or as something relative ?

2° *Opinions.*— a) Scotus and Suarez hold that the formal term of a relation is something absolute; v.g., paternity attains its term, which is a son, because the son is engendered by the father. Hence passive generation is that by which the relation of paternity attains its term, which is a son.

b) Thomists commonly teach that the formal term of a relation is something relative; v.g., paternity attains its term, which is a son, under the aspect of sonship.

In mutual relations, the term is a kind of real relation, i.e., the term is subjectively and intrinsically relative; v.g., the term of paternity in the son is the relation of sonship.

In non-mutual relations, the term is only extrinsically and terminatively relative; v.g., Peter who dislikes Paul has a

relation of unfriendliness to Paul, but, if Paul does not dislike
Peter, Paul is the term of that relation only in as much as he is
extrinsically or terminatively unfriendly, i.e., as he is disliked.

3° *Statement of the thesis.*

THESIS.— THE FORMAL TERM OF PREDICAMENTAL
RELATION IS SOMETHING RELATIVE.

A term which is essentially a *towardness* is something relative. But the formal term of predicamental relation is a *towardness*. Therefore the formal term of predicamental relation is something relative.

Minor.— The formal term of a predicamental relation as
such is essentially the term of another, i.e., it is essentially a
towardness.

661. Division of predicamental relation. — 1° *Accidental division. a)* Relation is accidentally divided into mutual
relation and non-mutual relation.

A mutual relation is a relation to which there corresponds
in another extreme a relation of the same entity, i.e., of the same
order; v.g., paternity, sonship.

A *non-mutual* relation is a relation to which there corresponds
in another extreme not a relation of the same entity, but of
another entity; v.g., corresponding to a real relation of the
speculative intellect to an object of knowledge there is, on the
side of the object of knowledge, only a relation of reason to the
intellect.

b) Mutual relation may be a mutual relation of the same
denomination (relatio mutua aequiparantiae) or a mutual
relation of different denomination (relatio mutua disquiparan-
tiae).

A mutual relation *of the same denomination* is a relation to
which corresponds in another extreme a relation of the same
entity and of the same species; v.g., the relation of likeness
between two white objects.

A mutual relation *of different denomination* is a relation to which corresponds in another extreme a relation of the same entity, but not of the same species; v.g., paternity and sonship.

2° *Essential division.*— Since predicamental relation is a relation to a term which results from a foundation, its essential or specific division is derived from the restriction of the foundation to the term, i.e., predicamental relation is divided according as the foundation is related to the terms of the relation.

If the foundation is considered, we have four sources of the essential division of relation:

1) unity and number;
2) measure and the measurable ;
3) action ;
4) passion.

Since action and passion do not belong to the same supreme genus, the relations which derive from them are specifically distinct ; v.g., paternity, which derives from active generation, is specifically distinct from sonship, which derives from passive generation.

If the term is considered, we find that relations are essentially or specifically distinct when their terms are essentially distinct ; v.g., the relation of likeness which one white object has to another white object is specifically distinct from the relation of unlikeness which this white object has to a black object.

3° *Numerical* division.— The numerical distiction of relations is derived from the numerical distinction of subjects, according to the principle : an accident which is specifically one cannot be numerically multiplied in the same subject. Thus, for example, in Peter, the father of ten children, there is only one relation of paternity which, according to its aspect *owards*, i.e., its *towardness*, is terminated in ten terms, but which, according to its aspect *in*, i.e., its *inherence*, is only one relation in Peter.

662. Properties of relations. — 1) Relations as such have no contraries : even relations which are most opposed can exist simultaneously in one and the same subject; v.g., paternity and sonship in one and the same man.

2) Relation as such does not admit of degrees ; v.g., Peter who is the father of ten sons is not a father to greater degree than Paul who has only one son.

The foundation of relation, however, admits of degrees ; v.g., the degree of likeness between two objects is proportionate to the degree of likeness of its foundations.

3) Relations are concomitant in the order of knowledge, that is to say, a relation can be known if its opposite is known at the same time.

4) Mutual relations are correlatives (ad invicem convertuntur), that is to say, a mutual relation in one extreme is explained by the relation corresponding to it in the other extreme, and vice versa ; v.g., paternity is explained by sonship, and sonship is explained by paternity.

5) Mutual relations are concomitant in nature (simul natura), for mutual relations exist at the same time, in as much as one cannot exist unless it is terminated in another.

POINTS FOR REVIEW

1. Define: relation, relation of reason, real relation, transcendental relation, predicamental relation, remote foundation of predicamental relation, proximate foundation of predicamental relation.

2. Distinguish between the aspect *in* and the aspect *towards* of predicamental relation.

3. Enumerate and briefly explain the requisites of predicamental relation.

4. Name the proximate foundations of predicamental relations.

5. Explain what is meant by unity as it is the first foundation of predicamental relation.

6. Name the principal relations founded on unity and number.

7. Explain briefly whether or not relations which derive from measure and the measurable are mutual relations.

8. Is the term of predicamental relation something relative ? Prove your answer.

9. Show how we derive a) the essential division, b) the numerical division of predicamental relations.

SPIRITUAL SUBSTANCE

663. Existence of spiritual sustances. — From revelation we know the existence of spiritual substances which are finite beings, that is to say, of angels. St. Thomas offers a number of arguments in proof of the existence of angels ([1]). Many Thomists maintain that these arguments are only probable, i.e., are not strictly demonstrative, whereas others hold that they are true demonstrations of the existence of angels. The latter opinion is the one that we follow. Though the scope of our present work does not call for a special tract on angels, there are a few observations that we wish to make in regard to the angelic nature.

664. Nature of spiritual substance. — Since spiritual substances, i.e., angels, are finite beings, they are composed of essence and existence as of two really distinct principles, and consequently admit of composition of substance and accidents, nature and subsistence. But, since angels are not spatio-temporal beings, they are not composed of first matter and substantial form, but are altogether simple in their essence, i.e., they are subsisting forms not united to matter ([2]). Moreover, since matter signed by quantity is the principle of the numerical distinction of one individual from another in the same species, angels do not admit of multiplication in the same specific nature, but differ specifically from each other, i.e., each angel is a species distinct from the species of each other angel ([3]).

---

(1) *Contra Gentes*, l. II, c. 91. — Quod sunt aliquae substantiae intellectuales corporibus non unitae.

(2) Creatura spiritualis est in sua essentia omnino simplex; sed remanet in ea compositio duplex: essentiae cum esse et substantiae cum accidentibus. — *Thesis VII* s. Thomae.

(3) *Thesis XI* s. Thomae.

—

Causes

Prologue. — In Philosophy of Nature, we defined cause in general: *a positive principle on which a thing really depends for its existence.* Causes are divided into material cause and formal cause, which are the intrinsic causes, and efficient cause and final cause, which are the extrinsic causes.

In this part of our work, we shall give a more complete development of the notions of the four causes than we did in Philosophy of Nature. First, we shall consider the intrinsic causes; secondly, efficient cause; and, thirdly, final cause. Hence there will be three chapters in this book.

Chapter   I.   Intrinsic causes

Chapter   II.   Efficient cause

Chapter III.   Final cause

—

CHAPTER I

INTRINSIC CAUSES

Prologue. — An intrinsic cause may be material or form-1. Hence there will be two articles in this chapter.

Material cause
- Notion of material cause
- Division of material cause
- Constituent of matter as a cause in first act
- Constituent of matter as a cause in second act
- Conditions required that matter actually exercise its causality
- Effects of matter

Formal cause
- Notion of formal cause
- Division of formal cause
- Constituent of formal cause as a cause in first act
- Constituent of formal cause as a cause in second act
- Conditions required that formal cause actually exercise its causality
- Effects of formal cause
- Exemplar cause

MATERIAL CAUSE

665. Notion of material cause. — Material cause is defined by Aristotle : *the cause out of which a thing is made, and which exists in it.*

a) *Out of which a thing is made*, as a statue is made out of marble.

b) *And which exists in it:* thus material cause is distinct from the privation of form, out of which a thing is made, but which does not exist in the thing produced, nor does it perdure in existence ([1]) ; v.g., a statue is made from a non-statue, i.e., from a subject in which is the privation of the form of the statue. But, when the statue is produced, the privation disappears and the form of the statue takes its place.

666. Division of material cause. — Under the name of material cause come :

a) first matter, which is pure potency ;

b) accidents which dispose matter for the reception of form — dispositive material cause ;

c) any potential subject which receives act : thus second matter, i.e., corporeal substance, in regard to accidental forms, spiritual substance in regard to its own accidents, essence in regard to existence, one accident in regard to another accident which it receives,— as quantity in regard to color,— nature with respect to supposit.

667. Constituent of matter as a cause in first act. — Matter is constituted a cause in first act by its own proper entity.

---

(1) JOANNES A SANCTO THOMA, *Cursus Phil.*, t. II, p. 223 (Reiser).

Every cause, indeed, is constituted a cause in first act by some potency. But the potency of matter is identified with the entity of matter. Therefore.

668. Constituent of matter as a cause in second act. Matter is constituted a cause in second act, i.e., actually exercises its causality. by its own entity as communicated, i.e., united, to form by an efficient cause.

669. Conditions required that matter actually exercise its causality. — In order that matter actually exercise its causality, the following are the requirements :

a) that matter exist as a real potency for the reception of form ;

b) that there be a concurrence of other causes by which matter is disposed to cause materially; v.g., the concurrence of efficient causes, of previous dispositions ;

c) that form be present in matter.

670. Effects of matter. — The effects of matter are two in number.

a) *The being, or at least the inherence (inesse), of form.*— Material forms are educed from the potency of matter. Therefore they are dependent on matter for being. An immaterial form, as the human soul, is not educed from the potency of matter, but is immediately created by God. Hence it is not dependent on matter in its being; but, when it exists in matter, it is dependent on matter for its *existence-in*, inherence (inesse).

b) *The being of the compound.*— Compounds, i.e., composite realities, are dependent on matter for being, in as much as a whole is dependent on its parts for its being.

The being of the compound and the being or existence-*in* of form are not disparate effects of matter : the being or existence-*in* of form is its first and immediate effect ; and from this effect results its secondary effect, which also is its principal effect, namely, the being of the compound.

POINTS FOR REVIEW

1. Define material cause, and give its divisions.

2. Explain how matter is constituted a cause in first act, and in second act.

3. State the conditions required that matter actually exercise its causality.

4. Enumerate and briefly explain the effects of matter.

FORMAL CAUSE

671. Notion of formal cause. — Formal cause is defined: *the intrinsic principle by which a thing is determined to a certain mode of being, and is constituted in its species.*

a) As an intrinsic principle, formal cause is distinct from efficient cause and final cause, which are extrinsic principles.

b) As a determining and specifying cause, formal cause is distinct from material cause, which is indeterminate.

672. Division of formal cause. — 1) Formal cause, in the strict sense, is divided into : *a*) substantial form, which is the principle which determines first matter ; *b*) accidental form, which is the act which determines second matter.

2) Every act received into potency can be reduced to formal cause ; v.g., a spiritual accident received into a spiritual substance, existence received into essence.

673. Constituent of formal cause as a cause in first act. — Formal cause is constituted as such in first act by its own proper entity : form is constituted a cause in first act, because it can give existence to a thing and can constitute it in its specific nature. But form can give existence to a thing and can constitute it in its specific nature by its own proper entity. Therefore.

Minor.— Form of itself is an entity which is an act, an act which of itself is transcendentally related to matter so as to give a thing its existence and to constitute it in its specific nature.

674. Constituent of formal cause as a cause in second act. — Formal cause is constituted a cause in second act by its own proper entity, not by something added to its entity.

Form actually exercises its causality in as much as it actually communicates with matter, i.e., informs matter. But it is by its own proper entity that form actuates matter, not by something added to its entity. Therefore.

675. Conditions required that formal cause actually exercise its causality. — The following conditions are required in order that formal cause actually exercise its causality:

a) that form exist concomitantly with its effect;

b) that there be the concurrence of an efficient cause which unites form to matter;

c) that matter be made disposed for form, and thus be made capable of receiving form.

676. Effects of formal cause. — Formal cause has two effects.

a) the actuation of matter, i.e., the actual existence of matter;

b) the being and existence of the compound.

The actuation of matter is the immediate effect of form; the being and existence of the compound is its principal effect, but yet a secondary effect which results from its immediate effect.

677. Exemplar cause. — 1° Exemplar cause is defined: *the form which an artificer uses as a pattern in his operation*, or *the form in imitation of which a thing is produced according to the intention of an agent that determines an end for itself.*

An exemplar cause *proximately* signifies an idea, an objective concept, existing in the mind of an artificer, because this is the proximate form on which the artificer patterns his artifact; *remotely* it signifies objects existing in nature, in as much as an artificer uses these objects for the formation of the ideas which he uses as patterns in his operation.

The question now arises: to what genus of cause does exemplar cause belong?

2° St. Bonaventure, Scotus, and Saurez hold that exemplar cause is properly reducible to the genus of efficient cause, in as much as it is the idea which completes the power of an intellectual agent, and determines this agent for operation.

Thomists hold that exemplar cause is, for the reasons already given, in a certain manner reducible to efficient cause; and that it is in a certain manner also reducible to final cause, in as much as an artificer is influenced by an idea to introduce the likeness of the idea into the thing he produces; but they affirm that exemplar cause is properly reducible to the genus of formal cause, because it is this cause which is the measure which gives determination to the intrinsic form which constitutes a thing in its species. Therefore exemplar cause is classified as *extrinsic formal cause.*

POINTS FOR REVIEW

1. Give the definition and divisions of formal cause.

2. Explain how formal cause is constituted a cause *a)* in first act, *b)* in second act.

3. Enumerate *a)* the conditions required that formal cause exercise its causality, *b)* the effects of formal cause.

4. Define exemplar cause, and state how it is classified by *a)* Scotus and Suarez, *b)* Thomists.

CHAPTER II

EFFICIENT CAUSE

Prologue. — In this chapter, we shall deal first with efficient cause in general; secondly, with instrumental efficient cause; thirdly, with the principle of causality; fourthly, with the existence of efficient causality in finite beings. Therefore there will be four articles in this chapter.

Efficient cause in general
- Notion of efficient cause
- Division of efficient cause
- Constituent of efficient cause as such in first act
- Constituent of efficient cause as such in second act
- Conditions required that efficient cause exercise its causality
- Effects of efficient cause

Instrumental cause
- Notion of instrumental cause
- Division of instrument
- Constituent of instrumental cause as such in first act
- Constituent of an instrument as a cause in second act
- Effect of instrumental cause

Principle of causality
- Notion of the principle of causality
- Origin of our knowledge of the principle of causality
- Metaphysical enunciation of the principle of causality
- Principle of causality according to Kant
- Principle of sufficient reason
- The principle of causality is a self-evident proposition

Existence of causality in finite beings
- Statement of the question
- Thesis: All finite beings are efficient causes
- Corollary
- Difficulties

_C_ **EFFICIENT CAUSE IN GENERAL**

678. Notion of efficient cause. — Efficient cause is defined: *the first positive extrinsic principle of motion* (¹).

a) *Principle:* the genus of efficient cause.

b) *Extrinsic:* to distinguish efficient cause from matter and form, which are intrinsic principles.

c) *Positive*: to distinguish efficient cause from privation, which is an accidental principle, i.e., a purely negative principle of motion.

d) *first*: to distinguish efficient cause from final cause, which is last in the *order of execution;* motion is properly dependent on the efficient cause in the *order of execution*, and is dependent on an end only in the *order of intention*, i.e., in as much as agents tend to an end.

e) *Motion:* motion is used in this definition to signify not merely the transition from preexisting potency to act, but the transition from absolute non-existence to existence, or, more briefly, any union of act with potency.

NOTE.— 1° Both matter and form are principles of motion, but not first principles. Matter and form do not exercise their own causality unless they are first united by an efficient cause, and hence efficient cause is the first principle of motion.

2° Efficient cause is the first principle of motion not in an *absolute manner*, but in relation to other genera of causes, i.e., to material cause and formal cause. Hence one efficient cause can be prior to another; v.g., a principal efficient cause is prior to an instrumental efficient cause as a principle of motion.

---

(1) JOANNES A SANCTO THOMA, *Cursus Phil.*, t. II, p. 248 (Reiser).

679. Division of efficient cause. An efficient cause may be a proper cause (causa per se) or an accidental cause (causa per accidens).

A *proper* cause is a cause which produces an effect with which it has a natural connexion; v.g., a sculptor is the proper cause of a statue.

An *accidental* cause is cause which produces an effect with which it has no natural connexion; v.g. a medical doctor sings.

An accidental cause can produce an effect in two cases:

a) when the proper cause of the effect is found united to the accidental cause in the same subject; v.g., when a medical doctor sings, the art of singing, which is the proper cause of singing, is found in the doctor united to his art of medicine;

b) when the accidental effect is found united to the proper effect of this cause; v.g., a man who, in digging a trench, discovers a treasure is the accidental cause of the discovery of the treasure, because the discovery is accidentally united to the work of digging the trench.

2° A proper efficient cause may be a principal cause or an instrumental cause.

A *principal* cause is a cause which acts by its own proper power; v.g., a man who speaks.

An *instrumental* cause is a cause which acts by the power of a principal cause by which it is elevated to produce an effect; v.g., a pen which is directed by a writer is the instrumental cause of a piece of writing.

3° A principal cause may be a first cause or a second cause.

A *first* cause is a cause which not only acts by its own power, but depends on no other cause for the actual exercise of its power; v.g., God is the only first cause.

A *second* cause is a cause which acts by its own power, but depends on the first cause for the actual exercise of its power. All created causes actually exercise their power only when moved by God, who is the First Cause. Therefore all created causes are second causes.

4° An efficient cause may be a universal cause or a particular cause.

A *universal* cause is cause which produces effects of different species; v.g., the sun as it produces light, life, etc.

A *particular* cause is a cause which produces effects of only one species; v.g., man as he engenders man.

5° An efficient cause may be an equivocal or analogous cause, or a univocal cause.

An *equivocal* or *analogous* cause is a cause which produces an effect dissimilar to itself in species; v.g., God with respect to creatures.

A *univocal* cause is a cause which produces an effect similar to itself in species; v.g., a man who engenders another man.

6° An efficient cause may be a total cause or a partial cause.

A *total* cause is cause which does not require the cooperation of other causes of the same order to produce its effect; v.g., a single horse which draws a wagon.

A *partial* cause is a cause which requires the cooperation of other causes of the same order to produce its effect; v.g., when several horses draw a wagon, each of the horses is a partial cause of the drawing of the wagon.

7° An efficient cause may be a natural cause or a free cause.

A *natural* cause is a cause which acts as a result of the determination of nature; v.g., a plant as it assimilates food.

A *free* cause is cause which acts as a result of election; v.g., an artificer is the free cause of his artifact.

8° An efficient cause may be a non-subordinated cause or a subordinated cause.

A *non-subordinated* cause is a cause which is dependent on no superior cause, v.g., the first cause, i.e., God.

A *subordinated* cause is a cause which is dependent on a superior cause; v.g., all created causes.

9° A subordinated efficient cause may be an essentially subordinated cause or an accidentally subordinated cause.

An *essentially subordinated* cause is a cause which requires the actual influence of the cause to which it is subordinated for its action; v.g., a child while writing as directed by the hand of his teacher; all second causes with respect to the first cause.

An *accidentally subordinated* cause is a cause which is not dependent on another cause for its action, but is subordinated to it in some other way; v.g., a son who is dependent on his father for his existence, but not for his operation.

10° An efficient cause may be a proximate cause or a remote cause.

A *proximate* cause is a cause which immediately produces an effect; v.g., a murderer is the proximate cause of a murder.

A *remote* cause is a cause which produces an effect by exercising an influence on its proximate cause; v.g., a man who gives orders for a murder is the remote cause of the murder.

There are many other divisions of efficient cause.

680. Constituent of efficient cause as such in first act. — 1° *Statement of the problem. a*) In our problem we are not concerned with the first cause, which is God, but with second or finite causes.

b) Finite supposit is the immediate principle-*which* of operation; the nature of supposit is the total remote principle-*by-which*; and substantial form is the partial remote principle *by which* supposit operates.

c) The question with which we are concerned is whether finite supposits, i.e., created substances, are of themselves immediately constituted efficient causes in first act, i.e., whether of themselves they are immediately capable of operation, or whether they require powers — forces, faculties, — really distinct from themselves in order that they may be able to operate.

In other words, is the operative or active power of a finite substance really and necessarily distinct from its nature ?

2° *Opinions.*— *a*) William of Ockam, Scotus, Suarez, and many others maintain that finite substances do not necessarily require powers really distinct from themselves, in order that they be capable of operation.

b) Thomists hold that finite substances cannot operate except by means of powers really distinct from themselves.

3° *Statement of thesis.*

THESIS. — Finite substances are constituted efficient causes in first act by operative powers which are really distinct from themselves.

A substance whose power of acting, i.e., operative power, is an accident is constituted an efficient cause in first act by an operative or active power distinct from itself. But all operative powers of finite substances are necessarily accidents. Therefore finite substances are constituted efficient causes in first act by operative powers which are really distinct from themselves.

The *major* is evident, for, if operative powers are accidents, they are really distinct from substance.

Minor.— A power which is completed and specified by an act which is an accident is itself an accident. But the action or operation of a finite substance, which is the act which completes and specifies its operative power, is an accident. Therefore the operative powers of created substances are necessarily accidents.

681. Constituent of efficient cause as such in second act. — An efficient cause is constituted as such in second act by its own operation, i.e., by the exercise of its own action or operation: a cause is a cause in second act when it actually exercises its causality, i.e., when it actually causes. But an efficient cause actually exercises its causality when it acts, i.e., when it actually exercises its action or operation. Therefore.

682. Conditions required that efficient cause exercise its causality. — The conditions required in order that efficient cause produce its effect, i.e., actually exercise its causality, are as follows:

1) the existence of an agent, either in itself or at least in some power left by it;

2) the presence in the effect of either the supposit of the agent, or of the power of the agent which attains the patient by means of its action; thus action at a distance is impossible, i.e., an effect cannot be produced unless the action of the efficient cause attains the patient; in other words, an efficient cause cannot produce an effect unless it attains that effect by its action;

3) and, if the efficient cause is a created or second cause, the concurrence of the first cause, i.e., of God.

a) God concurs in the operation of the creature by moving the creature to operation, i.e., by applying the active power of the creature to operation. The active power of the creature is of itself only in potency to act and cannot pass to act, i.e., cannot pass from the power of acting to actual action, unless God moves it to act.

b) God concurs in the operation of the creature by producing its operation as first cause, so that the operation is totally produced by the creature as by its second cause, and by God as by its first cause. The action of the creature is, indeed, a being by participation. But a being by participation is actually dependent on a being in which essence and existence are identified, i.e., on God, as we shall prove in Natural Theology. Therefore.

683. Effect of efficient cause. — The effect of an efficient cause is the thing produced.

Two questions:

1° Can a created efficient cause produce the subsistence of a substance which it produces ?

We reply *in the affirmative.* A created efficient cause produces substance as terminated. But subsistence is the term of substance. Therefore.

2° Can a created efficient cause produce existence?

a) A created efficient cause cannot be the principal cause of the production of existence.

No principal cause can produce an effect which is not found in its power. But existence is not found in the power of any created cause. Therefore no created efficient cause can, as principal cause, produce existence.

Minor.— There are three really distinct things in a created cause: essence, operative power, and existence. But the principles from which an effect is produced and in which it is virtually contained are the following: the operative power of the cause, which is the proximate principle; the essence, which is the remote principle. The existence, which is merely a condition required for the action or operation of the cause, is not a principle of the production of the effect. Therefore.

b) However, a created efficient cause can, as an instrumental cause employed by God, produce a particular kind of existence, i.e., a limited existence. A second cause can be elevated by divine power so as to attain the existence of its proper effect, and thus limit existence to a particular essence.

POINTS FOR REVIEW

1. Define: efficient cause, proper cause, accidental cause, first cause, univocal cause, analogous cause, subordinated cause, essentially subordinated cause, accidentally subordinated cause.

2. Are creatures first causes or second causes? Explain.

3. Explain how a finite substance is constituted an efficient cause in first act, and how an efficient cause in constituted as such in second act.

4. Enumerate the conditions required that an efficient cause exercise its causality.

5. Can a created efficient cause produce (*a*) the subsistence of a substance it produces, (*b*) the existence of an effect? Explain.

INSTRUMENTAL CAUSE

684. Notion of instrumental cause. — An instrument is defined: *a cause which acts by the power of another, i.e., of the principal cause* (¹).

Cause which acts is the genus of instrument, for an instrument is similar to a principal cause in as much as it is an efficient cause; the differentia of instrument is indicated by the other words of the definition, for an instrument is distinct from a principal cause in as much as the latter acts by its own proper power, whereas an instrument acts by an adventitious power, i.e., by the power of a principal cause.

Power is proper to an efficient cause:

a) when it is a property of the agent, i.e., is inherent in the agent; v.g., the intellect is a property of man;

b) when not a property of the agent, but subordinated to a radical power of acting which is a property of the agent; v.g., the light of glory is subordinated to the intellect of the blessed, and charity is subordinated to the will of the holy, even though they are not of themselves properties, i.e., inherent powers; therefore the blessed see God, and holy persons elicit acts of charity, as principal causes;

c) when not the property of another, but received into an agent as into a subject which supports and appropriates it; v.g., heat received into water. Water receives heat, i.e., the power of heating, which is a property of fire, from fire; but the hot water heats other things by its own power of heating, not by the heat of the fire by which it was itself heated; and thus it is as a principal cause that it heats other things.

---

(1) Goudin, *Primae Partis Physicae*, disp. 2, q. 4, a. 5.

685. Division of instrument. — 1° An instrument may be moral or physical.

A moral instrument is an instrument which either acts only morally, or is only morally moved by the principal cause. Thus, for example, a servant is only morally moved by his master by means of a command. Pacts, documents, and money act only morally in binding, instructing, and arousing men.

A physical instrument is an instrument which is moved physically and operates physically; v.g., a carpenter's hammer.

2° A physical instrument may be either a subjective instrument (instrumentum quod) or a mediatory instrument (instrumentum quo).

A subjective instrument is a supposit which acts in serving another; v.g., a bat used by a baseball player.

A mediatory instrument is either the instrumental power which is in the principal cause, as an accident given to it for action, as, for example, any active power or faculty; or it is the instrumental power which the instrument receives from the principal cause, as, for example, motion in a hammer. Only the *subjective* physical instrument is, properly speaking, an instrument; the *mediatory* physical instrument is only a quasi-instrument.

3° An instrument may be a natural, supernatural, or artificial: an instrument is *natural* which is produced by nature and destined to produce natural effects; *supernatural*, employed by God to produce effects which surpass the powers of nature; *artificial*, a product of art and destined for the production of works of art.

686. Constituent of instrumental cause as such in first act. — 1° *Statement of the problem.* We are at present concerned with physical instrument *in the strict sense*, i.e., with subjective physical instrument, as, for example, a hammer as employed by a workman.

The instrumental cause, i.e., a cause which acts by the power of the principal cause, has two characteristics which distinguish it from the principal cause:

a) as regards its effect: it produces, or at least can produce, an effect which surpasses its own active power;

b) as regards its power: it acts not only by its own power, but by the power of another.

How then, we may ask, is an instrument constituted capable of operation ?   In other words, how is an instrument constituted an efficient cause in first act ?

2° *Opinions.*— *a)* Suarez holds that an instrumental cause is formally a cause which produces an effect which surpasses its own active power.   Therefore he affirms that an instrument is constituted in first act by an active obediential power by which it can act in obedience to a superior agent, i.e., by a power of subserving the ends of a principal cause.   This power is elevated, he maintains, in as much as a superior cause moves it to act by concomitant concurrence (concursus).

b) Thomists hold that an instrumental cause produces, or can produce, an effect which surpasses its own proper power, but do not admit that an instrumental cause consists formally in its being a cause that produces such an effect ([1]).   Thus, for example, the intellect elevated by the light of grace or of glory produces supernatural acts which surpass its own proper power; but yet it is as a principal cause that it produces them, because these are vital acts.   According to Thomists, an instrumental cause is formally such in as much as it acts by the power of a principal cause;   and therefore the principal cause not only moves the power of the instrument to act, but it gives it the power by which it acts.

Therefore Thomists teach that there are two distinct active powers in an instrument:

1) the proper power of the thing which is the instrument, i.e., the previous power;

---

(1) JOANNES A SANCTO THOMA, *Cursus Phil.*, t. II, p. 514 (Reiser).

2) the properly instrumental power.

Previous power is the power which antecedes the instrumental power and disposes the instrument for an action proper and proportionate to it; v.g., the power by which a saw saws.

Properly instrumental power is the transitory motion received from the principal cause which intrinsically changes the instrument and elevates it to produce an effect which surpasses its own proper power; v.g., the power by which a saw produces an artifact.

An instrument is properly constituted in first act by this motion of the principal cause, which is a transitory and passing participation in the instrument of the power of the principal cause.

3° *Exposition of the Thomistic opinion.*

First part.— *A thing which is an instrument of necessity has a proper or previous power destined for its own proper operation.*

Every efficient cause of necessity has a proper power destined for its own proper operation. But a thing which is an instrument is an efficient cause. Therefore a thing which is an instrument of necessity has a proper power destined for its own proper operation .

Minor.— A thing which is an instrument is not a mere material subject, i.e., a mere medium through which the motion of the principal cause passes, but really operates; v.g., the saw used by a carpenter really saws.

NOTE.— When a thing which is an instrument operates by its own proper power, it does not operate properly as an instrument, i.e., is not properly an instrumental cause, but rather as a principal cause applied to action by a superior cause.

Second part.— *An instrument of necessity receives instrumental power, i.e., something by which it is intrinsically changed, from a principal cause.*

A cause which is elevated by the power communicated to it by a principal cause, to produce an effect which is beyond its own proper power, receives from the principal cause something by which it is intrinsically changed.   But an instrument is elevated by the power communicated to it by a principal cause, to produce an effect which is beyond its own proper power. Therefore an instrument of necessity receives something by which it is intrinsically changed, i.e., instrumental power, from a principal cause.

The *major* is evident from its very terms: if an instrument is elevated to produce an effect which surpasses its own proper power, it is by this very fact changed so as to be able to produce this effect.

The *minor* is clear from the statement of the problem.

Third part. — *Instrumental power is a transitory motion received from a principal cause.*

If instrumental power is not a transitory motion, it is a permanent power.   But instrumental power cannot be permanent.   Therefore.

Minor.— A permanent power is a power proper to a cause. But a proper power is a power which belongs to a principal cause.   Therefore.

687. Constituent of an instrument as a cause in second act. — An instrument is constituted a cause in second act by *its own action*, i.e., *by operation*.

An instrument has two operations:

a) an instrumental operation, which corresponds to its instrumental power;

b) a proper operation, which corresponds to its proper power ([1]).

The following points in regard to these two actions should be noted.

_____

(1) III, q. 62, a. 1, ad 1.

1) Sometimes the proper or previous operation and the instrumental operation are really distinct, because they produce really distinct terms. In this case, the proper operation of the instrument can produce an effect which is a disposition for the effect of the instrumental operation, and consequently for the operation of the principal cause.

2) Sometimes the proper operation and the instrumental operation are not really, but only formally distinct, because they produce terms which are not really, but only formally distinct; v.g., when a saw by its act of sawing produces a bed, the division of quantity and the form produced by art are not really distinct terms, but terms which are only formally distinct as regards certain relations and modes of figure, which is more perfect according to the greater perfection of the division of quantity. In this case, we say that the instrument, by its own proper power, acts *dispositively* in the production of the effect of the principal cause, not because it produces a term which is a disposition required for the effect of the principal cause, but because it modifies, as regards mode of operation, the action of the principal agent, so that the principal agent's operation is modified by the inferior cause; v.g., a saw modifies the action of the artificer who uses it in the production of an artifact (¹).

3) Sometimes an instrumental cause produces a proper effect which is not a disposition for the effect of the principal cause. In this case, we say that the instrumental cause operates *dispositively* in the production of the effect of the principal cause, because it modifies, as regards mode of operation, the action of the principal cause; v.g., the washing by water and the production of grace.

688. Effect of instrumental cause. — The effect of an instrumental cause is the thing produced considered as the product of the instrumental cause as moved by the principal cause.

---

(1) JOANNES A SANCTO THOMA, *Cursus Phil.*, t. II, pp. 527-529 (Reiser).

POINTS FOR REVIEW

1. Define: instrumental cause, moral instrument, physical instrument, subjective physical instrument, mediatory physical instrument, previous power of instrumental cause, properly instrumental power.

2. When is power proper to an efficient cause?

3. Distinguish between the teaching of Suarez and that of St. Thomas as regards the formal constituent of instrumental cause.

4. What are the two operations of an instrumental cause?

5. Explain how an instrumental cause acts dispositively in the production of the effect of a principal cause.

———————

PRINCIPLE OF CAUSALITY

689. Notion of the principle of causality. — The principle of causality is a principle which expresses a necessary nexus between a thing and its efficient cause. It is more accurately denominated the « principle of efficient causality », although antonomastically it is simply called the *principle of causality*.

690. Origin of our knowledge of the principle of causality. — Our first knowledge of the principle of causality is derived from *motion*, i.e., from *becoming*, as known from experience. Thus, according to common sense, our first enunciation of the principle of causality is as follows: *everything which becomes*, i.e., comes into being, is produced, *has a cause* (¹).

691. Metaphysical enunciation of the principle of causality. — The principle of causality, of which we derive our first knowledge from our experience with motion, derives its metaphysical enunciation from a resolution of becoming — *tou* fieri — into act and potency, which first divide being (Cf. n. 551-552).

1° Becoming (*To* fieri) essentially implies a union of act and potency. Hence the principle of causality may be metaphysically enunciated: *everything composed of potency and act has a cause*, or *every composite being has a cause* (²).

2° The essence and existence of a being composed of potency and act are really distinct, and therefore such a being is

---

(1) I-II, q. 75, a. 1, Sed contra.
(2) I, q. 3, a. 7, c.

a finite, participated being. Hence we have the following formulae of the principle of causality: *a being whose essence and existence are distinct is caused by another* ([1]); *every finite being has a cause; every being by participation has a cause.*

3° Scholastics also give the following enunciation of the principle of causality: *everything which moves,* i.e., is in motion, *is moved by another* ([2]).

Suarez explains this principle thus: everything which moves, i.e., passes from potency to act, is moved by another in this sense: it receives its motion or act from another, if it has only passive potency for act; otherwise, it receives from another the operative power by which it moves, as happens, for example, in the case of living beings ([3]).

Thomists are unanimous in teaching that this principle signifies that any union of potency and act whatsoever is effected by an extrinsic efficient cause. Hence even living beings, which have operative power, cannot move, i.e., operate, unless they are moved by another to the act by which they move. In other words, no created cause can operate unless its potency is applied to act by the first cause, i.e., by God.

The reason for this is obvious: a being which of itself has only potency for act has not act of its own, but must receive it from another.

NOTE.— *a*) If we use the term motion in its strict sense, the principle: everything which moves is moved by another, is not the metaphysical enunciation of the principle of causality, but rather the principle of causality as understood in Philosophy of Nature.

b) This principle is applicable not only to the order of execution, but also to the order of intention, and hence is valid for final cause, as well as for efficient cause.

4° We have also the following enunciation of the principle of causality: *act is absolutely prior to potency* ([4]).

---

(1) I, q. 3, a. 4, c.
(2) I, q. 2, a. 3, c.
(3) SUAREZIUS, *Disp. Met.*, d. 29, sect. I, n. VII.
(4) I, q. 3, a. 1.

We say that act is *absolutely* prior, i.e., prior in the order of efficient causality, to potency, because relatively, i.e., in the order of material causality, potency is prior to act.

Act is absolutely prior to potency, because a being in potency can be reduced to act only by a being in act ([1]).

Other formulae of the principle of causality:
> *A thing cannot be the efficient cause of itself* ([2]).
> *Every effect has a cause.*
> *Everything caused has a cause.*

692. Principle of causality according to Kant. — Kant gives the following enunciation of the principle of causality: *everything which begins has a cause.*

Is this a valid formula of the principle of causality?

Reply: the principle, according to Kant's formula, is quite true; but it is not the principle of causality in the whole of its universality. The principle of causality is not founded on time or on beginning in time, but on the composition of potency and act in being. Hence, even if a composite being existed from eternity, it would have been caused; v.g., if the world existed from eternity, it would have been produced from eternity by God.

693. Principle of sufficient reason. — The principle of sufficient reason is enunciated as follows: *nothing exists without a sufficient reason.*

We are indebted to Leibniz for this formula.

There are some philosophers who use the principle of sufficient reason rather than the principle of causality. Is this justifiable?

Reply: the principle of sufficient reason has greater extension than the principle of causality. It is applicable to the intrinsic causes, as well as to the extrinsic causes; v.g., the sufficient reason of motion is found only in potency. More-

---

(1) I, q. 3, a. 1.
(2) I, q. 2, a. 3.

over, this principle is applicable to God: God, as an uncaused being, has the sufficient reason of Himself in Himself, whereas a being by participation has the sufficient reason of its existence only in some other being.

694. The principle of causality is a self-evident proposition.— 1° *Preliminaries*. A self-evident proposition is a proposition in which the nexus between the subject and the predicate is clear from the very notion or analysis of the terms.

2° *Opinions*.— The Empirists, as Hume, and certain modern philosophers, as Leroy, deny the validity of the principle of causality.

3° *Confirmation.*

The first formula: *everything composed of potency and act has a cause*, is self-evident. Potency of itself is only potency, and can be reduced to act only by a being in act, i.e., by a cause.

The second formula: *every being by participation has a cause*, is also self-evident. A being by participation is a being which has not existence from itself, i.e., which is not determined of itself to exist. Therefore it must be determined to exist by another, i.e., by an extrinsic cause.

POINTS FOR REVIEW

1. How do we first come to a knowledge of the principle of causality?

2. Give the metaphysical enunciation of the principle of causality, and also Kant's formula of this principle.

3. Compare the explanation offered by Suarez with that given by Thomists of the principle: everything which moves is moved by another.

EXISTENCE OF EFFICIENT CAUSALITY IN FINITE BEINGS

1) **695. Statement of the question.**— 1° A finite being is any being, corporeal or spiritual, which is distinct from God.

2° *a)* Avicebron (1020-1070) denies that corporeal beings are endowed with any kind of activity, and attributes their production to some spiritual substance which pervades all bodies.

b) Descartes holds that the essence of bodies consists in quantity. Moreover, he teaches that no body is endowed with activity, for quantity is a principle of passivity, not a principle of activity.

c) Malebranche (1638-1715), for moral reasons, contends that only God can act efficiently, i.e., can be an efficient cause, and that creatures merely provide God, of Whom alone efficient causality is a prerogative, with occasions for His operation, i.e., for the exercise of His causality. This teaching is called Occasionalism.

d) Many modern philosophers, as the exponents of the experimental sciences, teach that the concept of causality is metaphysical, and therefore arbitrary. Hence they maintain that creatures are not true efficient causes, but merely antecedent phenomena from which other phenomena result, without any causal dependence.

e) Scholastics are unanimous in affirming that all finite . beings are endowed with activity.

2) **696. Statement of the thesis.**— We know from experience, both internal and external, that finite beings are true efficient causes. Our present purpose is to prove metaphysically that all finite beings are endowed with activity.

THESIS.— ALL FINITE BEINGS ARE EFFICIENT CAUSES.

Any being which is in act is an efficient cause. But all finite beings are in act. Therefore all finite beings are efficient causes.

Major.— A being which is an active principle, i.e., a principle of action, is an efficient cause. But every being which is in act is an active principle. Therefore.

The *minor* is evident: every being as such is in act.

697. Corollary.— The concept of causality is a metaphysical concept, because it signifies the dependence of a thing on another *for its existence.* Hence metaphysical causality may be ignored, overlooked by the experimental scientists, who are concerned only with the *empirical* union of objects; but it may not be legitimately denied by them.

698. Difficulties.— 1° An efficient cause is a cause on which a thing is necessarily dependent as an effect. But God is the only cause on which all finite beings, as effects, are necessarily dependent. Therefore God alone is an efficient cause (Malebranche).

Major.— On which a thing is necessarily dependent, by absolute or hypothetical necessity, *I concede;* by absolute necessity only, *I deny.*

Minor.— On which all finite beings are dependent by absolute necessity, *I concede;* by hypothetical necessity, *I deny.*

Absolutely speaking, God could have produced all the effects of second causes, i. e., of finite beings, without these causes. But, given the order established by God in the world, effects are necessarily dependent on second causes, i. e., on finite beings.

2° Efficient causes do not exist without necessity. But God can immediately produce all things. Therefore efficient causes do not exist (Malebranche).

Major.— Without absolute necessity or necessity of suitability, *I concede;* without absolute necessity only, *I deny.*

Minor.— God, absolutely speaking, can immediately produce all things, *I concede;* it is suitable or fitting that He do so, *I deny.*

Since finite beings, i. e., creatures, are active principles, it is fitting that they exercise their activity, i. e., that they be really efficient causes.

3° Accidents cannot be transmitted from one subject to another subject. But, if bodies were efficient causes, accidents could be transmitted from one subject to another subject.   Therefore bodies are not efficient causes (Leibniz).

Major.— The same accident cannot be transmitted from one subject to another subject, *I concede;* an accident cannot be produced by the action of an agent in another subject, *I deny.*

Minor.— The same accident cannot be transmitted from one subject to another subject, *I deny;* an accident cannot be produced by the action of a body in another subject, *I concede.*

When a body exercises its efficient causality on another subject, it produces a new accident in that subject, but does not transmit to that subject any individual accident of its own.

———————

CHAPTER III

FINAL CAUSE

Prologue.— In this chapter, we shall deal with final cause and with the principle of finality. Hence there will be two articles in the chapter. In an appendix, we shall discuss the relation of the four causes to each other and to their effects.

Final cause
- Notion of end
- Division of end
- Constituent of final cause in first act
- Constituent of final cause in second act
- Objection
- Condition required that an end exercise its causality
- Effects of final cause

Principle of finality
- Enunciation of the principle of finality
- The principle of finality is a self-evident proposition
- False formulae of the principle of finality
- Manners of acting for an end

Appendix
- Order of perfection of the four causes
- Mutual causation of causes
- Order of causality of causes
- Order of priority of cause and effect
- Order of perfection of cause and effect
- Concept of cause is analogous

FINAL CAUSE

699. Notion of end.— End signifies term. It can have two meanings:

a) that which terminates something; v.g., the effect obtained by an operation is the term of that operation *in the order of execution;*

b) that towards which an appetite tends. This is the meaning of an end *in the order of intention*, and thus understood it has the nature of a cause ([1]).

An end as a cause may be an *objective end* (finis qui, finis cuius gratia), a *subjective end* (finis cui), or a *formal end* (finis quo).

a) An *objective end* is the thing desired, or the good for whose sake an action is performed; v.g., the money for the sake of which a man works.

b) A *subjective end* is the subject for which a good is desired; v.g., a son for whom a father desires money.

c) A *formal end* is the attainment and possession of an objective end; v.g., the possession of money.

The objective end, the subjective end, and the formal end are not really distinct ends, but different aspects under which end is considered. An end is properly a cause when considered under the aspect of objective end.

700. Division of end.— 1° From the point of view of its object, an end may be proximate or remote.

---

(1) Finis, etsi postremus in exsecutione, tamen est primus in intentione agentis; et hoc modo habet rationem causae.— I-II, q. 1, a. 1, ad 1.

a) A *proximate end* is an end to which no other end is related, i.e., an end which an agent immediately intends. Health, for example, is the proximate end of a person who takes medicine.

A *remote end* is an end to which other ends are related i.e., directed as intermediaries. Study, for example, and not health, is the remote end of a student who takes medicine.

b) A remote end may be intermediate or ultimate.

An *intermediate end* is an end to which a proximate end is related, and which itself is related to another end. Study for example, which is intended for the acquirement of a B.A. degree can be the intermediate end of a student who takes medicine.

An intermediate end is not a *mere means*, because an intermediate end is a good which is sought for its own sake, whereas a means is not sought for its own sake, but solely for the sake of an end; v.g., the taking of a bitter medicine is a mere means to the restoration of health.

An *ultimate end* is an end to which other ends are subordinated, but which itself is not subordinated to any higher end.

c) An ultimate end may be such relatively or absolutely.

A *relatively ultimate end* is an end which is not subordinated to another end in its own order, but which can be subordinated to another end of a higher order. The acquirement of knowledge, for example, can be the natural ultimate end of a man who studies, and it can also be directed to the attainment of eternal life.

An *absolutely ultimate end* is an end which is ultimate in all orders, and so cannot be subordinated to any other end. The glory of God, for example, is the absolutely ultimate end of all creatures.

2° As regards influence, an end may be principal or secondary.

A *principal end* is an end which primarily moves an agent and is sufficient of itself to do so. The glory of God, for example, is the principal end which a saintly person has in view in studying.

A *secondary end* (accessory end) is an end which is annexed to a principal end, but in such manner that it does not primarily move the agent; v.g., spiritual delight can be the secondary end of a saintly person who studies.

3° End considered subjectively, i.e., in regard to the intention of the agent, is divided into the end of the work (finis operis) and the end of the agent (finis operantis).

The *end of the work* is the end to which the work tends or is destined of its very nature; v.g., the relief of the poor is the end of almsgiving.

The *end of the agent* is the end which the agent intends when acting. The end of the work may be the end of the agent, or it may differ from it; v.g., a person who gives alms may intend the relief of the poor, or he may intend his own glory.

4° An end is *natural* or *supernatural* according as it can or cannot be attained by natural powers.

701. Constituent of final cause in first act.— There are two questions which we must answer in order to determine how an end is constituted a cause in first act.

1) First question: is an end constituted a cause in first act only by good as such? In other words, is it also possible that an end be constituted a cause in first act by evil as evil?

William of Ockam, Durandus, and the Nominalists hold that sometimes an end is constituted in first act by evil as such. Scholastics commonly affirm that an end is constituted a cause in first act only by a good as such.

The truth of the Scholastic opinion is evident. For an end is a cause in as much as it attracts the appetite. But only a good as such can attract the appetite. Therefore.

2) Second question: is it by a good as such or by something apprehended as a good that an end is formally constituted as a cause in first act?

9

Scholastics commonly admit that an end is constituted a cause by a good apprehended as such, but point out that the apprehension of good is not the formal constituent of good as a final cause, for this apprehension is only a condition required in order that a good which of itself is an end exercise its function of final cause. For an end is constituted a cause in as much as it attracts the appetite. But an end attracts the appetite by its own goodness, not by the apprehension of its goodness. Therefore.

702. Constituent of final cause in second act.— An end is constituted a cause in second act by love of itself, i.e., by the love or desire it excites in the appetite. An act of love can be considered under two aspects:

a) as an act elicited by the appetite, i.e., as an act desiring, an act of the appetite proceeding from the appetite. In this sense, it is more an effect than the second act of an end;

b) as an act which is passively dependent on an end, i.e., as an act of being desired, a modification of the appetite by a good. It is in this sense that an act of love constitutes an end as a cause in second act, i.e., that it is the constituent of the actual causality of an end ([1]).

Proof.— An end moves in second act in as much as it attracts the appetite to itself. But an end attracts the appetite to itself by an act of love, not in as much as this act is dependent on the appetite, but in as much as it is dependent on the end. Therefore an end moves in second act, i.e., is constituted a cause in second act, by an act of love in as much as this act is dependent on an end; in other words, an end moves in second act because it is actually loved.

703. Objection.— If an end is a mover only in as much as it is desired, it is a mover only in a metaphorical sense, and hence is not a real cause.

---

[1] Sicut influere causae efficientis est agere, ita influere causae finalis est appeti et desiderari.— *De Veritate*, q. 22, a. 2.

Reply : an end does not move physically, as an efficient cause ; but it really moves in the intentional order, in as much as it is really intended. Thus it is a real cause on which all effects are dependent for existence.

704.— Condition required that an end exercise its causality.— Knowledge or apprehension of the end is the condition required that an end actually cause, i.e., exercise its causality. .

705. Effects of final cause.— The first effect of an end is an act of love in as much as this act is dependent on the appetite.

The other effects of final cause are all the operations of the appetite and of the other faculties in regard to ends and means, and the effects of these operations.

POINTS FOR REVIEW

1. Distinguish between end in the order of execution and end in the order of intention, and show whether or not the former is a cause.

2. Define objective end, subjective end, and formal end; and state whether or not they are distinct ends.

3. Define: proximate end, remote end, intermediate end, ultimate end, absolutely ultimate end.

4. Distinguish between end of the work and end of the agent.

5. Explain whether or not good is the only constituent of an end as a cause in first act, and whether this good may be only an apparent good.

6. How is an end constituted a cause in second act ?

7. Enumerate the effects of final cause.

PRINCIPLE OF FINALITY

706. Enunciation of the principle of finality.— The principle of finality may be enunciated in two ways :

a) it is enunciated in a formula derived from the consideration of the potentiality in finite beings : *all potency is for act,* that is to say, *all potency tends to act as to its good and its end ;*

b) it is enunciated absolutely, i.e., from the point of view of act, in the following formula : *every agent acts for an end,* i.e., every agent is for operation for which it is destined of its very nature, that is to say, a thing is for itself when in operation.

707. The principle of finality is a self-evident proposition. — 1° *Preliminaries.*— *a*) A self-evident proposition is a proposition in which the predicate is contained in the notion of the subject. Hence a self-evident proposition is universal, necessary, and certain, not a mere law based on experiment.

b) Certain philosophers of ancient times, as Democritus, and others of more recent years, as the Darwinists, deny the existence of finality in natural agents. They maintain that the principle of finality is a mere law based on the acts of the will, and which is illegitimately extended to all agents. Many modern philosophers, as the Cartesians, etc. hold this opinion.

Aristotle and all Scholastics teach that the principle of finality is a universal and necessary principle.

First formula : *all potency is for act.*

Potency as potency connotes a transcendental relation to act as to its good or end. Hence the proposition : all potency is for act, is a self-evident proposition.

Second formula : *every agent acts for an end.*

Every agent as such tends to a determinate action, and, in transitive action, to a determinate effect, as to the good which it desires for itself or for another. But the good which an agent desires is an end. Therefore every agent acts for an end, and this principle is a self-evident proposition ([1]).

708. False formulae of the principle of finality.— a) The principle of finality is enunciated by certain philosophers, as Janet ([2]), in the following formula : *everything is for an end.*

This formula is incorrect, because the concept of end derives from the concept of agent, not from the concept of thing.

b) Others use the formula : *every effect is for an end* ([3]).

This formula is inadmissible, for it is not applicable to chance : a thing which is produced by chance is not produced for an end ([4]).

709. Manners of acting for an end.— An agent acts for an end either formally, i.e., directively, or materially.

1° Intellectual agents, which have knowledge not only of the thing which is an end, but also of the end as properly an end, as attainable by determinate means, act formally for an end. Hence intellectual agents, properly speaking, move themselves to an end, because they can choose means for its attainment. Moreover, they can provide themselves with at least the end of the agent.

2° Sentient agents and natural agents act materially for an end.

a) Sentient agents, i.e., irrational animals, have no knowledge of an end as such, i.e., as attainable by means, but yet can have apprehension of the good which is the end, from

---

(1) I-II, q. 1, a. 2.
(2) P. JANET, *Les Causes finales,* p. 6.
(3) HUGON, *Met.,* 3a p.
(4) Omnia quae fiunt, aut fiunt a casu, aut fiunt propter finem. Quae enim accidunt praeter intentionem finis, dicuntur accidere casualiter.— *In Phys.,* I. II, l. 13.

which comes the impulse to the end. Hence they are said to act *apprehensively* for an end.

b) Natural agents have no knowledge whatsoever of their end, but tend to it in virtue of their natural appetite, in as much as they execute, i.e., carry out, the direction or inclination to their end received from an intellectual agent which knows their end as an end. Hence they are said to act only *executively* for an end.

POINTS FOR REVIEW

1. Give the enunciation of the principle of finality.
2. Is the principle of finality self-evident?   Explain.
3. Explain the ways in which agents act for an end.

RELATIONS OF THE FOUR CAUSES TO EACH OTHER AND TO THEIR EFFECTS

710. Order of perfection of the four causes.— 1° The extrinsic causes, i.e., efficient cause and final cause, are more perfect than the intrinsic causes, i.e., material cause and formal cause, for the latter are partial causes: our concept of an intrinsic cause is the concept of a part, which is an imperfection.

Hence it is impossible that God be a formal cause, even by analogy.

2° Formal cause is more perfect than material cause.

3° Final cause is more perfect than efficient cause, for it is the good to which efficient cause tends, that for which it operates.

711. Mutual causation of causes.— *Causes are causes of each other in different genera*, not in the same genus of causality. But yet this axiom cannot be verified in all combinations of causes.

Efficient cause and final cause are causes of each other: efficient cause is dependent on final cause for its causality, because an agent acts only for an end. The end or final cause is dependent on efficient cause for the attainment of its being, because an agent acts for the realization of an end.

Similarly, matter and form are causes of each other as regards their being: form is the cause of matter in as much as it gives matter its actual existence; and matter is the cause of form in as much as it sustains form (¹). But material cause

---

(1) *In Metaph.*, l. V, l. 5.

and efficient cause are not causes of each other, nor are formal cause and final cause causes of each other (¹).

712. Order of the four causes.— 1° The first place must be assigned to final cause, which is called the cause of causes, i.e., the cause of the other three causes. The other causes receive their causality from final cause: the efficient cause acts only for an end; and it is in dependence upon the action of the efficient cause that the formal cause (form) perfects the material cause (matter), and that matter supports form (²).

2° The second place belongs to efficient cause. Without the influx or causation of efficient cause, matter would not be actuated by form, nor would form be sustained in matter.

3° Form, i.e., formal cause, holds the third place, for it better corresponds to final cause and efficient cause than does matter, i.e., material cause.

4° In the last place comes matter, material cause.

713. Order of priority of cause and effect.— 1° Every cause is prior in nature to its effect, for an effect is dependent on its cause as on its principle.

2° A cause is not necessarily prior in time to its effect. Moreover, a cause as actually causing and its effect must exist at the same time: for in the instant when a cause actually causes, in that same instant must exist the effect in which the causality of the cause is terminated.

714. Order of perfection of cause and effect.— 1° A cause, considered as exercising its causality, is always more perfect than its effect. It is more perfect to give than to receive. But a cause always gives something to its effect, and receives nothing in return. Therefore a cause is more perfect than its effect.

---

(1) JOANNES A SANCTO THOMA, *Cursus Phil.*, t. II, pp. 209-213.
(2) *De Veritate*, q. 28, a. 7, c.

2° Not every cause is more perfect in entity, i.e., in nature, than its effect.

a) Matter and form are in nature less perfect than their effect, which is the compound: for the composite reality is a whole of which matter and form are the parts.

b) The principal efficient cause is not always more perfect than its effect: if it is a univocal cause, it is equal to its effect in perfection; if it is an anologous cause, it is more perfect than its effect.

The instrumental cause is not necessarily as perfect as its effect: it can be equal to its effect in perfection, or it can be less perfect than its effect.

c) Final cause, considered as the objective end of the work, is always more perfect than that of which it is the end, because it is naturally related to the appetite, as act, i.e., perfection, to potency.

Final cause, considered as the end of the agent, can be less perfect than that of which it is the end, for, if the desire of the agent is inordinate, i.e., sinful, the agent tends to something which is imperfect.

Similarly, the end, considered as an effect, can be less perfect than its efficient cause, because the effect is not of a higher order than its efficient cause.

715. Concept of cause is analogous.— The concept of cause is analogous. In the concept of cause, we can distinguish three elements:

a) the thing which is the cause;

b) causality;

c) the relation resulting from causality.

But these three elements are analogous:

a) The thing which is the cause can belong to different genera; and it can even exist outside all genera: God is a cause which does not belong to any genus.

b) Causality is analogous. Sometimes causality consists in action; sometimes it is a substantial or accidental entity, as matter and form. Causality in God, Who is pure act, is not action really distinct from His essence, but is the divine essence itself.

c) The relation resulting from causality is also analogous. Sometimes it is a real relation, and sometimes it is a relation of reason; v.g., the relation of the Creator to the creature is only a relation of reason, because in the Creator, Who is pure act, there can be no predicamental accident.

POINTS FOR REVIEW

1. Why are the extrinsic causes more perfect than the intrinsic causes? Why is final cause more perfect than efficient cause? Is matter less perfect than form?

2. Is mutual causation possible in the case of: *a*) efficient cause and final cause; *b*) material cause and formal cause; *c*) material cause and efficient cause? Explain.

3. Give the order of causality of the four causes.

4. Compare the causes and their effects as regards *a*) order of priority, *b*) order of perfection.

5. Is the concept of cause univocal or analogous? Explain.

METAPHYSICS OF INFINITE BEING

INTRODUCTION

716. Nominal definition of theology.— The part of Metaphysics which deals with infinite being is commonly called natural theology.

Etymologically, the word theology ($\theta\epsilon o\lambda o\gamma i\alpha = \theta\epsilon os$, $\lambda o\gamma os$) signifies science of God.

Both the ancient philosophers, as Aristotle, and the Fathers of the Church speak of theology. But the latter are concerned with supernatural theology, which, according to its nominal definition, is the *science of God which is based on Revelation.* Aristotle is concerned with natural theology, which, according to its nominal definition, is the *science of God which is based on things of which we can have natural knowledge.*

Many philosophers, following the example of Leibniz, call Metaphysics of infinite being Theodicy; but this name is inaccurate, for Theodicy ($\theta\epsilon os$, $\delta\iota\kappa\eta$) signifies the justification of God.

717. Real definition of theology. — Natural theology is defined: *the science of God, considered under the common aspect of being, acquired by the natural light of reason.* This definition contains:

a) the *material object:* God, i.e., infinite being.

b) the *formal object quod:* God under the common aspect of being, as He is the first and most perfect being, the first efficient cause of the beings of the natural order. Thus natural theology is distinguished from supernatural theology, which deals with God as the Deity, i.e., according to the mystery of

His intimate life, and as the author of the supernatural life (¹).

c) the *formal object quo:* the natural light of reason as it shines forth in the third degree of abstraction. Thus natural theology is again distinguished from supernatural theology, whose formal object quo is the light of Revelation together with the light reason, i.e., the light of reason illumined by faith.

718. Division of natural theology.— Natural theology answers the following three questions: does God exist ?   what is God ? how does God operate outside Himself ? Hence there will be three books in natural theology:

Book   I: Existence of God.

Book II: Essence and attributes of God.

Book III: Operation of God outside Himself.

---

(1) Theologia naturalis Deum cognoscit ab exteriori, dum Theologia supernaturalis, etsi obscure, vitam ejus intimam cognoscit. Differentia inter duas illas cognitiones est maxima, sicut maxima est differentia inter videre hominem ab exteriori et penetrare ejus cordis intima.— Cf. GARRIGOU-LAGRANGE, *De Revelatione*, t. I, p. 9, ed. 2a.

BOOK I

Existence of God

THE ONLY CHAPTER

Prologue.— In this chapter, we shall deal first with the question of whether the existence of God is immediately known. Secondly, having shown that the existence of God is not immediately known to us, we shall prove that the existence of God is demonstrable. Thirdly, we shall demonstrate the existence of God. Atheism will be discussed briefly in an appendix.

The existence of God is not immediately known

- Statement of the question
- Thesis: The proposition, *God exists*, is self-evident in itself, but not self-evident to us
- St. Anselm's argument
- Descartes' argument
- Leibniz' argument

The existence of God is demonstrable

- Statement of the question
- Opinions
- Thesis: The existence of God can be demonstrated, not a priori, but a posteriori
- Difficulties

Demonstration of the existence of God

- General preliminaries
  - I. Demonstration of the existence of an unmoved mover, which is God, from motion
    - Statement of the question
    - Demonstration
    - Corollaries
    - Difficulties
  - II. Demonstration of the existence of the first efficient cause, which is God, from essentially subordinated causes
    - Statement of the question
    - Demonstration
    - Corollaries
    - Scholion
    - Difficulties

THE EXISTENCE OF GOD IS NOT IMMEDIATELY KNOWN

719. Statement of the question. — 1° The term God, according to its nominal definition, is used to signify the first efficient cause of the world, i.e., of all finite beings.

Existence is the proper act of real being as such, or the act by which a thing is placed outside of nothing. Existence is predicated of God and creatures analogously.

2° It is commonly held by Scholastics, and especially by Thomists, that all men have a common and confused knowledge of God, in as much as they can easily perceive from the order which exists in the world that there is a supreme author of this order (¹).

But they affirm that the existence of God is never known by intuition (i.e., immediately), but always by some kind of scientific or confused reasoning. Their teaching may be stated as follows:

The proposition, *God exists*, is a proposition which is self-evident in itself, but not self-evident to us.

a) *A proposition self-evident in itself* is one in which the predicate is immediately contained in the notion of the subject, but this inclusion is not immediately perceived by us, because we have not sufficient knowledge of the subject and the predicate.

---

(1) Est enim quaedam communis et confusa Dei cognitio, quae quasi omnibus hominibus adest. . . quia naturali ratione statim homo in aliqualem Dei cognitionem pervenire potest; videntes enim homines res naturales secundum ordinem certum currere, quum ordinatio absque ordinatore non sit, percipiunt ut in pluribus aliquem esse ordinatorem rerum quas vidimus.— *Contra Gentes*, l. III, c. 38.

b) *A proposition self-evident to us* is one in which the immediate inclusion of the predicate in the notion of the subject is
immediately known by us, because we have sufficient knowledge of the subject and predicate; v.g., the whole is greater
than the part; being is not non-being, etc.

3° St. Anselm claims that the existence of God is self-
evident to us from a *divine illumination* (¹). Hence he sets
forth an argument to show that the existence of God is immediately known to us.

4° Descartes and Leibniz maintain that the idea of God
is innate in us. Therefore, according to their teaching, a
sound mind has knowledge of God's existence from the mere
apprehension of the terms, and without any process of reasoning (²).

5° The Ontologists, as Gioberti, Malebranche, and Rosmini, and the Neo-Platonists assert that God is the first known
by the human intellect, even in this life.

720. Statement of the thesis.

THESIS.— The proposition, god exists, is self-
evident in itself, but not self-
evident to us.

First part. — *The proposition, God exists, is self-evident in
itself.* — A proposition whose predicate is the same as its subject is a proposition self-evident in itself. But in the proposition, *God exists*, the predicate is the same as the subject.
Therefore the proposition, *God exists*, is self-evident in itself.

Minor.—We shall prove later that the existence of God is
identified with His quiddity.

Second part.— *The proposition, God exists, is not self-
evident to us.*— The proposition, *God exists*, is not self-evident

---

(1) Gratias tibi, bone Domine, gratias tibi; quia quod prius credidi, te
donante, jam sic intelligo, te illuminante, ut si te esse nolim credere, non
possim non intelligere.— *Proslogium*, c. IV.
(2) Billuart, *De Deo*, dissert. I, a. 1.

to us, if we know the quiddity of God only by means of demonstration. But we know the quiddity of God only by means of demonstration. Therefore the proposition, *God exists*, is not self-evident to us.

The *major* is evident from the statement of the question.

Minor.— The first and direct object of the human intellect is the abstracted quiddity of a material thing, from which we can arise, by means of the principle of causality, to a knowledge of the first efficient cause of the world, i.e., to a knowledge of God

721. St. Anselm's argument.— It may be stated as follows: The term *God* signifies a being greater than which none can be conceived. But a being greater than which none can be conceived exist in reality; for what exists in reality and in the intellect is greater than that which exists in the intellect only. Therefore the proposition *God exists*, is self-evident to us.

To this argument we reply as follows:

First, the term *God* does not necessarily signify a being greater than which none can be conceived, for some have believed that God is a body (¹).

Secondly, even though we concede the major, we must distinguish the minor. A being greater than which none can be conceived is apprehended by the intellect as including real existence in its notion, *I concede;* is affirmed by the intellect as having existence in reality, *I deny.*

St. Anselm confounds the *logical* order with the *real* order. A being which is conceived as having existence in the intellect and in reality is conceived to be greater in the logical order than a being which has existence in the intellect only; but it cannot be argued from this that this greater being exists in reality.

(1) I, q. 2, a. 1, ad 2.

722. Descartes' argument.— What is contained in a clear and distinct idea of a thing may be affirmed of that thing. But actual existence is contained in a clear and distinct idea of the most perfect being, which is God. Therefore actual existence may be affirmed by God.

We reply to this argument as follows:

Major.— It may be affirmed of it in the logical order, *I concede;* in the real order, *I subdistinguish:* if that thing is already known by the intellect as existing in reality, *I concede;* otherwise, *I deny.*

Minor.— Actual existence is contained in a clear and distinct idea of the most perfect being in the logical order, *I concede;* in the real order, *I subdistinguish:* if the most perfect being is already known as existing, *I concede;* otherwise, *I deny.*

Descartes, like St. Anselm, confounds the logical order with the real order.

723. Leibniz' argument.— An infinitely perfect being is possible. But, if an infinitely perfect being did not exist in reality, it would not be possible, because it could not be produced either by itself or by another. Therefore an infinitely perfect being, i.e., God, exists in reality.

Major.— It is possible, i.e., it is apprehended as negatively possible, i.e., as non-contradictory, *I concede;* is apprehended as positively possible, *I subdistinguish:* when it is already apprehended as actually existing, *I concede;* when it is not already apprehended as actually existing, *I deny.*

Minor.— It would not be possible, i.e., it would not be apprehended as negatively possible, i.e., as non-contradictory, *I deny;* it would not be apprehended as positively possible, *I concede.*

Leibniz is guilty of an unlawful transition from the logical order to the real order. Infinite being, its existence not being known, is apprehended as *logically* possible; but it is not apprehended as *really* possible, i.e., *positively* possible, unless its essence and existence are already known, for real potency is known only from act. Besides, we may not properly speak of the possiblity of God, since God is pure act, and therefore does not admit of potency.

POINTS FOR REVIEW

1. Can the existence of God be known without some kind of reasoning?

2. State the teaching of St. Anselm on our knowledge of the existence of God.

3. Explain why the proposition, *God exists*, is self-evident in itself, but not self-evident to us.

THE EXISTENCE OF GOD IS DEMONSTRABLE

724. Statement of the question.— A demonstration is a syllogism which engenders knowledge. Demonstration is either *a priori* or *a posteriori*.

An *a priori demonstration* is a demonstration which proceeds from cause to effect, that is to say, from things which are strictly prior.

An *a posteriori demonstration* is one which proceeds from effect to cause, that is to say, from things which are strictly posterior, i.e., posterior in being, although as regards us they may be prior, i.e., prior in knowledge.

725. Opinions.— 1° Moses Maimonides, among the ancient philosophers, held that God could be known only by faith.

Protestants, as represented by Calvin, Huxley, Gore, etc., hold the same opinion.

Jansenius taught that the knowledge of God which ethnics acquire was of no importance for a religious and moral life. His disciples, as Pascal, claim that God cannot be known by the natural light of reason (¹).

2° The traditionalists assert that the existence of God is known either from tradition received from our First Parents, who learned it from divine revelation (De Bonald, Lamennais, Bautin), or that it cannot be demonstrated without the aid of divine revelation (Bonetty, Ventura).

---

(1) Parlons maintenant selon les lumières naturelles. S'il y a un Dieu, il est infiniment incompréhensible. Nous sommes donc incapables de connaître ni ce qu'il est, ni s'il est.— *Pensées*, t. 2, p. 145, fragm. 133, 1904.

Yet some hold that Pascal denied the validity of only such demonstrations as are based on positive sciences.

3° The positivists (Comte, Condillac, Hume, Stuart Mill, Hobbes, Berkeley, Spencer), who hold that the principle of causality is a mere empirical law, likewise claim that the existence of God cannot be demonstrated. This opinion is supported by the idealists (Kant, Schelling, Hegel), according to whom the principle of causality is not objective, but a subjective form of the intellect.

4° This opinion is held too by modernists who profess the doctrine of *agnosticism*, according to which human reason cannot know any supersensible thing (Loisy, Tyrrell, Sabatier, William James, etc.).

5° It is the common teaching of Scholastics that the existence of God cannot be demonstrated a priori, but can be demonstrated a posteriori.

726. Statement of the thesis.— The Vatican Council defined that Holy Mother the Church holds and teaches that God, the beginning and end of all things, can be known with certainty by the natural light of human reason from created things.— *Dei Filius, c.* 1.

> **THESIS.**—The existence of God can be demon-
> strated, not a priori, but a poste-
> riori.

First part.— *The existence of God cannot be demonstrated a priori.*—An a priori demonstration is one that argues from cause to effect. But God has no cause. Therefore the existence of God cannot be demonstrated a priori.

Minor.— The term *God* is accepted as meaning the first efficient cause of the world.

Second part. — *The existence of God be can demonstrated a posteriori.*— If the existence of God can be demonstrated from the world, and especially from the sensible world, as from an effect, the existence of God can be demonstrated a posteriori. But the existence of God can be demonstrated from the world, especially from the sensible world, as from an effect. Therefore the existence of God can be demonstrated a posteriori.

The *major* is evident.

Minor.— We can demonstrate the existence of the proper cause of an effect, when that effect is better known to us than its cause. But the sensible world, whose existence is clearly known to everyone, is admitted to be an effect whose proper efficient cause is God. Therefore.

727. Difficulties.— 1° An article of faith cannot be demonstrated. But the existence of God is an article of faith. Therefore the existence of God cannot be demonstrated.

Major.— What is properly an article of faith, *I concede;* what is a preamble of faith, *I deny.*

Minor.— Is properly an article of faith, *I deny;* is a preamble of faith, *I concede.*

Since the existence of God can be known by natural reason, it is not properly an article of faith, but a preamble of faith. Yet there is nothing to prevent one who does not know the existence of God by natural reason from holding it on faith.

2° The means of demonstration is the quiddity of a thing. But, if we do not know the existence of God, we cannot know His quiddity. Therefore the existence of God cannot be demonstrated.

Major.— Of an a priori demonstration, *I concede;* of an a posteriori demonstration, *I subdistinguish:* the quiddity of the thing, *I deny;* the nominal definition, *I concede.*

Minor.— The real quiddity of God, *I concede;* the nominal definition, *I deny.*

POINTS FOR REVIEW

1. State the teaching of Moses Maimonides and modernists on the demonstrability of the existence of God.

2. Explain why it is possible to demonstrate the existence of God by an a posteriori argument, but not by an a priori argument.

3. Is the existence of God an article of faith?

DEMONSTRATION OF THE EXISTENCE OF GOD

GENERAL PRELIMINARIES

1° Since, on the one hand, all our knowledge begins with the senses, and, on the other hand, the term *God* is accepted as meaning the first efficient cause of the world, the existence of God is demonstrated, by means of the principle of causality, from some sensible fact.

2° The sensible facts from which St. Thomas proceeds to demonstrate the existence of God are the following:

a) motion perceived by the senses;

b) subordination of efficient causes;

c) contingency of things which are engendered and corrupt;

d) different degrees of beings;

e) finality of natural things.

3° The arguments for the demonstration of the existence of God proceed from effects to proper cause.

A proper cause is a cause on which the effect depends necessarily and directly:

a) as a cause on which the effect *necessarily* depends, it is opposed to an accidental cause. Thus singing proceeds accidentally from a doctor who sings;

b) as a cause on which the effect *directly* depends, it is opposed to a cause on which the effect necessarily depends, but does not depend directly and immediately. Thus a work of sculpture necessarily depends on an artificer, but it does not depend directly and immediately on an artificer as such, but rather on an artificer in as much as he is a sculptor.

4° Therefore, *a*) from motion we proceed to an unmoved mover;

b) from the subordination of efficient causes, to the first efficient cause.

c) from the contingency of the world, to a necessary being;

d) from the degrees of beings, to a sovereign being

e) from the finality of natural things, to the supreme author of their finality.

5° Unmoved mover, first efficient cause, necessary being, sovereign being, and supreme author of finality are five predicates, i.e., concepts, which designate one and the same being, which we call *God*.

6° Hence, in the demonstration of the existence of God, we abstract from all the perfections which are attributed to God, as unity, simplicity, etc.

7° The arguments used to demonstrate the existence of God are not free from all difficulty, because they are metaphysical demonstrations, which are regulated by the rules of artificial Logic.

8° Finally there is, apart from the knowledge of the existence of God deduced by Metaphysics, a certain natural and most certain knowledge common to all men; and in this common knowledge there is contained, as in a seed, the knowledge that is deduced by Metaphysics; v.g., the non-scientific knowledge of the existence of God from the order existing in the world. And besides the five arguments, called the *Five Ways*, presented by St. Thomas at the beginning of the Summa Theologica, there is an argument based on the desire for a universal good; we shall deal with it at the end of the chapter.

FIRST WAY

Demonstration of the existence of an unmoved mover, who is God, from motion.

728. Statement of the question.— 1° The first argument is based on motion perceived by the senses, and analyzed from the point of view of Metaphysics.

Motion, considered from the point of view of Metaphysics, is any transition, successive or instantaneous, from potency to act.

2° The argument concludes to the existence of an unmoved mover, because an infinite series of movers subordinated to one another in virtue of motion is impossible.

a) A mover is an agent which reduces a mobile being from potency to act.

b) An unmoved mover is used here to designate not a mover in potency, i.e., a mover having the immobility of potency, but a mover which actually moves without transition from potency to act, i.e., a mover that excludes all potentiality.

c) Movers subordinated to one another because of motion are essentially subordinated movers, and as such are distinct from accidentally subordinated movers.

Essentially subordinated movers are movers of which the inferior is moved by the superior to the act by which it moves; v.g., when a child's hand writes under the actual influence of his teacher's hand.

Accidentally subordinated movers are movers which are subordinated to one another not because of actual motion, but in virtue of some other nexus; v.g., a boy acting not under the actual influence of his father is as an agent, i.e., a mover, accidentally subordinated to his father, because he received from his father the operative power by which he acts.

729. Demonstration.— It is certain, and, indeed, testified by the senses, that some things move in this world. But everything which moves is moved by another, and ultimately by an unmoved mover. Therefore there exists an unmoved mover, which we call *God*.

First part of minor. — *Everything which moves is moved by another.*— A thing is moved in as much as it is in potency, and moves in as much it is in act; for to be moved is to be reduced from potency to act, and nothing is reduced from potency to act except by a being in act. But it is impossible that a thing be at the same time in potency and in act in the same respect (principle of contradiction). Therefore it is impossible that a thing at the same time be moved and move in the same respect, i.e., everything which moves is moved by another.

Second part of minor.— *Everything which moves is moved ultimately by an unmoved mover.*—Everything which moves is moved by another; and, if this mover moves, it is moved by another, and this latter is moved by another, etc. But an infinite series of essentially subordinated movers is impossible, because the secondary movers move only because actually moved by the first mover; and, if the first mover does not exist, neither secondary movers nor motion can any longer exist. Therefore everything which moves is moved ultimately by an unmoved mover (¹).

---

(1) Prima autem et manifestior via est, quae sumitur ex parte motus. Certum est enim et sensu constat, aliqua moveri in hoc mundo. Omne autem quod movetur ab alio movetur; nihil enim movetur, nisi secundum quod est in potentia ad illud, ad quod movetur. Movet autem aliquid, secundum quod est actu; movere enim nihil aliud est quam educere aliquid de potentia in actum. De potentia autem non potest aliquid reduci in actum, nisi per aliquod ens in actu: sicut calidum in actu, ut ignis, facit lignum, quod est calidum in potentia, esse actu calidum, et per hoc movet et alterat ipsum. Non autem est possibile ut idem sit simul in actu et potentia secundum idem, sed solum secundum diversa. Quod enim est calidum in actu, non potest simul esse calidum in potentia, sed est simul frigidum in potentia. Impossibile est ergo, quod secundum idem et eodem modo, aliquid sit movens et motum, vel quod moveat seipsum: omne ergo quod movetur, oportet ab alio moveri. Si ergo id a quo movetur, moveatur, oportet et ipsum ab alio moveri, et illud ab alio. Hic autem non est procedere in infinitum, quia sic non esset aliquod primum movens, et per consequens nec aliquod aliud movens; quia moventia secunda non movent nisi per hoc, quod sunt mota a primo movente, sicut baculus non movet nisi per hoc quod est motus a manu. Ergo necesse et devenire ad aliquod primum movens, quod a nullo moveatur: et hoc omnes intelligunt Deum.— 1, q. 2, a. 3.

730. Corollaries. — 1° The argument may be summarized as follows: Motion of any kind must be reduced to an unmoved mover as to its proper and immediate cause. Moreover, motion is composed of potency and act. But the proper cause of a compound of potency and act is pure act.

2° The first of the Five Ways abstracts from the eternity or non-eternity of the world, for it proves only that all motion actually proceeds from the first unmoved mover.

3° Since an unmoved mover does not admit of potency, God is pure act, and therefore is a being that is infinite, simple, all-perfect, immutable, etc.

731. Difficulties. — 1° *Against the conclusion.* — a) An impossible thing does not exist. But an unmoved mover is impossible. Therefore an unmoved mover, i. e., God, does not exist.

I concede the major.

Minor. — A mover which cannot move without passing from potency to act cannot be unmoved, *I concede;* a mover which actually moves without passing from potency to act is not unmoved, *I deny.*

For a mover as such is a being in act, and is movable only accidentally in as much as it must needs be reduced from potency to the act by which it is constituted a mover.

b) *I persist.* — God's operation has a beginning. But the operation of an unmoved mover has no beginning. Therefore God is not an unmoved mover.

Major. — God's operation has a beginning, *I deny;* the effect of God's free operation has a beginning, *I concede.*

Minor. — The effect of the free operation of an unmoved mover has a beginning, *I concede;* the operation of an unmoved mover has a beginning, *I deny.*

The operation of an unmoved mover, i. e., of God, is eternal; but God in His eternity can freely determine that this or that effect begin in time.

2° *Against the first part of the minor.* — A thing which moves itself is not moved by another. But a living creature moves itself. Therefore a living creature is not moved by another, i. e., not everything which moves is moved by another.

Major. — A thing which moves itself without first being moved by another, *I concede;* a thing which moves itself only if it is first moved by another, *I deny.*

Minor. — A living creature moves itself without first being moved by another, *I deny;* a living creature moves itself only if it is first moved by another, *I concede.*

A living creature has the operative power of moving itself; but, since it has only potency for act, it does not actually move itself without being moved by another to the act by which it moves itself. More briefly, a living creature moves itself as a secondary mover, not as the first mover.

SECOND WAY

DEMONSTRATION OF THE EXISTENCE OF THE FIRST EFFICIENT
CAUSE, WHICH IS GOD, FROM ESSENTIALLY SUBORDINATED
EFFICIENT CAUSES.

732. Statement of the question.— 1° The second argument is based on essentially subordinated efficient causes.

a) An efficient cause is the first principle, i.e., first source, of motion.

b) Essentially subordinated efficient causes are distinct from accidentally subordinated efficient causes.

Essentially subordinated efficient causes are causes which are subordinated to one another in virtue of their causality in such manner that the causality of the inferior cause actually depends on the causality of the superior; v.g., when a bat sets a ball in motion because it is set in motion by the hand, and the hand by another cause.

Accidentally subordinated efficient causes are causes which are subordinated to one another not because of their causality, but because of some other nexus; v.g., if in his work an artificer successively uses several hammers because he breaks one after the other, these hammers are subordinated to one another not because of their causality, but in time. Similarly, a son who engenders is an efficient cause subordinated to his father, not essentially subordinated, i.e., because of causality, but accidentally, in virtue of his origin.

2° The first efficient cause is that cause which depends on no other for its existence and operation, but on which others depend. It is an uncaused cause.

733. Demonstration.— We find in our observation of sensible things that there are essentially subordinated causes. But regress into infinity in essentially subordinated causes is impossible. Therefore there must needs be a first efficient cause, which all call God.

Major.— a) The *major* is evident from experience, for we see, for example, a bat set a ball in motion, and a hand set the bat in motion.

b) The *major* is also evident in virtue of the principle of causality. For everything composed of potency and act has a cause. But every sensible efficient cause, as actually efficient, is composed of potency and act: for its action is act which is really distinct from its operative power, because we see it pass from the state of repose to operation. Therefore every sensible efficient cause is constituted actually efficient by some other cause; in other words, it is essentially subordinated to a superior cause.

Minor.— If there is regress into infinity in essentially subordinated causes, there is no first cause. But there must be a first cause in a series of essentially subordinated causes; for the first is the cause of the intermediary, and the intermediary, whether one or many, is the cause of the last. To disallow the first cause is to disallow intermediary causes and effects. Therefore regress into infinity in essentially subordinated causes is impossible (¹).

734. Corollaries.— 1° A briefer exposition of the second argument may be made as follows: An efficient cause whose operation is act really distinct from its potency is essentially subordinated to a cause whose operation is not act really distinct from its potency, but which it its own operation. This is the principle of causality as applied in the order of efficient causes.

---

(1) Secunda via est ex ratione causae efficientis. Invenimus enim in istis sensibilibus esse ordinem causarum efficientium; nec tamen invenitur, nec est possibile quod aliquid sit causa efficiens sui ipsius, quia sic esset prius seipso, quod est impossibile: non autem est possibile, quod in causis efficientibus procedatur in infinitum, quia in omnibus causis efficientibus ordinatis primum est causa medii, et medium est causa ultimi, sive media sint plura, sive unum tantum. Remota autem causa removetur effectus. Ergo si non fuerit primum in causis efficientibus, non erit ultimum, nec medium. Sed si procedatur in infinitum in causis efficientibus, non erit prima causa efficiens, et sic non erit nec effectus ultimus, nec causae efficientes mediae, quod patet esse falsum. Ergo est necesse aliquam causam efficientem primam, quam omnes Deum nominant.— I, q. 2, a. 3.

2° Therefore, since the first efficient cause is its own operation, it is pure act, and therefore simple, infinite, all-perfect, etc.

3° Therefore God operates in everything that is in operation, since He constitutes everything in actual operation.

735. Scholion. — Although an infinite series of accidentally subordinated causes is possible, an infinite series of such causes would have a superior and uncaused cause. For such an infinite series would be made up of finite beings composed of potency and act, hence of beings produced by a being which is pure act (fourth way). Hence, if the world had existed from eternity, it would have been produced from eternity.

736. Difficulties.— It is falsely posited in the demonstration that God operates in everything that is in operation. Therefore the demonstration is false (¹).

1° We must not attribute any insufficiency to God. But, if God operates in everything that is in operation, He operates sufficiently in each one of them. Therefore the operation of a created agent would be superfluous.

Let us disregard the major.

Minor.— Sufficiently operates as first cause, *I concede;* as second cause, *I deny.*

2° *I continue.*— One and the same operation does not derive from two distinct agents. But, if God operates in everything that is operation, one and the same operation simultaneously derives from God and from the creature. Therefore God does not operate in everything that is in operation.

Major.— Does not derive from two agents of the same order, *I concede;* from two agents of different orders, *I deny.*

Minor.— From God and from the creature as from agents of the same order, *I deny;* of different orders, *I concede.*

The operation of the creature derives from the creature as from its second cause, and from God as from its first cause.

3° *I persist.*— An agent which has the power of operating can operate without God's operating in it. But the creature has the power of operating from the beginning, i. e., from the time when it was produced. Therefore God does not operate in everything which has operation.

Major.— An agent which has the power of operating *can* act without God's operating in it, *I concede; actually* operates without God's operating in it, *I deny.*

Minor.— Always has the act by which it operates, *I deny;* has the power by which it operates, *I concede.*

An agent which has the power of acting is only in potency for operation, and can be reduced to act only by a being in act, and ultimately by God.

(1) I, q. 105, a. 5.

THIRD WAY

737. Statement of the question. — 1° *a*) A contingent being is a being which can exist or not exist. *b*) The third argument is not based on the contingency of any being whatsoever, v.g., on the contingency of the angel, but on the contingency of beings which we see engendered and corrupt.

2° A necessary being is a being which cannot not exist, i.e., a being whose existence is indefectible. There are two kinds of necessary being: necessary being of caused necessity (ens necessarium *ab alio*), and necessary being of uncaused necessity, i.e., being necessary of itself (ens necessarium *a se*).

a) A necessary being *of caused necessity* is a being which once existing cannot not exist, but which receives its existence from another; v.g., the angel, the human soul. Such a being is contingent in as much as it can be produced, although absolutely necessary in as much as it is incorruptible.

b) A necessary being *of uncaused necessity* is a being which cannot not exist, because it is uncaused and incorruptible. This being is necessary of itself, and is called God.

738. Demonstration. — Contingent beings which are engendered and corrupt exist. But the proper cause of a contingent being which is engendered and corrupts is a necessary being. Therefore a necessary being exists. But, if this necessary being is a being whose necessity is caused, its proper cause is a necessary being whose necessity is uncaused. Therefore there exists a necessary being whose necessity is uncaused, i.e., a necessary being of uncaused necessity, which we call God (¹).

---

(1) Tertia via est sumpta ex possibili et necessario, quae talis est. Invenimus enim in rebus quaedam quae sunt possibilia esse et non esse; cum quaedam inveniantur generari et corrumpi, et per consequens possibilia esse

The *major* is evident from experience, for we see bodies engendered and corrupt.

First minor.— The proper cause of a being produced from preexisting potency is a being in act not produced from preexisting potency: act is always prior to potency (principle of causality). But a contingent being which is engendered is produced from preexisting potency, i.e., from first matter. Therefore the proper cause of a contingent being which is engendered is a being which neither is engendered nor can be engendered from first matter, and therefore is incorruptible and necessary.

Second minor.—An infinite series of necessary beings whose necessity is caused is impossible, because, in virtue of the principle of causality, the proper cause of a necessary being whose necessity is caused is a necessary being whose necessity is not caused. This proposition is evident from its very terms.

739. Corollary.— Necessary being of uncaused necessity has no cause, and therefore is pure act.

740. Difficulties.— 1° Every demonstration proceeds from necessary beings. But the foregoing demonstration does not proceed from necessary beings. Therefore the foregoing demonstration is invalid.

Major.— Either from necessary beings or from the necessary formalities of contingent being, *I concede;* only from necessary beings, *I deny.*

Minor.— It does not proceed from the relations of the necessary dependence of contingent being on necessary being, *I deny;* from necessary beings, *I concede.*

2° The demonstration concludes to the existence of a necessary being. But a necessary being can be either the world or matter. Therefore the demonstration does not conclude to the existence of the necessary being which is God.

---

et non esse. Impossibile est autem omnia, quae sunt talia, semper esse quia quod possibile est non esse, quandoque non est. Si igitur omnia sunt possibilia non esse, aliquando nihil fuit in rebus. Sed si hoc est verum, etiam nunc nihil esset: quod patet esse falsum. Non ergo omnia entia sunt possibilia, sed oportet aliquid esse necessarium in rebus. Omne autem necessarium vel habet causam suae necessitatis aliunde, vel non habet. Non est autem possibile quod procedatur in infinitum in necessariis, quae habent causam suae necessitatis, sicut nec in causis efficientibus, ut probatum est (in isto art); ergo necesse est ponere aliquid quod sit per se necessarium, non habens causam necessitatis aliunde, sed quod est causa necessitatis aliis: quod omnes dicunt Deum.— I, q. 2, a. 3.

Minor.— *a*) The world, as an aggregate of contingent beings, cannot be a necessary being, because contingent beings cannot constitute necessary being. *b*) Second matter, as corruptible, is not necessary being, nor can first matter, which is pure potency, be necessary being from which other beings receive their existence as from their efficient cause.

FOURTH WAY

DEMONSTRATION OF THE EXISTENCE OF A MOST PERFECT BEING, WHICH IS GOD, FROM THE DEGREES OF PERFECTION.

741. Statement of the question. — 1° The fourth argument is based on the different degrees of goodness, truth, and similar perfections found in things; v.g., a living being has more goodness and truth than a non-living being; likewise, a knowing being has more goodness and truth than either a living or a non-living being, because a knowing being has all the perfections of a living and a non-living being, and others as well.

2° Although goodness, truth, and similar perfections are not of themselves sensible notions, yet they are accidentally such, in as much as the intellect perceives that a thing known by the senses is good, true, etc. Hence the fourth argument, like the others, is founded on sense knowledge, according to the principle: all knowledge begins with the senses.

3° Goodness, truth, and similar perfections are absolute perfections (*perfectiones simpliciter simplices*), and are distinct from mixed perfections (*perfectiones secundum quid simplices*).

a) An *absolute perfection* is a perfection whose formal concept admits of no imperfection; v.g., every perfection which is convertible with being, as goodness, truth, unity, etc., and also every perfection which has a transcendental relation to being as such, as the intellect, the will, etc.

b) A *mixed perfection* is a perfection whose formal concept admits of imperfection; v.g., extension, vegetative being, etc.

4° The fourth argument proceeds, in virtue of the principle of causality, from the degrees of perfections to the being

10

which possesses the fulness of perfection. An absolute perfection has different degrees in as much as it is participated and is limited, i.e., is received as act into potency which is really distinct from it and which limits it. The cause of any being composed of potency and act is a being which is not a compound of potency and act, i.e., pure act, which is being possessing the fulness of perfection.

742. Demonstration.— Various degrees of goodness, truth, and nobleness are found in things. But the proper cause of beings which are more or less good, more or less true, and more or less noble is a being which possesses goodness, truth, and nobleness in an unlimited degree, and consequently is sovereign being.   Therefore there exists a sovereign being which is the cause of the being, the goodness, and all the other perfections of things; and this being we call God (1).

The *major* is evident from the statement of the question.

Minor.— The proper cause of a participated perfection is a being which is essentially this perfection. But goodness, truth, and nobleness have different degress in as much as they are participated in different ways.   Therefore the proper cause of beings which are more or less good, more or less true, more or less noble, is a being which of its essence is goodness, truth, and nobleness, i.e., a being which is sovereignly being: for a being which of its essence is good, true, and noble is pure act, for these perfections do not admit of potency in their formal concept.

743.— Scholia.— Since every mixed perfection admits of imperfection, i.e., of composition of potency and act, in its

----

(1) Quarta via sumitur ex gradibus, qui in rebus inveniuntur. Invenitur enim in rebus aliquid magis et minus bonum, et verum, et nobile, et sic de aliis hujusmodi. Sed magis et minus dicuntur de diversis, secundum quod appropinquant diversimode ad aliquid quod maxime est: sicut magis calidum est, quod magis appropinquat maxime calido. Est igitur aliquid quod est verissimum, et optimum, et nobilissimum, et per consequens maxime ens. Nam quae sunt maxime vera, sunt maxime entia, ut dicitur. Quod autem dicitur maxime tale in aliquo genere, est causa omnium quae sunt illius generis; sicut ignis, qui est maxime calidus, est causa omnium calidorum, ut in eodem libro dicitur. Ergo est aliquod quod omnibus entibus est causa esse, et bonitatis, et cujuslibet perfectionis; et hoc dicimus Deum.— I, q. 2, a. 3.

formal concept, every mixed perfection has a cause. But we cannot proceed from a mixed perfection to a being which possesses the fulness of this perfection in the same genus, i.e., in the same order of perfection. For a mixed perfection cannot exist as the fulness of perfection, i.e., as pure act. Thus, for example, the proper cause of man is not a being which is the fulness of man, i.e., sovereign man ; since man is a limited and participated being, his proper cause is a being which has no limitation, i.e., is being of its very essence.

2° This fourth argument was presented before the time of St. Thomas by Plato. But Plato proceeded in virtue of exemplar causality, whereas St. Thomas argued from efficient causality.

744. Corollaries.— 1° Therefore God possesses all absolute perfections in the state of pure act, i.e., God is sovereign goodness, sovereign truth, etc.

2° Since God is pure act, He is of His very essence being; therefore He is intelligent and personal being.

3° Therefore all finite beings, i.e., beings by participation, are dependent on God, Who is being by His very essence.

FIFTH WAY

DEMONSTRATION OF THE EXISTENCE OF THE SUPREME INTELLIGENT AUTHOR OF FINALITY, WHO IS GOD, FROM THE FINALITY OF NATURAL THINGS.

745. Statement of the question.— 1° Natural things are things which lack knowledge.

2° The fifth way proceeds from the finality of natural things, that is to say, from the fact that natural things are directed to an end which is their operation, and consequently to the object to which their operation tends.

3° Natural things are in potency to the operation to which they are directed as to their end. Hence this fifth way argues from composition of potency and act, from the point of view of finality, appealing to the principle: all potency refers, i.e., has a transcendental relation, to act.

746. Demonstration.— Natural things, i.e., things which have no knowledge, act for an end. But things which have no knowledge do not tend to an end unless directed to it by some being which has knowledge and intelligence. Therefore there exists some supreme intelligent being by which all natural things are directed to their end; and this being we call God (1).

Major.— a) *A posteriori.*— Natural things always, or at least in the majority of cases, act in the same way, in order to attain what is best for them; v.g., vegetative being acts for the attainment of the assimilation, nutrition, conservation, etc., proper to it. Therefore it is not by chance, but as a result of intention, that natural things tend to their end.

b) *A priori.*— Natural things have operation, i.e., they operate. But every agent acts for an end. Therefore natural things operate for an end.

Minor.— The directing of a thing to an end can be accomplished only by a being which apprehends the end as future and possible, and knows the relation and proportion of the things directed to this end. But only an intelligent being can know an end as future and know the proportions of several

---

(1) Quinta via sumitur ex gubernatione rerum: videmus enim quod, aliqua quae cognitione carent, scilicet corpora naturalia, operantur propter finem. Quod apparet ex hoc quod semper aut frequentius eodem modo operantur ut consequantur id quod est optimum. Unde patet quod non a casu, sed ex intentione perveniunt ad finem. Ea autem quae non habent cognitionem non tendunt in finem nisi directa ab aliquo cognoscente et intelligente, sicut sagitta a sagittante; ergo est aliquid intelligens, a quo omnes res naturales ordinantur ad finem, et hoc dicimus Deum.— I, q. 2, a. 3.

S. Thomas is here appealing to the fact of internal finality, not external; to the finality which is observable in things destitute of intelligence taken separately; as that the eye is directed to seeing, the ear to hearing, wings to flight. External finality, the purpose of some noxious animal, such as a viper, or of a disease germ, is often difficult to discover; whereas internal finality, such as the purpose of the organs of the body, is plain.—PHILLIPS, *Modern Thomistic Philosophy*, Burns Oates & Washbourne Ltd., 1935, vol. II, p. 291. — Added by the Translator.

things to one another. Therefore things which have no knowledge do not tend to an end unless directed to it by some being which has knowledge and intelligence (¹).

747. Scholia. — 1° Natural things are directed to their end in virtue of natural inclination. Hence the fifth way concludes to an Intelligent Being Who is the author of natural things in as much as they *are directed* to an end.

2° This argument does not conclude explicitly to the existence of a being which is the Supreme Intelligence, infinite, unique, etc. Explicit proof of the infinity and unicity of the Intelligent Being Who is the author of natural things will be given later; and implicit proof of them is found in the fifth way in as much as the Author of the finality of natural things is also the author of the finality by which all potency is related to act, and therefore is pure act.

3° The argument by which we conclude to the existence of the Supreme Legislator from the existence of moral obligation is contained in the fifth way. For the human will is subject to moral obligation in as much as it is of its very nature directed to something as to an end. But the fifth way concludes to the existence of the Intelligent Being Who directs all natural things to their end. Therefore.

ARGUMENT FROM THE DESIRE FOR A UNIVERSAL GOOD

PROOF OF THE EXISTENCE OF A UNIVERSAL GOOD, WHICH WE CALL GOD, FROM THE NATURAL DESIRE OF THE WILL FOR A UNIVERSAL GOOD

748. Statement of the question. — 1° The other arguments prove the existence of God as the first efficient cause of

---

(1) *Contra Gentes*, L. II, c. 24.

the world; this argument proves the existence of God, as the final cause of the will.

2° The present argument sets out from the natural desire of the will for a universal good, and it reaches its conclusion in virtue of the absolute value of the principle of finality. Just as it is absolutely repugnant that finite being has no efficient cause, so too it is absolutely repugnant that the will naturally desires a good which does not exist in reality.

749. Demonstration. — If the will of its very nature is directed to, i.e., naturally desires, a universal good as its end, this universal or infinite good exists in reality. But the will naturally desires a universal good as its end. Therefore a universal or infinite good, which we call God, exists in reality.

Major.— The will of its very nature tends towards good as it exists in reality. Hence, if it naturally desires a universal good as its end, this good must exist in reality; otherwise the will of its very nature would naturally desire what is naturally impossible; or, in other words, a natural desire would be in vain, which is repugnant.

Minor.— The will of its very nature tends to a good known by the intellect. But the intellect knows universal good, i.e., good under its universal aspect. Therefore the will of its very nature naturally desires a universal good as its end.

750. Scholion. — Many authors prove the existence of God from the common consent of all peoples. But this argument is not a scientific argument. The criterion of the consent of mankind can be reduced to the extrinsic criterion of authority: it is the authority of the human race. Hence it can produce an act of faith, but cannot engender science, that is to say, it has no scientific value.

Moreover, the consent of mankind has no value unless it is concerned with truths which are immediately evident, or at least almost immediately evident. And this is something which must be proved by the philosopher, in order that we be placed under obligation to accept the consent of mankind in regard to some particular truth.

All men can easily, though in a confused manner, know the existence of God either from the order of the world, or from the existence of the moral law, or from the natural desire of the will for a universal good.

POINTS FOR REVIEW

1. Define: unmoved mover, essentially subordinated movers, accidentally subordinated movers, essentially subordinated efficient causes, accidentally subordinated efficient causes.

2. Explain why it is impossible to have *a*) an infinite series of essentially subordinated movers, *b*) an infinite series of essentially subordinated efficient causes.

3. Why must an engendered being have a cause? What is the proper cause of such a being? Why?

4. Distinguish between absolute perfection and mixed perfection. What is the proper cause of a participated absolute perfection?

5. Explain whether or not *a*) the fourth argument of St. Thomas is based on exemplar causality, *b*) the fifth argument is based on composition of potency and act.

6. Name the Five Ways of St. Thomas. Which of these arguments do you like best? Why?

7. Show why a universal good desired by the will must exist in reality.

8. Is it true that an argument based on the common consent of mankind has no scientific value? Explain.

READING.— Cette preuve de l'existence de Dieu, souverain Bien, par le désir du bonheur revient donc à ceci en énonçant d'abord le principe qui est sa majeure.

Un désir naturel, et non pas fondé sur l'imagination ou l'égarement de la raison, *ne peut être vain, chimérique*, tendre à un bien irréel ou inaccessible. Car il tendrait à la fois vers quelque chose ou vers rien, contrairement au principe de finalité: « tout agent agit pour une fin ». Ce principe n'aurait plus aucune valeur métaphysique certaine avant d'avoir prouvé l'existence de Dieu. En réalité, sa nécessité et sa certitude métaphysiques sont égales à celles du principe de causalité efficiente; bien plus l'efficience ne peut se concevoir sans finalité, autrement elle n'aurait aucune direction déterminée, elle ne tendrait vers rien, ou ne produirait rien.

Enfin le principe de finalité n'est pas seulement vrai des tendances et des désirs qu'on *voit* se réaliser, mais aussi des désirs *naturels* dont la *réalisation n'apparaît pas encore;* car ce principe n'est pas seulement une loi empirique, comme: la chaleur dilate le fer, mais une loi métaphysique qui énonce ce qui est et *ce qui doit être* sous peine d'absurdité: la tendance proprement naturelle, immédiatement fondée sur la nature d'une chose, surtout sur la nature de notre esprit, ne peut être vaine, ou chimérique. Autrement la tendance de notre intelligence à connaître le vrai pourrait être également trompeuse, illusoire, et notre intelligence ne pourrait s'assurer de la vérité de son jugement par réflexion sur la nature de son acte et sur sa nature à elle, *faite pour se conformer aux choses*, comme le dit saint Thomas. L'intelligence voit dans sa nature même sa propre finalité essentielle (c'est capital en épistomologie), elle voit aussi dans la nature de la volonté le finalité de celle-ci.

Or (c'est la mineure de la preuve) *tout homme désire naturellement être heureux*, et l'expérience comme la raison montrent que *le vrai bonheur ne se trouve en aucun bien limité ou fini*, car, notre intelligence concevant le bien universel et sans limites, l'amplitude de notre volonté, éclairée par l'intelligence, est elle-même sans limites.

De plus il s'agit ici non pas d'un désir conditionnel et inefficace comme celui de la vision béatifique, fondé sur ce jugement conditionnel: cette vision serait la béatitude parfaite pour moi, s'il est possible que j'y sois élevé et si Dieu voulait bien m'y élever. Il s'agit ici d'un désir naturel *inné*, fondé non pas sur un jugement conditionnel, mais immédiatement sur la nature même de notre volonté et sur son amplitude universelle. Pas de désir naturel, sans bien désirable, et sans bien de même amplitude que ce désir naturel.

Donc il faut qu'il existe un Bien sans limites, Bien pur, sans mélange de non-bien ou d'imperfection, car en lui seul se trouve *réellement* le bien universel qui spécifie notre volonté. Sans l'existence du Souverain Bien, l'amplitude universelle de notre volonté ou sa profondeur, qu'aucun bien fini ne peut combler, serait une absurdité radicale, ou non-sens absolu.

Il y a là une impossibilité qui est inscrite dans la nature même de notre volonté, dont le désir naturel tend non pas vers l'idée du bien, mais vers un *bien réel* (car le bien est non dans l'esprit, mais dans les choses) et vers un bien réel non restreint, qui ait la même amplitude que le désir naturel qui se porte vers lui. GARRIGOU-LAGRANGE. *Le Réalisme du principe de Finalité*. Desclée, 1932, pp. 274-277.

APPENDIX

———

ATHEISM

751. Statement of the question. — a) Atheists, generally speaking, are persons who do not recognize the existence of God.

b) Atheists are of two kinds: practical and theoretical.

Practical atheists are persons who recognize God with their *minds*, but not with their *hearts*, i.e., they live as if God did not exist.

Theoretical atheists are persons who do not recognize God even with their *minds*.

c) Theoretical atheists are *negative*, if they are destitute of all notion of God; *positive*, if they know what we mean by God, but yet either deny that He exists (dogmatic atheists), or doubt that He exists (critical atheists), or affirm that, even though God may exist, we cannot come to a knowledge of whether He exists or not (agnostic atheists).

752. Possibility and existence of atheism. — The following is a brief summary on the possibility and existence of atheism:

I. The existence of *practical* atheists is a lamentable fact of experience.

II. In regard to *theoretical* atheists, a distinction must be made between negative atheists and positive atheists:

1° *Negative* atheists.— a) It is certain that there can be, and, indeed, that there actually are men who are destitute of a clear and distinct notion of God as the supreme author of all nature. This is confirmed by experience, v.g., among pagan peoples. *b*) It is certain that it is impossible that men endowed with reason are destitute of an implicit and confused notion of God. For the human mind, in virtue of an almost natural process of reasoning, concludes from the order of the world that a Supreme Author of this order exists, from the moral law, that a Supreme Legislator exists, and from the natural desire of the will for a universal good, that a Supreme Good exists.

2° *Positive* atheists.— *a*) It seems certain that there cannot be positive atheists who hold, without any fear of error, that God does not exist. For the implicit and confused notion of God, which is quasi-innate in all men, seems so firm as to exclude an opinion which, without fear of erring, can deny that God exists. *b*) It seems certain that there can be atheists who seriously adhere over a long period of time to the opinion (opinionative judgment) that God does not exist, as experience seems to prove. But it is only in the case of grave imprudence and negligence that this opinion can be held for an indefinite period of time.

Essence and attributes of God

Prologue. — We turn now from our study of the existence of God to the study of His essence and attributes.

Since God is absolutely simple, there can be no real distinction between His essence and attributes. But, since our knowledge of God derives from comparing God to finite beings, our knowledge of Him is imperfect: we attribute to God perfections which exist as separate and varied in creatures, but which in God are identified. This is the root of the distinction between God's essence and His attributes, according to our mode of knowledge of them .

In virtue of two different points of view from which we consider God's essence, we make a distinction between God's entitative attributes, which are concerned with the very being of God, and His operative attributes, which relate to His operations.

Hence there will be three chapters in this book:

Chapter   I. Essence of God.

Chapter   II. God's entitative attributes.

Chapter III. God's operative attributes.

CHAPTER I

ESSENCE OF GOD

Prologue. We may consider God's essence either as it exists in reality, or as it is known in the abstract. Considered from the first point of view, it is called the physical essence of God; and, from the second point of view, the metaphysical essence of God. God's metaphysical essence may be understood in a wide sense as signifying that by which increate being is first distinct from created being, or the divine from the creature; or it may be understood in a strict sense as signifying God's nature, that is to say, that which we conceive as the essential differentia of God, and as the first root of the divine properties, just as we conceive rationality as the essential differentia of man and the first root of his properties.

Therefore there will be three articles in this chapter.

Physical essence of God
- Statement of the question
- Thesis: The physical essence of God is the Deity as possessing formally and in an infinite degree all absolute perfections in its sovereign simplicity
- Distinction between the divine perfections

Metaphysical essence of God
- Statement of the question
- Thesis: The metaphysical essence of God is Subsisting Being

Nature of God
- Statement of the question
- Thesis: The nature of God is Subsisting Intellection

PHYSICAL ESSENCE OF GOD

753. Statement of the question. — 1° Physical essence is essence understood in the concrete, i.e., as it exists in reality. It is distinguished from metaphysical essence, which is essence as known in the abstract.

2° In the thesis, we state that the physical essence of God is the Deity as possessing formally and in an infinite degree all absolute perfections in its sovereign simplicity (¹).

a) The Deity is the same in reality as God. However, it is not the same in its signification: the term God signifies a person, i.e., a being whose essence is divine, whereas Deity signifies the divine essence itself (²).

b) Sovereign simplicity is simplicity which admits of no composition of potency and act, and consequently of no composition of essence and existence, nature and supposit, substance and accident, matter and form, genus and species, etc.

c) An absolute perfection is a perfection whose formal concept admits of no imperfection; v.g., goodness, truth, intelligence. It is distinct from a mixed perfection, which admits of imperfection in its formal concept; v.g., reasoning sensation.

d) We say that the Deity formally possesses all absolute perfections, because every absolute perfection according to its proper and formal concept is found in God; v.g., God is properly good and wise, and not metaphorically good and wise, nor merely *casually* good and wise in as much as He produces goodness and wisdom in creatures.

---

(1) Quapropter in absoluta ipsius esse ratione unus subsistit Deus, unus est simplicissimus.— *Ex thesi III* s. Thomae.
(2) I, q. 39, a. 5, c.

e) Finally, we say that absolute perfections are found in God in an infinite degree, i.e., eminently: they exist in Him without any actual limitation, whereas they never exist in creatures without some limitation. Therefore God is infinite in act, in as much as He is act without limitation, and not infinite in potency, as would be a potency always capable of receiving some act, as, v.g., first matter.

3° Our adversaries are all who affirm that perfections are attributed to God only causally, as Maimonides; or metaphorically, as Agnostics; or who deny the infinity of God, as Renouvier, William James, Wells, and Bradley; or who deny God's absolute simplicity, as pantheists.

The thesis, as it is enunciated, is the common teaching of Scholastics.

754. Statement of the thesis.

THESIS.— THE PHYSICAL ESSENCE OF GOD IS THE DEITY AS POSSESSING FORMALLY AND IN AN INFINITE DEGREE ALL ABSOLUTE PERFECTIONS IN ITS SOVEREIGN SIMPLICITY.

1° God is pure act. But the physical essence of pure act possesses formally and in an infinite degree all absolute perfections in its sovereign simplicity. Therefore the physical essence of God is the Deity as possessing formally and in an infinite degree all absolute perfections in its sovereign simplicity.

The *major* is evident from the arguments used to demonstrate the existence of God, and especially from the first argument, by which we demonstrate that God is an unmoved mover.

Minor.— Pure act is absolutely simple, and is all-perfect and infinite.

2° God is subsisting being. But the physical essence of subsisting being possesses formally and in an infinite degree all absolute perfections in its sovereign simplicity. Therefore the physical essence of God is the Deity as possessing formally and in an infinite degree all absolute perfections in its sovereign simplicity.

The *major* is self-evident from the arguments used to demonstrate the existence of God, and especially from the second, third, and fourth. For God is His own operation (second way), and therefore His own being. God is a necessary being of uncaused necessity (third way), and therefore does not receive His being, but is His own being. God is sovereign being (fourth way) and absolutely simple, and therefore has not participated being, but is His own being.

Minor.— Since subsisting being is not received into potency, it is in no way limited, and therefore is absolutely simple and all-perfect, because being admits of no imperfection in its formal concept.

755. Distinction between the divine perfections.—

1° *Preliminaries.* a) God possesses mixed perfections *virtually* and in an *eminent manner* because He has the power of producing these perfections in creatures, and because an absolute perfection in God can produce all the effects produced by a mixed perfection in creatures. Thus God knows by a simple act of His intellect a truth which man knows by reasoning.

Absolute perfections are formally attributed to God. Hence arises the problem : how can multiplicity of perfections be reconciled with God's sovereign simplicity, i.e., how are God's perfections distinguished from each other ?

b) Distinction is lack of identity ; it is *real*, if it obtains in reality, independently of the consideration of the mind; *of reason* (logical), if it obtains only between concepts of one and the same thing.

A distinction of reason is called a distinction of reason *reasoning*, if it is made without foundation in reality; v.g., the distinction between Tullius and Cicero; and of reason *reasoned*, if it is made with foundation in reality ; v.g., the distinction between genus and species.

A distinction of reason, considered in reality, which is its root, is called virtual, and has a twofold foundation : *a)* the eminence of the thing which identifies in its simplicity perfections which are really distinct in its inferiors ; *b)* the imperfection of our intellect which, unable by a single act to conceive these perfections united, conceives them by distinct acts and as if they were distinct.

A distinction of reason obtains with total abstraction (penes præcisionem totalem) of one from another, when several concepts of one and the same thing are perfectly prescinded from one another ; v.g., when we say : *rational animal ;* as the implicit and the explicit, when several concepts of one and the same thing are only imperfectly prescinded from one another, because one actually includes the other, but in a confused manner. Thus the notion of being is not perfectly prescinded from the notions of goodness and truth, because it actually contains them, but in a confused manner (in actu confuso). The notion of divine wisdom is not perfectly prescinded from the notion of divine love, because divine wisdom, which is infinite, contains all absolute perfections.

2° *Opinions.* — *a)* Nominalists teach that God's perfections are distinguished by a distinction of reason reasoning.

b) Gilbert de la **Porrée** seems to affirm that the divine perfections are really.distinct from each other.

c) Scotus teaches that his peculiar formal distinction (distinctio formalis a parte rei) distinguishes the divine perfections.

d) Thomists teach that God's perfections are distinct from each other by a distinction of reason reasoned as the implicit and the explicit.

3° *Proof of the Thomistic opinion.*

THESIS.— The divine perfections are distinguished from each other by a distinction of reason reasoned as the implicit and the explicit.

First part. — *The divine perfections are distinguished from each other by a distinction or reason reasoned.* —Things which are not distinguished in reality, but whose objective concepts are intrinsically different, are distinguished from each other by a distinction of reason reasoned. But the divine perfections are not distinguished from each other in reality, but their objective concepts are intrinsically different. Therefore the divine perfections are distinguished from each other by a distinction of reason reasoned.

Major. — Since they are not distinct in reality, they do not admit of a real distinction; and, since their objective concepts are intrinsically different, they admit of a distinction of reason reasoned.

Minor. — *a)* The divine perfections are not distinguished in reality, because God is pure act and absolutely simple.

b) The objective concepts of the divine perfections are intrinsically different, because divine wisdom, divine mercy, etc. have not the same definitions.

Second part. — *The divine perfections are distinugished as the implicit and the explicit.*—Perfections whose objective concepts are imperfectly prescinded from each other are distinguished as the implicit and the explicit. But the objective concepts of the divine perfections are imperfectly prescinded from each other. Therefore the divine perfections are distinguished as the implicit and the explicit.

The *major* is evident from the statement of the question.

Minor. — Every divine perfection exists in the state of pure act, i.e., is pure act, is infinite, and therefore each one of the divine perfections actually, though in a confused manner, contains all the other divine perfections.

756. Scholia. — 1° In the present state of union, there are three ways by which we come to a knowledge of God: *the way of affirmation and causality,* by which we attribute to God as First Cause all the perfections of creatures; *the way of* *remotion and negation* by which we do not admit in God any of the imperfections of creatures ([1]) ; *the way of excess and eminence*, by which we assert that all the perfections of creatures are possessed by God in an infinite degree, i.e., eminently.

2° Absolute perfections are predicated of God and creatures according to analogy of proper proportionality, because they are found properly and intrinsically in God and creatures, but in modes that are essentially different: they preexist united and infinite in God, whereas in creatures they are received divided and in finite mode ([2]). The way in which all perfections exist united and in infinite mode in God must remain a mystery to the human intellect, for our knowledge of it must depend on the way of negation, by which we disallow in God a real distinction between existence and operation, intellect and will, justice and mercy, intellection and love, etc. ([3]).

POINTS FOR REVIEW

1. Define: physical essence of God, the Deity, distinction of reason reasoned as the implicit and the explicit.

2. Explain whether or not absolute perfections are formally predicated of God.

3. By what kind of distinction are God's perfections distinct? Briefly explain.

---

(1) Hoc ipsum, quod scimus de Deo quid non est, supplet in divina scientia (in scientia de Deo) locum cognitionis quid est; quia, sicut per quid est distinguitur res ab aliis, ita per hoc quod scitur quid non est.— *De Trin.*, q. 2, a. 2, ad 2.

(2) 1, q. 13, a. 4, c.

(3) Cum hoc nomen sapiens, de homine dicitur, quodammodo circumscribit et comprehendit rem significatam; non autem cum dicitur de Deo, sed relinquit rem significatam ut incomprehensam et excedentem nominis significationem.— 1, q. 13, a. 5.

METAPHYSICAL ESSENCE OF GOD

757. Statement of the question. – 1° God's physical essence, as we have seen, is absolutely simple. Yet, on account of God's eminence and the imperfection of the human intellect, we know God by concepts that are intrinsically different. Hence arises the question of the order that obtains among these intrinsically different concepts, and, in particular, which of these concepts corresponds to that absolute perfection in God which holds first place and is the source of all His other perfections. Such, indeed, is the question of God's metaphysical essence.

2° The metaphysical essence of God may be considered under a twofold aspect :

a) as His essence in a wide sense, that is to say, that divine perfection by which the divine, according to our mode of knowledge, is distinguished from the creature, infinite being from finite being ;

b) as His nature in the strict sense, that is to say, that divine perfection which we conceive as God's essential differentia and the first root of His operations.

We shall deal with God's nature in the next article.

Hence in this article we are concerned only with the question of what divine perfection, according to our mode of knowledge, first distinguishes the divine from the creature.

3° *a*) According to Ockam, the Nominalists, Descartes, and Leibniz, the metaphysical essence of God consists in the sum-total of all perfections, so that out first definition of God should be : *the sovereignly perfect being.*

b) Scotus holds that God's metaphysical essence is constituted by radical infinity, and therefore, according to him, God ought to be defined: *being infinite in every way.*

c) Modern Thomists commonly affirm that the perfection by which God is first distinguished from the creature is subsisting being, i.e., being whose essence and existence are identified (ens a se) ([1]).

Subsisting being is being whose existence subsists of itself, i.e., is not received into essence as act into potency.

Being whose essence and existence are identified is being which does not derive from another as from its root, even according to our mode of understanding it.   Hence God's eternity derives from another, because, according to our mode of knowledge, it is the effect of the divine immutability.

Subsisting being, being whose essence and existence are identified, and pure act have the same formal signification, and hence are distinct from each other only by a distinction of reason reasoning, for they all signify identity of essence and existence in God.

758. Statement of the thesis.

THESIS.— THE METAPHYSICAL ESSENCE OF GOD IS SUBSISTING BEING.

1° The first and fundamental perfection which distinguishes God from the creature is subsisting being.   But the metaphysical essence of God is that first and fundamental perfection which distinguishes God from the creature.   Therefore the metaphysical essence of God is subsisting being.

Major. — The creature is constituted as such by real composition of essence and existence.   Therefore that which first distinguishes God from the creature is the real identification of His essence and existence, i.e., God's subsisting being.

---

(1) Divina essentia, per hoc quod exercitae actualitati ipsius esse identificatur, seu per hoc quod est ipsum esse subsistens, in sua veluti metaphysica ratione bene nobis constituta proponitur, et per hoc idem rationem nobis exhibet suae infinitatis in perfectione.— *Thesis XIII* s. THOMAE.

The *minor* is evident from the statement of the question.

2° That perfection which we conceive in God as His most common predicate and as transcending all His other perfections is the metaphysical essence of God. But subsisting being is the perfection which we conceive in God as His most common predicate and as transcending all His other perfections. Therefore subsisting being is the metaphysical essence of God.[1].

Major. — The perfection which is conceived in God as His most common predicate and as transcending all His other perfections is the perfection by which *the divine* is first distinguished from the creature.

Minor. — a) *Subsisting being is the perfection which we conceive in God as His most common predicate.* — All other predicates which are attributed to God are either less common than subsisting being, v.g., justice and mercy, or, if convertible with it, add a logical aspect to it, v.g., goodness, truth, etc.

b) *Subsisting being is the perfection which we conceive in God as transcending all His other perfections.* — Just as being is transcendent with respect to everything which exists or can exist, so too subsisting being is transcendent with respect to everything found in God, so that everything which is divine is formally and intrinsically subsisting being: divine wisdom is formally and intrinsically subsisting being, and so too are the divine will, divine justice, and divine mercy; moreover, each of the three divine Persons is formally and intrinsically

---

(1) Respondeo dicendum quod hoc nomen *Qui est* triplici ratione est maxime proprium nomen Dei. Primo quidem, propter sui significationem...

Secundo, propter ejus universalitatem. Omnia enim alia nomina vel sunt minus communia; vel, si convertantur cum ipso, tamen addunt aliqua supra ipsum secundum rationem; unde quodammodo informant et determinant ipsum. Intellectus autem noster non potest ipsam Dei essentiam cognoscere in statu viae, secundum quod in se est: sed quemcumque modum determinet circa id quod de Deo intelligit, deficit a modo quo Deus in se est. Et ideo, quanto aliqua nomina sunt minus determinata, et magis communia et absoluta, tanto magis proprie dicuntur de Deo a nobis. Unde et Damascenus dicit quod *principalius omnibus quae de Deo dicuntur nominibus, est qui est; totum enim in seipso comprehendens, habet ipsum esse quoddam pelagus substantiae infinitum et indeterminatum.* Quolibet enim alio nomine determinatur aliquis modus substantiae rei: sed hoc nomen *Qui est* nullum modum essendi determinat, sed sese habet indeterminate ad omnes; et ideo nominat ipsum *pelagus substantiae infinitum.*— I, q. 13, a. 11, c.

subsisting being : the Father is formally and intrinsically Subsisting Being, and so too are the Son and the Holy Spirit.

3° *Rejection of other opinions.* — *a*) The sum-total of all perfections is God's physical essence, but does not constitute His metaphysical essence. For, according to our mode of knowledge, God is all-perfect being because He is subsisting being, just as the creature is limited being, because the existence of the creature is received into its essence, as act into potency.

b) Infinity is an intrinsic mode of the divine entity, and, according to our mode of knowledge, presupposes the divine entity already constituted. God is infinite being, because His existence is not received into the divine essence as into a distinct potency, but is identified with the divine essence ; in other words, God is infinite being because He is subsisting being(¹).

POINTS FOR REVIEW

1. How is God's metaphysical essence distinguished from His physical essence ?

2. Is it true that God's metaphysical essence may be considered under different aspects ?   Explain.

3. State the teaching of Scotus on God's metaphycial essence, and the Thomistic teaching on the metaphysical essence of God in the wide sense.

---

(1) *Contra Gentes,* I, 1, c. 43.

NATURE OF GOD

759. Statement of the question. 1° As we have already pointed out, a distinction must be made between God's metaphysical essence in a wide sense and His metaphysical essence in the strict sense, i.e., the divine nature.

The metaphysical essence of God in a wide sense is that first and fundamental perfection by which infinite being as such, i.e., increate entity, is formally constituted, and by which the divine is distinct from the creature.

The metaphysical essence of God in the strict sense is that perfection which we conceive as God's essential differentia and the first root of all His operative attributes, as rationality is man's essential differentia and the first root of his operative attributes [1]. It is with God's metaphysical essence in the strict sense, i.e., with the divine nature, that we are concerned at present.

2° The metaphysical essence of God in the wide sense is an attribute common to all His perfections. God's metaphysical essence thus understood is that perfection by which, as we understand it, increate entity is formally constituted as increate entity. For every perfection of God is formally constituted as increate entity. Moreover, every perfection of God is formally increate entity.

But the nature of God cannot be an attribute *common* to every perfection of God, but is a *special* divine perfection, distinct from and the first root of God's other *operative* perfections [2].

---

(1) BILLUART, *De Deo*, dissert. II, a. 1.
(2) JOANNES A SANCTO THOMA, *Cursus Theol.*, t. II, p. 336 (Sol.).

3° *a*) Molina teaches that God's nature is subsisting being. Capreolus, Bannez, Ledesma, and Contenson, among the older Thomists, incline to this opinion, but do not expressly teach it ([1]).

Modern Thomists commonly support this opinion.

b) There are others, as Arrubal, Ferre, and Godoy, who affirm that the formal constituent of the divine nature is intellectuality in first act, i.e., the degree of intellectuality which is the root of intellection in second act.

c) The older Thomists, as Gonzalez, Nazarius, Zamel, and John of St. Thomas, commonly teach that the divine nature is subsisting intellection, i.e., the second act of intellection not received into any potency. This the opinion of Aristotle([2]).

760. Statement of the thesis.

THESIS. —THE NATURE OF GOD IS SUBSISTING INTELLECTION.

The most perfect of all natures is subsisting intellection. But the nature of God is the most perfect of all natures. Therefore the nature of God is subsisting intellection [3].

Major — Intellective nature is the most perfect of all natures. Moreover, the most perfect of all intellective natures is that nature which admits of no potentiality whatsoever, i.e., which is the very act of intellection, i.e., subsisting intellection.

Minor. — The nature of God is the nature of pure act, i.e., of subsisting being.

761. Entitative attributes, operative attributes.—
Since we have already made a distinction between God's metaphysical essence in the wide sense and the divine nature, we

---

(1) JOANNES A SANCTO THOMA, *Cursus Theol.*, t. II, p. 337a (Sol.).
(2) *Metaph.*, l. XII, c. 9. 1074b 30.
(3) I, q. 18, a. 3, c.

can now understand the distinction between God's entitative attributes and His operative attributes.

The entitative attributes of God are divine perfections which we conceive as resulting from subsisting being; v.g., infinity, immensity, etc.

The operative attributes of God are divine perfections which we conceive as resulting from the divine nature; v.g., divine volition, justice, mercy, etc.

POINTS FOR REVIEW

1. Define God's nature.

2. Distinguish between: God's nature and His metaphysical essence in the wide sense; entitative attributes and operative attributes.

3. Explain why subsisting being is not the formal constituent of the divine nature.

4. Prove that the divine nature is subsisting intellection.

CHAPTER II

GOD'S ENTITATIVE ATTRIBUTES

Prologue. — The entitative attributes of God are absolute perfections formally existing in God which, according to our manner of conceiving them, necessarily result from God's metaphysical essence, i.e., from subsisting being.

These perfections are God's infinity, simplicity, unity, distinction from the world, immutability, and eternity.

We dealt with God's infinity and simplicity in our study of His physical essence. In this chapter, we shall deal first with God's immutability, eternity, and unity; and, secondly, with His distinction from the world, which is the question of pantheism.

Therefore there will be two articles in this chapter.

God's immutability, eternity, and unicity	Statement of the question Opinions Thesis: God is absolutely immutable, eternal, and unique Scholia
Pantheism	Statement of the question Thesis: God is entirely distinct from the world.

GOD'S IMMUTABILITY, ETERNITY, AND UNICITY

762. Statement of the question.— 1° Proper or intrinsic immutability is the remotion of every kind of intrinsic mutability. A thing can be changed intrinsically either because it has real potency to some act which it can acquire or lose, or because its essence and existence are really distinct from each other: and, in this case, it can be created and annihilated. Therefore mutability presupposes composition of potency and act, whereas immutability does not admit of such composition.

2° Eternity is the duration of an immutable being in its existence and operation. Therefore eternity does not admit of beginning, succession, or end([1]).

3° The term unicity, as used in the thesis, signifies numerical unity in virtue of which nature admits of no division, i.e., of multiplication in inferiors.

God is unique (absolutely one) in as much as the divine nature does not admit of any other being similar to itself either in species or in genus. The angelic nature admits of other beings similar to it in genus, but not in species ; God alone does not admit of another being similar in genus.

---

(1) Eternity is defined by Boetius: the total, simultaneous, and perfect possession of interminable life (*interminabilis vitae tota simul et perfecta possessio*). This definition is obtained by comparing eternity to time as *measure*. The total, simultaneous, and perfect possession of interminable life is the *measure* of the duration of an immobile being in its existence and operation.

Explanation of Boethius' definition: Eternity is called *life*, to signify perfect existence and operation. This life is *interminable*, i. e., without beginning or end. Eternity is said to be the *total simultaneous* possession of this life, i. e., without succession; and is called the *perfect* possession, to distinguish it from the present time (the *now* of time), which also is total-simultaneous, but is such in virtue of its imperfection, for it is an incomplete being.

763. Opinions. 1° The immutability and eternity of God are generally recognized by everyone. *Pantheists*, in teaching that the reality of the spatial world is a part of God, call into question God's independence of place and time, and consequently His immutability.

Polytheism, which was an essential part of paganism, denies the unity of God. The Manicheans taught that there are two supreme first principles : the principle of good, venerated under the name of God ; and the principle of evil.

2° The thesis contains the doctrine taught by all Scholastics, and generally admitted by all others.

764. Statement of the thesis.

THESIS.— God is absolutely immutable, eternal, and unique.

First part. — *God is absolutely immutable.* — Subsisting being is absolutely immutable. But God is subsisting being. Therefore God is absolutely immutable.

Major. — Subsisting being is absolutely simple and pure act. Therefore it admits of no composition of potency and act whatsoever, and consequently of no mutability whatsoever.

Second part. — *God is eternal.* — Absolutely immutable being is eternal. But God is absolutely immutable. Therefore God is eternal.

The *major* is evident from the statement of the question.

Third part. — *God is unique,* i.e., *absolutely one.* — Infinite being is unique. But God is infinite being. Therefore God is unique, i.e., absolutely one.

Major. — *a)* Infinite being has no genus in common with any other being. *b)* Beings differ in as much as one has not all the perfection of another. But a being which is in any way deficient in perfection is not infinite. Therefore infinite being in unique, i.e., absolutely one.

Minor. — God is subsisting being, i.e., pure act.

765. Scholia.— 1) We may speak of extrinsic change in God in this sense : the extrinsic change is a mere extrinsic denomination deriving from the fact that intrinsic change takes place in an extrinsic subject, not in God. Thus the Word is said to be united to the humanity of Christ, to which It was not united before, not because the Word acquired a new perfection and a real relation to Christ's humanity, but because Christ's humanity acquired a new perfection and a real relation to the Word: therefore the whole change took place in the humanity.

2) Not only is God eternal, but He is His own eternity, because both His existence and His operation are immutable.

3) Mobile being is individuated by matter, the angel by the subsistence of form, and God by the subsistence of His own being. Hence God has absolute individuation, and is a personal being.

PANTHEISM

766. Statement of the question.— 1 Pantheism, in general, is the name given to any system that identifies God and the world.

The term *world* is used here to signify all these things whose existence is immediately manifest to us either from sen ible knowledge (the external, corporeal world), or from reflexion of the intellect (the internal world, the human soul).

2° Pantheism is either partial (semipantheism) or total (monism).

Partial pantheism teaches that God is a part of the world.

David of Dinant very foolishly claimed that God is first matter; the Stoics and Amoury of Chartres (d. 1204) held that God is the soul of the world; Eckhart (d. 1329) and Rosmini taught that God is the existence of the world.

Total pantheism, i.e., monism, teaches that God is the whole of the world.

The supporters of monism explain the system in different ways. Some claim that all things are composed of matter and material forces, and teach that this mat er is God; such is the teaching of Vogt, Moleschott, and Buchner. Others maintain that the psychic (the spiritual world) is a phenomenon concomitant to the physical, which alone is real and the constituent of every real essence; this is the opinion of Haeckel.

Such is the teaching of *materialistic monism*.

Some affirm that the only being which exists is a unique matter which manifests itself externally as extension, i.e., as the corporeal world, and internally as thought, i.e., as the spiritual world; such is the teaching of Spinoza, Parmenides, Zeno, Melissus, and Giordano Bruno (1548-1600). Others hold that the only reality is some principle higher than the physical and the psychic which evolves by immanent evolution, and whose two sides are the psychic and the physical; this is the opinion of Bain, Spencer, Taine, Hoffding, and Bergson.

Such is the teaching of *materialistico-spiritualistic* monism.

Some claim that the only reality is the psychic (the spiritual world), of which the physical is a concomitant phenomenon. Some conceive this psychic reality as the intellect, i.e., the cognitive principle, (Hegel, Fechner); others conceive it as the will, i.e., the appetitive principle (Schopenhauer, Wundt, Paulsen); and others conceive it as the cognitive principle and the appetitive principle (Eduard von Hartmann, Drews).

Such is the teaching of *spiritualistic* monism.

3° What we have already learned from Philosophy of Nature, Metaphysics, and the arguments by which we demonstrated that God is the efficient cause of the world demonstrate that pantheism is false. But, because of the errors so rampant in the world today, we offer now a special exposition of the teaching that God is distinct from the world.

The church condemned pantheism at the Council of the Vatican.

767. Statement of the thesis.

THESIS.— GOD IS ENTIRELY DISTINCT FROM THE WORLD.

1° Being which is infinite simple, immutable, all-perfect, necessary, and unique is entirely distinct from being which is neither infinite, nor simple, nor immutable, nor all-perfect, nor ncessary, nor unique. But God is a being which is infinite, simple, immutable, all-perfect, necessary, and unique; the world, on the other hand, is neither infinite, nor simple, nor immutable, nor all-perfect, nor necessary, nor unique. Therefore God is entirely distinct from the world.

Major. — Infinite being cannot be finite being, nor can it be either its formal or material part, nor can it have existence in common with it, because the existence of finite being is received into its essence as into a distinct potency, whereas the existence of infinite being is subsisting existence.

Minor. — God is subsisting being, and therefore is infinite, simple, immutable, all-perfect, necessary and unique; but the world, since it is composed of beings whose existence is distinct from their essence, is finite, composite, mutable, imperfect, contingent, and not unique (¹).

2° Pantheism is opposed to the testimony of conscience by which each one perceives that he is a substance distinct from others; and it is subversive of the moral order, because it leads to the denial of personality, liberty, and the immortality of a personal soul. Therefore we must reject pantheism, and must affirm that God is a being entirely distinct from the world.

768. Rejection of the arguments of pantheists.) 1° The finite cannot be added to the infinite. But God is infinite. Therefore the world cannot be added to God, i. e., God is all things.

Major. — The finite cannot be added to the infinite in the same order, that is to say, to the infinite cannot be added a finite mode which limits and confines it, *I concede;* to the infinite cannot be added a finite being of a different order, that is to say, to an infinite cause cannot be added, in an inferior order, a finite effect produced by it, *I deny.*

Minor. — A finite mode cannot be added to God, *I concede;* a finite effect cannot be added to God, Who is the Supreme Cause, *I deny.*

If the foregoing argument were accepted, God could not produce any effect, and God would no longer be the first and supreme cause of all things that exist, i. e., God would no longer be God.

2° Ouside of being nothing exists, since non-being is nothing. But God is being. Therefore outside of God nothing exists, i. e., God is all things.

Major. — Outside of those things which are certain beings, *I concede;* outside of some determinate being, *I deny.*

Minor. — God is not some determinate being, *I deny;* He is a determinate being, *I concede.*

The argument confounds the common concept of being as understood in the logical order with real being.

3° Being is a single concept, and cannot be multiplied by the addition of differentiae to it. Therefore only one being exists, and this being is God.

---

(1) Ipsa igitur puritate sui esse, a finitis omnibus rebus secernitur Deus. — *Thesis XXIV* s. THOMAE.

Antecedent.— Being is absolutely a single concept, *I deny;* is relatively a single concept, *I concede.*

Being cannot be multiplied by differentiae inherent in itself, *I deny;* by differentiae extraneous to itself, *I concede.*

The answer is evident from what has been said on the transcendence and analogy of being.

4° Substance is a being to which it appertains to exist in itself, and not in another. But it appertains to God alone to exist in Himself. Therefore God alone is a substance, i.e., one and only one substance exists, and that substance is God.

Major.— To exist in itself, i. e., not to exist in another as in a subject of inherence, *I concede;* to exist in itself, i.e., to have existence from another as from a cause, *I deny.*

Minor.— It appertains to God alone to exist in Himself, i. e., not to exist in another as in a subject of inherence, *I deny;* not to have existence from another, *I concede.*

5° An infinite being cannot be a personal being, since personality is limitation. But God is an infinite being. Therefore God is not a personal being.

Major.— Finite personality limits, *I concede;* personality in itself, formally understood, *I deny.*

In finite being, subsistence limits, since it is the ultimate perfection by which nature is rendered capable of receiving existence, as « standing » by itself, and therefore it is in the order of nature, which has a relation to existence as potency to act, as we have already seen; but personality, i. e., subsistence according to its formal concept, is an absolute perfection, since it renders something « standing » by itself (subsisting), and therefore it admits of no imperfection in its formal concept.

6° Simplicity cannot be the cause of multiplicity. But God is simple. Therefore God cannot be the cause of multiplicity, i. e., God alone exists.

Major.— Cannot be the cause of multiplicity in simple being, *I concede;* it cannot be the cause of multiplicity in beings which are produced as distinct from simple being, *I deny.*

READING.— Pantheism objects. . . ; but nothing can be added to the infinite. If, therefore, the world is added as a new reality to the being of God, the being of God is not infinite.

It is easy to answer this objection. We agree that nothing can be added to the infinite in the same order. But the contradiction of Pantheism consists in adding finite modes to the infinite, in such a way that the infinite is at the same time finite. But reason does not reject the idea that in an inferior order something may be added to the infinite, just as the effect is added to the eminent cause producing it. To deny such a possibility would be refusing to infinite Being the perfection of causality, and hence He would be no longer infinite.

But Pantheism maintains that, after the production of created beings, there is *more being* than there was before. Thus we find ourselves maintaining what we imputed as an error to the Evolutionists, namely, that the greater comes from the less.

There is not more being or more perfection as a consequence of creation; rather there are many beings; just as when a teacher has trained a pupil, there is not an increase in the sum of knowledge, but an increase of the number learned.   Yet this is but a faint analogy.   No matter how excellent a teacher may be, he and his school are more perfect than he is alone.   But if a cause is infinite, it already contains eminently all the perfections of its effects.

In the order of quantity, it is true to say that infinity plus one is still infinity. If we suppose that the series of days had no beginning, or that it is infinite *a parte ante* (regressively), then the addition of other days is possible *a parte post* (successively).   It is only from the finite point of view (in ratione finiti) that the series admits of increase inasmuch as it is finite in one direction. Inasmuch as the series is infinite, it admits of no incresae.

If we speak of the infinity of perfection (which means plenitude not of quantity or extent, but of being, of life, of wisdom, of love, of holiness), then with greater reason we must declare it to be evident that, as a consequence of creation, there is not more perfection, more being, more life, more wisdom, more holiness.   But that presupposes that being is analogous and not univocal.   Only on this condition do we find that the First Being contains within Himself the plenitude of being.— GARRIGOU-LAGRANGE, *God: His Existence and Attributes*, (Translated from the Fifth French Edition, by Dom Bede ROSE, O. S. B., S. T. D.), vol. II, pp. 48-50.

CHAPTER III

GOD'S OPERATIVE ATTRIBUTES

Prologue.— God's operative attributes are absolute perfections which result necessarily from the divine essence considered as the divine nature, i.e., from subsisting intellection, and they are the following: God's knowledge, will, and omnipotence. Since divine omnipotence is the principle of God's operation outside Himself, we shall study it in the book dealing with God's operation outside Himself. Hence there will be two articles in this chapter.

God's knowledge
- Statement of the question
- Thesis: God possesses perfect knowledge; moreover, He is His own eternal act of intellection by which He comprehends Himself, and has perfect knowledge of all things other than Himself in Himself, not in themselves
- God's knowledge in conjunction with His will is the cause of all created things
- God's foreknowledge of future contingent things
- Futurables
- Possibles
- Corollaries
- Division of God's knowledge

God's will
- Statement of the question
- Thesis: God possesses a will, which is not potency, nor habit, but act
- Object of God's will
- Formal constituent of God's free act
- Division of God's will
- Corollaries
- Difficulties

GOD'S KNOWLEDGE

769. Statement of the question. — 1° The term knowledge, i.e., science, may be used in a wide sense and in a strict sense. Knowledge in the wide sense is any certain and evident knowledge. Knowledge in the strict sense is certain and evident knowledge of things through their causes. God has knowledge in the wide sense and in the strict sense, and He possesses most perfect knowledge, i.e., knowledge in an eminent or infinite degree. Therefore God's knowledge does not admit of the imperfection found in human knowledge, such as composition of truths or of concepts.

2° We say that God is His own eternal act of intellection, and therefore that He is subsisting intellection. Hence God's knowledge does not admit of any of the potentiality found in created intellective knowledge. In other words, in God the intellect, the object of the intellect, the form of the intellect, and the act of the intellect are absolutely one and the same thing (¹).

God's intellection, in its absolute sense, is the divine nature; in its restricted sense, as connoting this or that particular object, it is a divine attribute.

3° We say that God comprehends His own essence, because God knows Himself to the degree that he is knowable (²).

4° We say that God has perfect knowledge of all things other than Himself, because not only has He knowledge of all finite things: things which actually exist and things which

---

(1) I, q. 14, a. 4, c.
(2) I, q. 14, a. 3.

exist only in the state of possibility; past, present, and future
things; corruptible things and incorruptible things; but His
knowledge of all these things is not a mere general knowledge
of them, i.e., a knowledge of them as regards their common
characteristics, but is a knowledge of them as regards all their
individual differentiæ, i.e., as individuals.

5° We say that God knows all things other than Himself
not in themselves, because He does not know them by means
of their proper (intentional) species; and that He knows them
in Himself, because God in knowing His own essence knows all
things other than Himself in His essence, because the simili ude
of all things other than God is found in the divine essence.

Therefore the divine essence is the proper object of God's
knowledge, and all things other than God are its secondary
objec .

770. Statement of the thesis.

THESIS.— God possesses perfect knowledge;
moreover, he is his own eternal
act of intellection by which he
comprehends himself, and has perfect knowledge of all things
other than himself in himself, not
in themselves.

First part. — *God possesses perfect knowledge.*— 1° All
absolute perfections are found in God in an eminent degree.
But knowledge is an absolute perfection. Therefore knowledge
is found in God in an eminent degree, i.e., God has perfect
knowledge.

2° A being which is at the summit of immateriality is at
the summit of knowledge. But God is at the summit of immateriality, since He is subsisting being and pure act. Therefore
God is at the summit of knowledg> (¹).

---

(1) I, q. 14, a. 1.

Major.— A being's degree of knowledge corresponds to its degree of immateriality.

Second part. —*God is His own eternal act of intellection.*— If God were not His own eternal act of intellection, He would not be pure act. But God is pure act. Therefore God is His own eternal act of intellection.

Major.— If God were not His own eternal act of intellection, intellection would be received as a perfection into God as act into potency. Hence God would not be pure act ([1]).

Third part. — *God comprehends Himself.*— God comprehends an object which is perfectly proportionate to His cognitive power. But the divine essence is perfectly proportionate to God's cognitive power. Therefore God comprehends His own essence, i.e., Himself.

Major.— An object which is perfectly proportionate to a cognitive power is known by that power to the degree that it is knowable.

Minor.— God's knowableness is perfectly proportionate to His cognitive power, because God is knowable in as much as He is pure act, and God is capable of knowledge in as much as He is free from all potency ([2]).

Fourth part. — *God has knowledge of all things other than Himself in Himself.*— God has knowledge in Himself of all things which have an intelligible mode of existence in Him. But all things other than God have an intelligible mode of existence in God. Therefore God has knowledge of all things other than Himself in Himself.

The *major* is evident.

Minor.— All things other than God have existence in God as in their first cause. But everything which has existence in

---

(1) I, q. 14, a. 4.
(2) I, q. 14, a. 3, c.

God has an intelligible mode of existence in Him: because God's being is His intellection.   Therefore ([1]).

Fifth part. —*God has no knowledge of things other than Himself in themselves.*— If God had knowledge of things other than Himself in themselves, there would be imperfection in Him. But there can be no imperfection in God.   Therefore God has no knowledge of things other than Himself in themselves.

Major.— If God had knowledge of things other than Himself in themselves, i.e., through their proper (intentional) species, He would be informed by these species as potency by act, and consequently there would be imperfection in Him.

Sixth part. — *God has perfect knowledge of things other than Himself.*— God has knowledge of things other than Himself as these things are represented in Him.   But things other than God are perfectly represented in God.   Therefore God has perfect knowledge of things other than Himself.

Minor.— All things other than God exist in God as in the first cause of every being and of every mode of being, and therefore they necessarily preexist and are perfectly represented in Him, i.e., in all their modes of being: general, special, and singular.

771. God's knowledge in conjunction with His will is the cause of all created things. —1° *Preliminaries.*— *a)* We are concerned here with things as actually existing in time, i.e., in the past, present, or future.

b) Knowledge can be the cause of things in two ways: *directively,* in as much as it directs the effective powers by proposing modes in which a thing can be or ought to be done; *effectively,* in as much as it effects externally what it conceives internally.

We teach that God's knowledge in conjunction with His will is the cause of all created things both directively and effectively.

---

(1) I, q. 14, a. 5.

2° *Proof.*— *a*) *God's knowledge is the effective cause of all created things.*— God's knowledge is the cause of all created things, just as the artificer's knowledge is the cause of artifacts. But the artificer's knowledge is both the directive and effective cause of things. Therefore God's knowledge is the effective cause of all created things.

The *major* is certain, because God produces things by acting through His intellect.

Minor.— Properly speaking, art is an operative habit, which not only perfects powers in relation to operation, but puts the form conceived in the artifact (¹).

a) *God's knowledge in conjunction with His will is the effective cause of all created things.*— Knowledge is an effective cause only when it has an inclination to the effect. But this inclination in God is His will. Therefore God's knowledge in conjunction with His will is the effective cause of all created things.

Major.— Knowledge as knowledge is not an active cause, but is the bare concept of an object. Hence knowledge is an active cause only when it has an inclination to the effect.

The *minor* is evident.

772. God's foreknowledge of future contingent things.

— 1° *Preliminaries.* — *a*) We have already learned that God's act of intellection is eternal, and that His knowledge in conjunction with His will is the cause of all created things. Hence we may conclude:

1) God knows in His eternity all things which exist in time;

2) God knows these things in the decree of His will; for all things other than God exist because God *wills* that they exist.

b) We are confronted with a special problem, according to our mode of knowledge, in regard to future contingent things. Since a future contingent thing, as future, does not exist, but will exist, how can it be present to God's eternity? Again, since

---

(1) BILLUART, *De Deo*, diss. V, a. III.

a future contingent thing, as contingent, is not necessarily determined to exist, how can God have certain and infallible knowledge of it ?

c) A future thing is a thing which is determined in its causes to have existence in the course of time, i.e., in the future.

A future *necessary* thing is a thing which of its nature, i.e., in its second causes, is determined to exist in the future, and cannot be impeded from doing so.

A future *contingent* thing, *in the wide sense*, is a thing which of its nature is determined to have existence, but can be naturally impeded from doing so by the concurrence of second causes; v.g., longevity from robust health.

A future *contingent* thing, *in the strict and proper sense*, is a thing which of its nature is indifferent to existence or non-existence; v.g., free acts, things of chance, fortuitous thing.

We are concerned here with contingent things which are strictly and properly future contingent.

d) The Thomistic school explains God's foreknowledge of future contingent thing as followss:

1) God knows future contingent things as they are physically present to His eternity, i.e., present in their real being, and not merely intentionally.

2) God knows future contingent things in the decrees of His will, i.e., He has knowledge of them because He has decreed their existence.

There are many who do not accept the Thomistic teaching, especially because of the difficulty of reconciling human liberty with the infallible decree of God's will. Hence they do not admit that God knows future contingent things in the decree of His will, and teach that God knows them eith r in His super-comprehension of second causes, in as much as God has perfect knowledge of the contingent cause (v.g , the free will), so that He knows how it would act if placed in a particular set of circumstances — this is the opinion of Molina; or in their objective and formal truth, for in the case of two contradictory propositions, — this will be or will not be, — the one is determinatedly false, and the other determinately true before any decree of the divine will — this is the opinion of Cardinal Mazella; or in the presence to God's eternity before the decree of the divine will — this the opinion of Janssens.

e) We hold the Thomistic opinion as certain; but we consider the reconciling of human liberty with the divine decree as a mystery; we shall discuss it in the article on divine motion.

2° Proof of the *Thomistic opinion.*

a) *God knows future contingent things as they are physically present to His eternity.*—God knows future contingent things as they are present to His eternity. But future contingent things are physically present to God's eternity. Therefore.

Major.— God's knowledge is measured by eternity.

Minor.— Eternity, total, simultaneous possession, is physically equivalent to all succession and embraces all times, just as immensity physically exceeds all differences of places. Hence all time, whether past, present, or future, is physically present to God's eternity.

b) *God knows future contingent things in the decree of His will.*— God knows all things other than Himself in as much as He is their cause. But God is the cause of future contingent things by the decree of His will. Therefore God knows future contingent things in the decree of His will.

The *major* is evident from what we have already said.

√ *Minor.*— Before the decree of the divine will, things exist only as possible; but some of these things are future contingent things, because God wills that they exist in the future, for God's knowledge in conjunction with His will is the cause of things which exist in time, as we have already proved.

c) *Rejection of the other opinions:* 1) God cannot know future contingent things *in the supercomprehension of their causes,* because future contingent things are not determined in their causes before the decree of God's will. 2) God does not know future contingent things *in their objective truth.* Certainly two contradictory propositions are not at the same time true and false. But, before the decree of the divine will, one is not determinately false and the other determinately true. 3) Finally, future contingent things *are physically present in God's eternity,* only because God wills that they exist in time.

773. Futurables. — 1° *Preliminaries.* — *a*) A futurable, i.e., a conditional future event, is an event which never will take place, but which certainly would take place if some condition were fulfilled.

There are three kinds of futurables: 1) the futurable which has a necessary connexion with the fulfillment of a condition; v.g., if Peter would commit mortal sin, he would lose sanctifying grace; 2) the futurable which has only a contingent connexion with the fulfillment of a condition, and therefore could be foreseen only conjecturally; v.g., if the Gospel were preached to the people of Tyre, they would do penance; 3) the futurable that has no connexion whatsoever with the fulfillment of a condition; v.g., if Joas had struck the earth, he would have destroyed Syria.

b) There is no doubt about God's having certain and infallible knowledge of futurables, because futurables are mentioned in Sacred Scripture. Our present question, therefore, concerns the medium of God's knowledge of futurables which have no necessary connexion with the fulfillment of a condition.

c) Thomists teach that God knows these futurables in the decree of His will, which is *subjectively* absolute and *objectively* conditional; v.g., I will the conversion of Peter, if he prays. Such a decree is subjectively absolute, because, on God's part, there is a firm and certain act of the will, not a mere disposition to will; objectively conditional, because it depends on the fulfillment of a condition on the part of the object.

The Molinists, who do not accept the Thomistic teaching, are unanimous in teaching that God, before any decree of His will, knows futurables by *middle knowledge* (scientia media).

Middle knowledge is defined : *the knowledge by which God, before any decree of His will, knows from all eternity how a cre-*

ated free will would act, if placed in a particular set of circumstances.

According to the Molinists, there are three states of divine knowledge : *a*) the state of necessary knowledge : God necessarily knows all possible things ;

b) the state of middle knowledge : God knows, before any decree of His will, how the created free will would act in a particular set of circumstances ;

c) the state of free knowledge : God decrees that He will place the will in a particular set of determinate circumstances, and thus knows in His decree how the free will will act.

To explain how God, before any decree of His will, has knowledge of futurables, the Molinists have recourse to the supercomprehension of causes, to the opinion of objective and formal truth, etc.

2° **Proof of the** *Thomistic opinion.*

God knows futurables in the decree of His will, which is subjectively absolute and objectively conditional. — God knows all things other than Himself in as much as He is their first cause. But God is the first cause of futurables by a decree of His will, which is subjectively absolute and objectively conditional. Therefore.

The *major* is evident from what has been said.

Minor. — God acts by His intellect and will. Hence some event would take place, if some condition were fulfilled with which it has no necessary connexion, only because God decreed this event from eternity, i.e., God is the first cause of futurables by a decree of His will, which is subjectively absolute and objectively conditional.

774. Possibles. — 1° *Preliminaries.* — *a*) Being connotes a relation to existence : for being signifies essence which is related to existence. Since relation to existence can be either *actual* or *non-actual*, we make a distinction between actual being and possible being.

An actual being is a being which has existence in act, i.e., it is either act or actuated potency. A possible being is a being which, though not possessing existence in act, can exist.

b) Since possibility is *relation to existence*, it is of two kinds : external and internal.

External possibility is capacity for receiving existence founded on a cause capable of producing a thing ; v.g., a picture is extrinsically possible because of a painter who is a cause capable of producing it.

Internal possibility (*objective, logical, pure* possibility) is capacity for receiving existence, which capacity essentially appertains to a thing, i.e., capacity which derives from the essence of a thing. Hence the internal possibility of a thing is constituted by the essence of the thing. Since we do not conceive essence as something simple, but rather as composed of several notes, internal possibility is formally constituted of real notes which are compatible with each other, i.e., from the compatibility of real notes. Hence there are two ways in which a thing can lack real possibility : *a*) it can be made up of notes which are compatible, but not real : being of reason with foundation in reality ; *b*) it can be made up of notes which are real, but incompatible, i.e., mutually destructive : a square circle.

c) We say that internal possibility is *fundamentally* constituted by the divine essence, because a thing is possible in as much as it can be an imitation of the divine essence ; and *formally* constituted by the divine intellect, because possible things are considered as having distinct formal constituents, only in as much as they are conceived by the divine intellect as different terms of the imitability of the divine essence. Therefore God has knowledge of possible things in as much as He has knowledge of the divine essence as imitable outside Himself.

Our opinion is opposed to the teaching of fatalists, who hold that only a thing which actually exists is at any time possible ; is opposed also to the teaching of all who maintain that the internal possibility of things depends either on the power of God (Ockam), or on the free will of God (Descartes), or on the human intellect (Protagoras) ; and is opposed to the teaching of certain Scholastics who affirm that possible things formally depend on the divine essence, not on the divine intellect.

2° Statement of the thesis.

THESIS.— THE INTERNAL POSSIBILITY OF THINGS DEPENDS FUNDAMENTALLY ON THE DIVINE ESSENCE, AND FORMALLY ON THE DIVINE INTELLECT.

First part. — *The internal possibility of things depends fundamentally on the divine essence.*— The modes in which being can be participated depend fundamentally on the divine essence. But the internal possibility of things is a mode in which being can be participated. Therefore the internal possibility of things depends fundamentally on the divine essence.

Major.— Participated being, both actual and possible, depends fundamentally on being in which essence and existence are identified, i.e., on the divine essence.

Minor.— Possibility intrinsically considered is a relation to being, i.e., a mode in which being can be participated.

Second part. — *The internal possibility of things depends formally on the divine intellect.*— The internal possibility of things depends formally on the first principle by which possible things are constituted as formally distinct. But the first principle by which possible things are constituted as formally distinct is the divine intellect.   Therefore.

The *major* is evident from the preliminaries.

Minor.— The degrees of the participability of the divine essence as such, i.e., possible things, eminently exist in the divine essence as identified with this essence; and possible things are constituted as distinct only by the intellect which first knows the different modes in which the divine essence can be imitated outside itself.   But the intellect which first knows the divine essence is the divine intellect.   Therefore.

Rejection of false opinions.— *a*) Possible things do not depend on things existing in the world, for mundane things are contingent, whereas possibles are necessary.

b) Possible things do not depend on the power of God, because in that case God's omnipotence would be destroyed: a thing would be impossible because God could not produce it.

c) Possible things do not depend on the free will of God, because God's free will presupposes possible things: God freely produces what His intellect proposes to His will as possible.

d) Possible things do not depend on the human intellect, because the human intellect is measured by things, but does not measure them: therefore it presupposes possible things as already constituted.

775. Corollaries. — 1° Therefore God has ideas, according to the strict meaning of idea as the concept of an artificer to the likeness of which he produces or can produce an artifact.

2° God's ideas are not only many in number, but they are infinite. Multiplicity of ideas is not opposed to God's simplicity, because in God ideas are only perceived aspects of the divine essence to whose likeness He produces or can produce things other than Himself, but not different subjective concepts which are really distinct from each other.

3° The divine essence is the exemplar cause of possible things, just as the object contemplated by the artificer is the exemplar cause of the idea to the likeness of which he can produce an artifact.   The divine ideas are the exemplar causes to the likeness of which God produces or can produce things outside Himself.

4° The whole metaphysical order (the essences of things and a priori truths that flow from the essences of things) depends on the divine intellect, whereas the physical order (the existence of things and truths concerning the existences of things) depends on the divine will in conjunction with the divine intellect.

776. Division of God's knowledge.— Divine knowledge in itself is unique, simple, unlimited, and comprehensive of all things by a single act.   Nevertheless, as it is conceived by us, it is divided according to its objects.

1° God has speculative knowledge and practical knowledge.

God's *speculative knowledge* is the knowledge by which He only contemplates things; v.g., God's knowledge of Himself, the knowledge by which God considers what things are.

God's *practical knowledge* is the knowledge by which He considers how things can be produced; or that by which He actually produces things.

Though God cannot do evil, yet He has practical knowledge of it, in as much as He permits, corrects, or directs it to some end.

2° God has necessary knowledge and free knowledge.

God's *necessary knowledge* is the knowledge which precedes God's free determination and is concerned only with necessary objects, as the quiddities of things which cannot be otherwise than they are.

God's *free knowledge* is that knowledge which presupposes a decree and is concerned with objects that depend on His free will, as are things existing in the past and present, future things, and futurables.

3° God has knowledge of simple intelligence and knowledge of vision.

God's *knowledge of simple intelligence* is the knowledge which He has of realities which neither exist, nor have existed, nor will exist.

God's *knowledge of vision* is the knowledge which He has of realities which exist, or have existed, or will exist.

God's knowledge of vision is knowledge of *approbation*, as it is concerned with good things, and presupposes a decree of the divine will approving of them; or is knowledge of *disapprobation*, as it is concerned with sin, and presupposes a decree of the divine will disapproving of it, and merely permitting it.

POINTS FOR REVIEW

1. Define: knowledge in the strict sense, future thing, contingent thing in the strict sense, divine ideas.

2. Prove that God possesses perfect knowledge, that He is His own eternal act of intellection, that He comprehends Himself, that He knows all things other than Himself in Himself, and that He has perfect knowledge of all things other than Himself.

3. Explain and prove the following statements: God has no knowledge of things other than Himself in themselves; God's knowledge is the cause of things; God's knowledge is the effective cause of things only when in conjunction with His will.

4. State the Thomistic teaching on God's foreknowledge of future contingent things.

5. Prove that the internal possibility of things depends fundamentally on God's essence, and formally on His intellect.

6. Does God possess many ideas? If so, does His possession of them militate against divine simplicity? Explain.

GOD'S WILL

777. Statement of the question.— 1° The will is the inclination of an intellectual nature to a good proposed to it by the intellect.

2° In man, the will is a faculty, i.e., a power; in God, the will cannot be a power or a habit, but is act ([1]).

778. Statement of the thesis.

THESIS.—GOD POSSESSES A WILL, WHICH IS NEITHER A POWER, NOR A HABIT, BUT ACT.

First part. — *God possesses a will.*— 1° A being endowed with an intellect possesses a will. But God is endowed with an intellect. Therefore God possesses a will.

The *major* is evident from what has been said in Philosophy of Nature.

2° The will is an absolute perfection. But God possesses all absolute perfections. Therefore God possesses a will.

Major.— The will is an inclination to a universal good, not to a limited good.

Second part. -- *The will of God is neither a power, nor a habit, but act.*— God's will is one and the same as His essence. But the essence of God can be neither a power, nor a habit, because it is pure act. Therefore the will of God is neither a power, nor a habit, but is pure act.

---

(1) *Contra Gentes*, l. IV, c. 15.

779. Object of God's will.— 1° *Preliminaries.* — *a*) The object of the will is twofold: proper and secondary.

The *proper* object of the will is the goodwhich is first and directly attained by it and which is also the end of all other objects of the will.

The *secondary* object of the will is the good attained by it in dependence on its proper object, and related to it as means to the end.

b) We state in the thesis that God necessarily wills His own essence as the proper object of His will. Therefore it is impossible for God not to will and to love His own essence. Secondly, we affirm that God freely wills things other than Himself as the secondary object of His will, i.e., as means to the attainment of His essence as to their end, but means which are in no way necessary.

2° Statement of the thesis.

> **THESIS.**—GOD NECESSARILY WILLS HIS OWN ESSENCE AS THE PROPER OBJECT OF HIS WILL; GOD FREELY WILLS THINGS OTHER THAN HIMSELF AS THE SECONDARY OBJECT OF HIS WILL.

First part. — *God wills His own essence as the proper object of His will.*— 1° The proper object of any will is the good first and directly attained by it, as an end. But the good first and directly attained by God's will as an end is the divine essence. Therefore the proper object of God's will is the divine essence, i.e., God wills His own essence as the proper object of His will.

Minor.— The good first and directly attained by God's will as an end is a good which is proportionate to it. But the divine essence is the only good which is proportionate to God's will. Therefore.

2° The good primarily known by God is the divine essence. But the good primarily known is the good primarily willed. Therefore the good primarily willed by God is the divine essence.

The *major* is evident from what has been said.

Minor.— The will is an inclination which follows the intellect.

Second part. — *God necessarily wills His own essence.*— When God's will is in act, He necessarily wills His own essence. But God's will is always in act. Therefore God necessarily wills His own essence.

Major.— A faculty has such a necessary relation to its proper object that, when it is in act, it is necessarily drawn to it. But the proper object of God's will is the divine essence. Therefore.

Minor.— God's will is identified with the divine essence, which is pure act, and therefore it is always in act.

Third part. — *God wills things other than Himself,* i.e., *creatures.*— Everything is inclined to its proper object and tends, in the measure in which it is perfect, to communicate its goodness to others, for goodness is diffusive of itself. But the divine nature is most perfect. Therefore God tends to communicate His own goodness, in so far as possibilities permit this, by means of created likenesses; in other words, God wills things other than Himself.

Fourth part. — *God wills things other than Himself as the secondary object of His will.*— The secondary object of the will is the object which it desires in dependence on its proper object, and which is related to the proper object as means to an end. But God wills things other than Himself in dependence on His own goodness and as means to it. Therefore God wills things other than Himself as the secondary object of His will.

Minor.— The goodness which exists in things is a participation of God's goodness, and therefore all such goodness is related to God's goodness as to its end.

Fifth part. — *God freely wills things other than Himself.*— The will is not necessarily drawn to things which are means to its end, if its end can be attained without them. But God wills things other than Himself as means related to His own goodness as to their end, but not as means without which His goodness is rendered impossible. Therefore God freely wills things other than Himself.

Minor.— God's goodness is of itself perfect and immense.

780. Formal constituent of God's free act.—1° *Preliminaries.*— The difficulty which here confronts us may be introduced by the following question: how can we reconcile God's liberty with His immutability? Either God could have been or could not have been without His free act. If He could not have been without His free act, how can He be free? If He could have been without His free act, how can He be immutable? The difficulty of the problem lies in the mystery of God's absolute simplicity. Hence its complete solution seems to exceed the capacity of human reason.

b) Divine liberty is not the same as human liberty.

Human liberty is the indifference of a potency to several acts of volition and nolition.

Divine liberty is not the indifference of a potency, for potency is absolutely alien to God; but it is the indifference of one most simple and pure act to several objects. Hence God, by one and the same most simple act, wills the being and the non-being of creatures, this and that.

2° *Opinions.*— There is great diversity of opinion among authors in regard to the formal constituent of God's free act.

a) Some hold that God's free act is constituted by some intrinsic and defectible reality in God, which is necessarily superadded to His act. We may not hold this opinion, for it destroys God's simplicity.

b) Others maintain that God's free act is constituted by something purely extrinsic, namely, the production of creatures. This opinion is untenable, because God is free from all eternity, and therefore before the production of created things, and also

because God's free act, as vital and immanent, must be constituted by something intrinsic to God.

c) Others contend that God's free act is constituted by a
relation of reason to creatures. This opinion is untenable because God's free act, as the cause of real being, cannot be a being
of reason.

d) Thomists commonly teach that God's free act is His
necessary act as connoting a non-necessary transcendental relation to creatures, i.e., a non-necessary termination in creatures.
This is the opinion that we follow.

3° Statement of the thesis.

> **THESIS.**— GOD'S FREE ACT IS HIS NECESSARY ACT
> AS CONNOTING A NON-NECESSARY TER-
> MINATION IN CREATURES.

God's free act is something intrinsic to God and in a certain
sense defectible. But God's necessary act as connoting a non-
necessary termination in creatures is something intrinsic to
God and in a certain sense defectible. Therefore God's free
act is His necessary act as connoting a non-necessary termination in creatures.

Major.— God's free act, as vital and immanent, is intrinsic to God; and, as free, is in a certain sense defectible, for in a
certain sense it admits of the possibility of non-existence ([1]).

Minor.— Since God's necessary act is identified with His
essence, it is something intrinsic to Him; and, though this act is
entitatively necessary, it is in a certain sense defectible: it is
defectible if it is understood formally as connoting a termination in creatures, in as much as this termination would be lacking if the creatures which admit of the possibility of non-existence did not exist. ([2]).

---

(1) To be more explicit, this means that God's free act is nothing else
but the necessary act by which He loves His goodness, in so far as this connotes
a non-necessary relation to creatures, and so it is only extrinsically defectible
by reason of the defectibility in the thing willed.— GARRIGOU-LAGRANGE,
The One God (Translation by Dom. Bede ROSE, O. S. B., S. T. D.), London,
Herder, 1943 p. 515.— Added by Translator.

(2) BILLUART, *De Deo*, diss. VII, a. 4.

781. Division of God's will.— Although the will of God as such is unique, we designate it by different names according to the different material objects with which it is concerned. Hence the divine will, according to our mode of conceiving it, has divisions.

1° Will of good pleasure and will of expression.

The *will of good pleasure* is the very act of the divine will; hence it is found properly and formally in God.

The *will of expression* is something extrinsic; hence it is not found properly and formally in God. In the case of man, the will of expression is an expression of his willing something, and therefore, properly speaking, it is the effect of the will, and only in a metaphorical sense it is the will, i.e., the expression or effect of the will is designated the will. Example: when God produces an exterior effect, — an effect which man is wont to produce by willing it, — v.g., when He gives a command, this exterior effect is God's will of expression, in the sense that the expression is designated the will.

2. Antecedent will and consequent will.

The *antecedent will* is the will of God as directed to an object considered in itself and prescinded from its circumstances.

The *consequent will* is the will of God as directed to an object with all its circumstances.

Example: By His antecedent will God wills that all men be saved; by His consequent will He wills that the wicked suffer damnation.

782. Corollaries.— 1° Therefore God is Subsisting Love, since He always actually wills Himself and things other than Himself, and since His act of volition is the divine essence.

2° Since God's will is most perfect, God is justice, mercy, goodness, etc.

3° The divine goodness is the reason, not the cause, of God's willing things other than Himself, for there can be nothing caused in God: something caused in God would imply evolution and imperfection in Him.   Therefore God is not moved to act by an end, but acts for an end.   In other words, God's operation, which is Himself, is not finalized by an end, i.e., it is not for an end as for a cause, because God is the ultimate end of all things.   Nevertheless, the term of God's operation (things other than God) is finalized by an end, i.e., is for the divine goodness as for its final cause.

783. Difficulties.— 1° A being endowed with an immutable will does not freely will things other than itself.   But God is a being endowed with an immutable will.   Therefore God does not freely will things other than Himself.

Major.— Does not freely will, i. e., wills of hypothetical necessity, I *concede;* of absolute necessity, I *deny.*

Minor.— And God wills of hypothetical necessity; I *concede;* always of absolute necessity; I *deny.*

God of hypothetical necessity wills whatever He wills in this sense: on the supposition that God wills a thing, He necessarily wills it because His will is immutable, in the same way as Socrates, on the supposition that he is seated, is necessarily seated as long as he is seated.   But since the divine goodness can exist without other things, God does not will things other than Himself as means necessarily directed to an end, i. e., of absolute necessity, but He freely wills them.

2° But God of absolute necessity wills things other than Himself.   Therefore.

A being whose volition is its absolutely necessary act wills of absolute necessity things other than itself.   But God is a being whose volition is His absolutely necessary act. Therefore.

Major.— Act absolutely necessary in itself and in the term which it connotes, I *concede;* act absolutely necessary in itself, but not in its term. I *deny.*

Minor.— Volition which is absolutely necessary in itself, I *concede;* as regards its term, I *subdistinguish:* as regards the divine essence, I *concede;* as regards things other than God, I *deny.*

3° But divine volition which is absolutely necessary in itself is also absolutely necessary in the term which it connotes.   Therefore.

If another act of the will is required, in order that the divine will have another term, divine volition which is absolutely necessary in itself is also absolutely necessary in the term which it connotes.   But another act of the will is required in order that divine volition have another term.   Therefore.

Major.— If another act is required in all wills, I *concede;* if it is required only in a will which is not pure act, i. e., in the created will, I *deny.*

Minor.— In a will which is pure act, I *deny;* in a will which is not pure act, I *concede.*

4° But any will requires another act, in order that it have another term, i. e., liberty requires mutability of the act of the will.   Therefore.

The active indifference in virtue of which the will has dominative power over its own act requires mutability of the act of the will.   But liberty is that active indifference in virtue of which the will has dominative power over its own act. Therefore.

Major.— The active indifference in virtue of which the will has power over the egression or non-egression of the act, *I concede;* over the act only as connoting a term, *I deny.*

Minor.— The active indifference in virtue of which the will has power only over the egression and the non-agression of its act, *I deny;* either over the egression and the non-agression of its act, or over its act as connoting a term, *I concede.*

POINTS FOR REVIEW

1. Prove that God possesses a will.

2. Explain why God's will is pure act.

3. State the proper object and also the secondary object of God's will.

4. Explain why God necessarily wills His own essence, and freely wills all things other than Himself.

5. Define: God's free act, the will of good pleasure, the will of expression.

6. Distinguish between the antecedent will and the consequent will of God.

BOOK III

———

God operation outside Himself

———

THE ONLY CHAPTER

Prologue.— In this book, which contains only one chapter, we shall consider first God's power, and, secondly, God's operations outside Himself, namely, creation, divine concurrence in the actions of creatures, the conservation of creatures, and divine providence. We shall study too the problem of divine providence and evil, and the problem of miracles. Therefore there will be seven articles in this chapter.

God's power

{
Statement of the question
Thesis: God possesses power, which is omnipotence; and this power consists in His intellect in conjunction with His will
God's absolute and ordained power
}

Creation

{
Statement of the question
Thesis: The world was created by God
Active creation, passive creation
No finite being can be either the principal cause or the instrumental cause of creation
}

Appendix

{
Statement of the question
Opinions
Exposition of the teaching of St. Thomas:
Finite being did not necessarily exist from eternity
The impossibility of creation from eternity cannot be demonstrated
It was fitting that God would create the world at the beginning of time, not from eternity.
}

Divine concurrence
- Statement of the question
- Opinions
- Thesis: God cooperates in the actions of creatures by simultaneous concurrence and also by moving them to their operation
- Divine motion and created liberty

Conservation of things
- Statement of the question
- Thesis: Creatures require that they be directly and immediately conserved in their being by God
- God's immensity and ubiquity
- Corollaries

Divine providence
- Statement of the question
- Errors
- Thesis: Divine providence exists, and extends to all things as individuals.
- Scholia

Divine providence and evil
- Statement of the question
- Errors
- Thesis: Divine providence wills no evil directly, wills physical evil indirectly, and cannot will moral evil as such even indirectly, but merely permits it; and this permission is a good

Miracles
- Statement of the question
- Adversaries
- Thesis: Miracles, as sensible facts, can be known with physical certitude; as supernatural facts, some can be known with metaphysical certitude, others only with moral certitude.
- Possibility of miracles
- Difficulties

GOD'S POWER

784. Statement of the question. — 1° The term *power* is used here to signify the active power of acting outside its subject.

2° Omnipotence is power which is capable of producing all absolutely possible things, i.e., all things which are not contradictory (¹), or in which the notion of being can be realized.

3° We state in the thesis that God's power consists in His intellect in conjunction with His will, not in as much as the operation of the intellect is considered formally immanent, but in as much as this operation is considered as virtually transitive. Even in us, the intellect and will operate transitively, in as much as they immediately move the phantasy, and, by means of the phantasy, all other powers subordinated to it.

785. Statement of the thesis.

> **THESIS.** — GOD POSSESSES POWER, WHICH IS OM-
> NIPOTENCE; AND THIS POWER CONSISTS
> IN HIS INTELLECT IN CONJUNCTION
> WITH HIS WILL.

First part. — *God possesses power.* — The being which is the first unmoved mover and the first efficient cause possesses power of acting outside itself. But God is the first unmoved mover and the first efficient cause. Therefore God possesses power.

The *major* is manifest from its very terms.

---

(1) I, q. 25, a. 3.

The *minor* is evident from the arguments used to demonstrate the existence of God.

Second part.—*God's power is omnipotence.*—Power which is infinite is omnipotence. . But God's power is infinite. Therefore God's power is omnipotence.

Major.—Infinite power is capable of producing any being whatsoever, and therefore it is omnipotence.

Minor.— Every divine perfection is infinite.

2° Power which is capable of producing anything whatsoever in which the notion of being is realized is omnipotence. But God's power is capable of producing anything whatsoever in which the notion of being is realized. Therefore God's power is omnipotence ([1]).

Major.— Such power is capable of producing anything which is not contradictory. For it is only in a contradictory thing that the notion of being is not realized.

Minor.— A power is capable of producing anything which comes within the scope of its proper effect. But the proper effect of God, Who is essentially being, is being. Therefore God's power is capable of producing anything which comes within the score of being, i.e., anything in which the notion of being is realized.

Third part. — *God's power consists in His intellect in conjunction with His will.* — The power of a purely spiritual being consists in its intellect in conjunction with its will. But God is a purely spiritual being. Therefore God's power consists in His intellect in conjunction with His will([2]).

Major. — A spiritual being possesses spiritual faculties only, i.e., intellect and will. Hence a spiritual being has power only in as much as the will commands what knowledge directs ([3]), i.e., power in a purely spiritual being consists in its intellect in conjunction with its will.

---

(1) *Contra Gentes*, l. II, c. 22.
(2) *De Malo*, q. 16, a. 1, ad 14.
(3) I, q. 25, a. 1, ad 4.

Minor.— God is subsisting being.

786. God's absolute and ordained power.— God's power, according to our mode of conceving it, is divided into His absolute power and His ordained power.

God's absolute power is His power considered in itself and without relation to the other divine attributes, in as much as its object is all possible things, i.e., everything in which the notion of being can be safeguarded.

God's ordained power is His power as subject to and regulated by divine wisdom, i.e., God's power of executing what His will, in the light of His knowledge, has decreed.

Thus God by His absolute power can do things other than those of which He has had foreknowledge and which He has preordained He would do ; but by His ordained power He can do only those things of which He has had foreknowledge and which He has preordained He would do, because His *actual doing* is subject to His foreknowledge and preordination, but not His *being able to do, His power* to do, which is His nature ; therefore God does things, because He wills to do them ; nevertheless, the power to do them comes not from His will, but from His nature[1].

POINTS FOR REVIEW

1. Define: omnipotence, God's absolute power, God's ordained power.
2. Prove that God possesses power, and that this power is omnipotence.
3. In what does God's power consist ? Prove your answer.

---

(1) I, q. 25, a. 5, ad 1.

CREATION

787. Statement of the question.— 1 A causation, i.e,
a production, is the emanation of an effect from its efficient
cause.   There are two ways in which an effect can be produced
by its efficient cause:

a) from a preexisting subject ; v.g., a statue is produced
from wood ;

b) from no preexisting subject, i.e., from nothing; and
this kind of production is creation.

Therefore creation, in its strict sense, is the production
of a thing from nothing, i.e., neither from itself, nor from any
preexisting subject.   In this definition:

a) from does not signify a material cause, but only a
relation of reason between non-being and created being, just
as when we say : from morning comes midday, i.e., after
morning comes midday([1]).

b) neither from itself designates the element common to
every particular production, v.g., to generation, and to universal production, which is creation ; thus, if this man is engendered, he did not exist as this man before he was engendered,
but is engendered from a non-man as from a subject, that is
to say, not from himself, but from a seed([2]) ;

c) nor from any preexisting subject designates the element
proper to creation, in as much as a created thing is not produced
from a preexisting subject.

Hence creation, from the point of view of its term-to-
which, is defined: the production of the whole substance of

---

(1) I, q. 45, a. 1, ad 3.
(2) *Ibid.,* c.

a thing, i.e., the production of the whole being of an effect ([1]);
from the point of view of its term-from-which, it is the production of the whole being of an effect from non-being which is
nothing([2]) ; from the point of view of both its term-from-which
and its term-to-which, it is the production of the whole being
of something from no preexisting subject([3]).

2° The term world is used in the thesis to signify all
beings other than God, corporeal and spiritual.

3° a) The philosophers of antiquity could not arrive at
the concept of creation.   Hence they held that there existed
an increate matter from which the world was produced.   Even
Aristotle, it would seem, held this opinion.

b) Pantheists, as a result of their system, are forced to
deny the creation of the world.

788. Statement of the thesis.— The thesis is of faith,
for the Council of the Vatican, Can. V. Cap. I, Sess. III, defined that the world was created by God.

THESIS. — THE WORLD WAS CREATED BY GOD.

All things other than God were caused by God.   But, if
the world was not created by God, all things other than God
were not caused by God.   Therefore the world was created
by God.

Major. — All beings other than God are beings by participation, and therefore have been caused by God, Who is essentially being, i.e., Who is the universal cause of all being.

Minor. — If the world was not created by God, it would
have been produced from a preexisting subject which would
not have been caused by God([4]).

---

(1) I, q. 45, a. 3, *Sed contra.*
(2) I, q. 45, a. 1, c.
(3) I, q. 65, a. 3.
(4) I, q. 45, 1. 2, c.

789. Active creation, passive creation.— 1° Creation, in its active meaning, signifies God's operation, which is the divine essence, with a relation (of reason) to creatures.

2° Although creation, in its passive meaning, is conceived by us as a change, properly speaking, it is not a change at all. Every change presupposes a subject which passes from one mode of being to another mode of being. But in creation there is no such subject. Hence God in creating produces things without motion. Action and passion without motion are only relation : action and passion are merely motion with different relations.

Therefore creation in its passive meaning, i.e., creation in the creature, is merely a real relation (predicamental) of the creature to the Creator as to the principle of its being[1].

790. No finite being can be either the principal cause or the instrumental cause of creation.— 1° *Preliminaries.* — a) A principal cause is a cause which operates by its own power ; an instrumental cause is a cause which operates by motion received from the principal cause.

b) Durandus asserted that God could communicate the power of creating to a creature, i.e., to a finite being, as to a principal cause, within certains limits.

Peter the Lombard (surnamed *Magister Sententiarum*), Suarez, and others hold that the creature can be used by God as the instrument (physical) of creation.

St. Thomas and many doctors teach that the power of creating is proper to God alone, and that it cannot be communicated to a finite being either as principal cause or as instrumental cause [2].

2° *Proof of the teaching of St. Thomas.*

---

(1) I, q. 45, a. 3, c.
(2) Ipsa igitur puritate sui esse, a finitis omnibus rebus secernitur Deus. Inde infertur primo, mundum nonnisi per creationem a Deo procedere potuisse, deinde virtutem creativam, qua per se primo attingitur ens in quantum ens, nec miraculose ulli finitae naturae esse communicabilem.— *Thesis XXIV* s. THOMAE.

a) No finite being can be the principal cause of creation. —
1° No finite being can be the principal cause of the production
of being in its totality. But creation is the production of
being in its totality. Therefore no finite being can be the
principal cause of creation.

Major.— Being in its totality is the first and most universal of all effects, and therefore it must be attributed to the
first and most universal of all causes, as to its proper cause.
But finite being is not the first and most universal of all causes,
but is a second and particular cause. Therefore.

Minor.— In creation, no being is presupposed from which
the thing created is produced ; therefore being in its totality
is produced in the act of creation. In other productions, i.e.,
in generation and alteration, a being is presupposed: in generation, a preexisting being is substantially changed, the subject
remaining the same, i.e., from a preexisting subject a new being
is engendered, as, v.g., a man ; in alteration, a being is only
accidentally changed, the substance remaining the same ; v.g.,
an object is made white.

2° No finite being has infinite power. But the principal
cause of creation has infinite power. Therefore no finite being
can be the principal cause of creation.

Minor. — Creation is the production of a being from no
preexisting potency as subject. But an agent which produces
a being from no preexisting potency, i.e., from no pre-existing
subject, has infinite power : since greater power is required
in an agent in the measure in which its potency is removed
from act, the power of an agent which produces a being from
no preexisting potency must be infinite. Therefore.

b) No finite being can be the instrumental cause of creation.
— An instrumental cause either operates dispositively in a
pre-existing subject, or it modifies the action of the principal
agent. But both dispositive operation in a pre-existing subject
and modification of the action of the principal cause are repugnant in creation. Therefore instrumental causality in crea-

tion is repugnant, i.e., no finite being can be the instrumental cause of creation.

Minor. — *a*) An instrumental cause cannot operate dispositively in a preexisting subject : for in creation there is no preexisting subject. *b*) An instrumental cause cannot modify the action of the principal cause : for an instrumental cause, in modifying the action of a principal cause, would contract, i.e., limit, the mode of acting of the principal cause. But action thus limited in creation is repugnant, for the creative act attains its effect under an unlimited aspect, i.e., being in its totality.

791. Difficulties. — 1° Nothing is made from nothing.   But creation is production from nothing.   Therefore creation is impossible.

Major.— In particular productions, *I concede;* in the universal production of a being in its totality, *I deny.*

Minor.— Creation is a particular production, *I deny;* is the universal production of a being in its totality, *I concede.*

2° But in any production whatsoever nothing is made from nothing. Therefore.

Every production is a change.   But every change presupposes a subject. Therefore every production presupposes a subject.

Major.— Either a real change or a change according to our mode of conceiving it, *I concede;* a real change only, *I deny.*

Minor.— Every real change, *I concede;* a change which is not real, but only conceived by us as such, *I deny.*

Although creation is conceived by us a change, it is not a change at all, as we have already pointed out.

POINTS FOR REVIEW

1. Define: creation, active creation, passive creation.

2. Prove that the world was created by God.

3. Explain why no finite being can be the principal cause or the instrumental cause of creation.

CREATION OF THE WORLD FROM ETERNITY

792. Statement of the question.— 1° According to the Fourth Council of the Lateran, it is an article of faith that the world did not always exist, but was created at the beginning of time.

2° We are here concerned with the question : can it be demonstrated by human reason that the world did not always exist, i.e., is creation from eternity repugnant ?

793. Opinions.— 1° The philosophers of ancient times, as Democritus, taught that the world necessarily existed from eternity.

2° Anaxagoras, Empedocles, and Plato held that the world did not exist from eternity. St. Augustine, St. Albert the Great, and St. Bonaventure denied the possibility of its creation from eternity.

3° St. Thomas teaches that human reason can demonstrate that the world did not necessarily exist always. But he affirms that human reason cannot demonstrate that it was impossible that the world exist from eternity. Hence creation in time is a truth of faith only.

According to this opinion, if any creature existed from eternity, it would have been produced from eternity. Therefore the eternity proper to it would be participated eternity, not essential eternity.

Essential eternity, which is the duration of an immobile being in being and in operation, does not admit of beginning, end, succession, or production of eternal being.

Participated eternity is the duration of produced being, which does not admit of beginning (regressively) or end (successively), but does admit of succession either in operation, as in the case of the angels, or in operation and in being.

794. Exposition of St. Thomas' opinion.

First proposition. — *The world did not necessarily exist from eternity.* — The world did not necessarily exist from eternity if God freely created it. But God freely created the world. Therefore the world did not necessarily exist from eternity[1].

Major. — If God freely created the world, the world came into existence when God willed it.

Minor. — God acts by His intellect and is free in regard to beings other than Himself.

Second proposition. — *The impossibility of creation from eternity cannot be demonstrated.* — If the impossibility of creation from eternity could be demonstrated, it would be demonstrated either from a consideration of the creative action, or from a consideration of the created effect. But it cannot be demonstrated from either of these considerations. Therefore the impossibility of creation from eternity cannot be demonstrated.

Minor. — 1° *Not from a consideration of the creative action:* the creative action, entitatively understood, is the divine essence, and therefore is from eternity.

2° *Not from a consideration of the created effect :* a) first, an effect, though posterior in nature to its cause, is not necessarily posterior to it in time ;

b) secondly, if an infinite series in the corruptible beings which constitute the world were repugnant, this would not prove that an incorruptible being, v.g., an angel, could not exist from eternity.

---

(1) I, q. 46, a. 1.

795. It was fitting that God would create the world at the beginning of time, not from eternity.— The end of God's will in the production of things is His goodness as manifested by the things produced. But God's goodness and power are manifested above all by the fact that things other than God did not always exist : for from this it is clearly manifest that creatures receive their being from God, because they did not always exist. Therefore it was fitting that God would create the world at the beginning of time, not from eternity (1).

---

(1) *Contra Gentes*, l. II, c. 38.

DIVINE CONCURRENCE

796. Statement of the question.— 1° Divine concurrence is the cooperation of God, as the first cause, in the operation and the effect of secondary causes.

2° There are two kinds of divine concurrence : moral and physical.

a) *Moral concurrence* is the concurrence by which God exercises an influence on the created will in the order of finality by proposing a good, by counseling, by persuading, etc.

b) *Physical concurrence* is the concurrence by which God, as the first efficient cause, cooperates in the action and the effect of secondary causes. Here we are concerned with physical concurrence.

3° Physical concurrence is of two kinds : simultaneous concurrence and motion or, as Thomists contend, premotion, i.e., previous concurrence.

a) *Simultaneous concurrence*, which is immediate, is the action by which God, as the first cause, immediately produces the operation (and the effect) of secondary causes, so that the operation is wholly produced by God acting as first cause, and wholly produced by the creature acting as second cause.

Simultaneous concurrence is called immediate, because God not only exercises an influence on the operation of the secondary cause by producing or conserving the created agent's power of acting, — such concurrence would be only mediate,— but because God, as the first cause, immediately produces this operation, just as the creature, as the second cause, immediately produces it.

l Divine motion is the action by which God applies the created agent's power, i.e., potency of acting, and moves it to operation, which is the second act of this potency.

797. Opinions.— 1° Scholastics commonly admit God's simultaneous concurrence. But Durandus does not agree with this opinion : he teaches that a creature, once having received its power of acting from God, is the one and only cause of its operation and effect.

2° St. Thomas and his disciples affirm that God concurs in the operation of creatures not only by simultaneous concurrence, but also by motion, by which He applies the creature's power of operating to act. Suarez and some Molinists deny the necessity of divine motion, and admit only simultaneous concurrence.

798. Statement of the thesis.

> **THESIS.**— God cooperates in the actions of creatures by simultaneous concurrence, and also by moving them to their operation.

First part. — *God cooperates in the actions of creatures by simultaneous concurrence.* — God is the immediate efficient cause of every being, in as much as the most universal aspect of being is found in the actions (and in the effects) of creatures. But in the actions (and in the effects) of creatures is found the most universal aspect of being. Therefore God cooperates as the immediate efficient cause of the actions (and of the effects) of creatures, i.e., God cooperates in the actions of creatures by simultaneous concurrence.

Major. — The most universal aspect of being is the most universal of all effects. But only God, Who is the most universal of agents, is the immediate efficient cause of the most universal of all effects. Therefore.

Minor. — The action (and the effect) of the creature not only is a particular kind of being, but also is being as such, i.e., there is found in it, besides the contracted aspects by which it is a being of a particular kind, the most universal aspect of being.

Second part. — *God cooperates in the actions of creatures by moving creatures to operation.* — 1° Everything which moves is moved by God. But creatures operate only when moved to operate. Therefore creatures operate only when moved to operation by God, i.e., God cooperates in the actions of creatures by moving them to operation.

The *major* is evident from the first argument used in the demonstration of the existence of God.

Minor. — Everything which passes from potency to act is moved. But the creature operates by passing from potency to act : for the creature's power of acting is really distinct from its operation, as potency is really distinct from its act.

2° In its operation, the creature exercises an influence on the being of its operation and of its effect. But the creature can exercise an influence on the being of its operation and of its effect only when, as instrumental cause, it is moved by God as principal cause. Therefore the creature operates only when moved by God([1]).

The *major* is evident, because, by acting, the creature gives existence to its operation and effect.

Minor. — Being is the most universal of all effects, and it can be produced only by God, as its proper and principal cause. Hence the creature, as instrumental cause, can exercise an influence on being only when moved by God as principal cause.

799. Divine motion and created liberty. — 1° *Preliminaries.*

---

(1) Ipsa igitur puritate sui esse, a finitis omnibus rebus secernitur Deus. Unde infertur... nullum... creatum agens in esse cujuscumque effectus influere, nisi motione accepta a prima causa.— *Thesis XXIV* s. THOMAE.

a) We know from the preceding thesis that God moves every created agent to its act, and therefore He moves even the created free will to its act.

b) Divine motion can be mediate or immediate.

Mediate divine motion is that motion by which God moves a created agent, i.e., a second cause, to its act by means of some other second cause ; v.g., a baseball bat is immediately moved by the hand, but is moved ultimately by God.

Immediate divine motion is that motion by which God moves a second cause to its act, without the concurrence of a second cause.

c) The influence of divine motion on the created will is *immediate*, because no finite agent can act, as efficient cause, on the human will([1]) ; it is *physical*, because God, as first efficient cause, moves the will ; it is *intrinsic*, because God, in moving the will, changes it intrinsically in as much as He alters its potentiality ; it is *infallible*, because the divine operation is perfectly efficacious and can be in no way impeded.

Hence arises the problem : how can we reconcile created liberty with divine motion ? To solve this problem, we would have to have perfect knowledge of the nature of God's operation. But we have only imperfect knowledge of it, knowledge which derives from analogy to the operation of creatures. Hence we have here a mystery which we cannot solve.

Therefore we shall pass over the controversies which have arisen in regard to this problem, and we shall prove, in so far as natural reason can, that divine motion can be reconciled with created liberty.

2° *Statement of the proposition.*

Proposition. — *God moves the created will to its free act, leaving its liberty intact.* — An agent which moves all things according to their condition moves the created will to its free act, leaving its liberty intact. But God moves all things according to their condition. Therefore([2]).

---

(1) We are concerned with the natural order.
(2) I-II, q. 10, a. 4, c.

Major. — An agent which moves all things according to their condition, i.e., in a manner in conformity with their nature, moves necessary causes in such a way that their effects are necessary, and free causes in such a way that their effects are free.

Minor. — It appertains to divine providence to safeguard the nature of things, not to destroy it.

POINTS FOR REVIEW

1. Define: divine concurrence, moral concurrence, physical concurrence, simultaneous concurrence, and divine motion.

2. Explain why God's simultaneous concurrence is necessary for the operation of creatures.

3. Prove that divine motion is necessary for the operation of creatures.

4. Why is the influence of divine motion on the human will immediate?

5. Can created liberty be reconciled with divine motion? Explain.

ARTICLE IV

CONSERVATION OF THINGS

800. Statement of the question. — 1° Conservation, in general, is the influence in virtue of which a thing is maintained in existence.

2° There are two kinds of conservation : indirect and direct.

Indirect conservation is conservation by which causes which could destroy or corrupt a thing are removed from it ; v.g., the removal of fire from a thing, so that it will not be burned.

Direct conservation is the positive influence of a cause on an effect in such manner that, without this influence, the effect could not continue in existence. Thus the air is illuminated by the sun, and this illumination of the air lasts only as long as it is under the influence of the sun.

3° God conserves things *immediately*, in as much as He conserves them in their very being, without the cooperation of second causes.

801. Statement of the thesis.

> **THESIS.** — CREATURES REQUIRE THAT THEY BE CONSERVED DIRECTLY AND IMMEDIATELY IN BEING BY GOD.

1° A thing which depends on a cause not only for its *becoming*, but also for its *being*, requires that it be conserved directly and immediately by that cause. But creatures depend on God not only for their becoming, but also for their being. Therefore creatures require that they be conserved directly and immediately in being by God.

Major. — Just as the becoming of a thing cannot endure if the action of the agent which is the cause of the effect in its becoming ceases, so too the being of a thing cannot endure if the action of the agent which is the cause of the effect both in its becoming and in its being ceases.

Thus, v.g., if the action of a builder who is the cause of a house in its becoming ceases, the building of the house, not the being of the house, ceases; but, if the action of the sun which is the cause of the illumination of the air both in its becoming and in its being ceases, illuminated air ceases to be.

Minor. — The being of creatures is participated being, and therefore is caused directly and immediately by a being which is such by its essence, as by its proper cause ; and this being is God.

2° Contingent being, as being, requires that it be conserved directly and immediately in being by a being which is such by its essence. But creatures are contingent beings. Therefore creatures require that they be conserved directly and immediately in being by God.

Major. — Contingent being is not its own existence, but, under the universal aspect of being, depends directly and immediately on a being which is such by its essence : for the union of its essence and existence, which are really distinct, can be effected only by a being whose proper effect is being. Since a contingent being always remains contingent, it is not only produced by a being which is such by its essence, but it continues in being only because a being which is such by its essence is continually uniting its essence and existence : for a contingent thing is never its own existence. Therefore God's conservation of creatures is rightly called *continued creation.*

802. God's immensity and ubiquity. — Immensity is the attribute in virtue of which God can be in all bodies and generally in all things, without being defined by them.

Ubiquity is the attribute in virtue of which God is actually intimately present in all bodies and generally in all things, i.e., it is the actual omnipresence of God in all things. God's ubiquity is distinct from His immensity, as second act from first act.

2° God is *everywhere*, i.e., He is intimately present in all things other than Himself, because He has created them and continually conserves them in their being.

God is in all things *by His essence*, because His operation is His essence ; *by His power*, because all things are subject to His power ; *by His presence*, because all things are naked and open to His eyes.

3° God is immense, because He has unlimited power of producing things other than Himself, in which He would operate.

4° Finally, the special modes of God's presence in certain things must be distinguished from the general mode of His presence in all things ; v.g., God is present in the souls of the just as an object experimentally and supernaturally known and loved.

803. Corollaries.— 1° God also conserves corruptible things indirectly, in as much as he removes corrupting agencies from them.

2° God immediately conserves all things in their being as such ; but He also conserves some things mediately, in as much as He conserves the second causes by which they are directly conserved in a particular mode of being ; v.g., accidents, as accidents, are immediately conserved by substance as by the second causes from which they continually receive their being ; and they are mediately conserved by God Who immediately conserves substance.

POINTS FOR REVIEW

1. Define: conservation, indirect conservation, and direct conservation.
2. Distinguish between God's immensity and His ubiquity.

3. Prove that God directly and immediately conserves all things.

4. Under what aspect is God's conservation of some things mediate? Explain.

READING.— If the doctrine of creation is understood, then we see that the preservation of creatures follows as a consequence of this (Ia, q. 104). If, for one moment, God ceased to preserve creatures in their being, they would immediately fall into nothingness, just as the sun's ray disappears when it ceases to give light.

The imagination does not perceive this necessity for the preservation of beings. The imagination pictures many sensible effects which do not have to be preserved by the sensible cause which brought them into being. The father and mother of a child may die after it is born, and the child continues to live.

The imagination is unable to distinguish between agents which are directly the causes merely of the becoming of their effects, and those which are causes not only of the *becoming* but also of the *being itself* of their effects. This distinction can be made only by the intellect, that faculty which is concerned with being. Some examples, however, will help to make this point clear.

The father is directly the cause of the passive generation of his son, and only indirectly of the being of his son. He may die, too, and the son may continue to live. On the contrary, other agents are causes directly both of the becoming and of the being of their effects; also, there can be no cessation of their action without a cessation of the effect. The generation of an animal depends not only upon the male parent of the animal, but also upon a vast number of cosmic influences which are also necessary for its preservation. Take away atmospheric pressure and solar heat, and the most vigorous animal will not survive for one second. In the physical order general agents are necessary for the preservation of beings, upon which these agents exert a beneficent influence.

Likewise, sensation or the sensible impression can subsist only so long as the object which produced it, preserves it in being. This is because it is the cause not only of its appearance but also directly of its being. Our visual sense perception of red continues to last only because of the influence exerted by the object which causes the perception in us. A virtual focus disappears when the real focus which maintained it ceases to act.

Likewise, in the intellectual life, the knowledge of a conclusion, resulting from certain principles, disappears if we forget the principles. Why? Because they are a higher cause, a direct cause not only of becoming, but of the being of the effect. It is only because of its actually depending and not merely because of its having depended upon the principle, that the conclusion remains in force.

So too, in the volitional order, the desire continues to assert itself only so long as the good which brought it into being, attracts it. If we cease to will an end, by that every fact we cease to will the means chosen for attaining it.

It is the characteristic of a cause which is of the same species as its effect, for it to be the only cause of the becoming of this effect. It is quite evident that the being of the effect cannot depend directly upon this cause, for it is as poor as the effect, participating like it in a perfection which neither of the two can have except by reason of a higher cause.

On the contrary, it is the characteristic of a cause which is of a higher order than its effects, for it to be the direct cause not only of their becoming but also of their being. Of such a nature is either the principle with regard to the consequences, or the validity of the end with regard to that of the means.

God is the supreme cause, who is the self-subsisting being, and every creature is being by participation. Therefore it follows that the creature not only depends upon God for its becoming, at the moment when it is produced, but also depends upon Him for its very being, and this at every moment of its existence. It would immediately fall into nothingness if, for one moment, God ceased to preserve it in its being; just as the scientific knowledge of a conclusion disappears when the principle upon which it rests is forgotten, and when the objective light which causes this knowledge in us is lost to view.

If the inferior cause which accounts for the becoming of its effect, ceases to act, there is a stop to becoming. If the higher cause which directly accounts for the very being of its effect ceases to act, at this very moment the effect ceases to be.

« The preservation of things by God is not effected by a new divine action, but it is a continuation of that creative action whereby He gives existence. This divine action is without either motion or time » (Ia, q. 104, a. 1, ad 4um). « Nor does He preserve things in existence otherwise than by continually pouring out existence into them » (*Ibid.*, a. 4).

God, who freely created all things, by reason of His absolute power could annihilate all creatures by ceasing to preserve them in being. But *de facto* nothing is annihilated by God, neither spirits nor matter. He does not do so, either according to the ordinary course of things in nature, or even by working a miracle, for He has no motive for doing so. Annihilation would not be a manifestation of any divine perfection (Ia, q. 104, a. 4).

Such is the Thomistic and classical teaching of the theologians concerning the preservation of creatures.— GARRIGOU-LAGRANGE, *God: His Existence and Attributes*, (Translated from the Fifth French Edition by Dom Bede ROSE, O. S. B., S. T. D.), vol. II, pp. 141-144.

DIVINE PROVIDENCE

804. Statement of the question.— 1° All understand that God, by His providence, directs created things to a determinate end. But creatures are also directed to their end by law. However, this does not mean that providence and law are one and the same : for they are distinct. Law is an ordination which determines how the creature naturally or freely should act. Providence in the manuduction of things to a determinate end. Therefore providence presupposes law, i.e., the eternal law in God, and it carries into execution what this law dictates.

2° Providence may be considered in God and in creatures (¹).

In God, providence is something eternal, and is defined: *the plan,* i.e., the conception in the divine intellect, *of the order of things to their end* (²), order being understood as the manuduction of things to their end.

In creatures, providence is something temporal, and is defined : the execution of that order whose plan is in the mind of God ; and it is called divine governance(³).

805. Errors.— 1° Pantheists, as a result of their system, are led into fatalism, i.e., the absolute necessity to which even God would be subjected, and deny providence. Providence is denied too by all deists, as Tindal, Shaftesbury, Voltaire, etc., who, though they admit that God is distinct from the world, teach that He pays no attention to the world.

(1) MONSABRÉ, *Conf. N. D.,* 1876.
(2) I, q. 22, a. 1, c.
(3) *Ibid.*

Deists are opposed, according to our modern manner of speaking, to theists, who admit providence.

2° Some of the philosophers of old taught that God extends His providence only to incorruptible things. Some attribute this opinion to Aristotle, but wrongly, it seems to us, for it cannot be proved from his words.([1]).

3° Others claim that God's providence extends to all things, but only as to *genus* and *species*, not to things as individuals.

806. Statement of the thesis.

THESIS.— DIVINE PROVIDENCE EXISTS, AND EXTENDS TO ALL THINGS AS INDIVIDUALS.

First part. — *Divin providence exists.* — The plan of the order of things to their end exists in the mind of God. But divine providence is the plan, i.e., the conception in the divine intellect, of the order of things to their end. Therefore divine providence exists.

Major. — All the goodness there is in things was created by God. But, in created things, goodness is found not only in their substance, but also in their order to an end, especially to their ultimate end, which is the goodness of God. Therefore this goodness of order was created by God. But since God acts through His intellect, there must preexist in the mind of God the plan of all things which He creates. Therefore the plan of the order of things to their end exists in the mind of God.

The *minor* is the definition of divine providence.

Second part. — *Divine providence extends to all things as individuals.* — The extension of God's providence is equal to that of His causality. But God's causality extends to all things not only as to their generic and specific principles, but

[1] *Contra Gentes*, l. III, c. 75.

also as to their individualizing principles. Therefore God's providence extends to all things as to their individualizing principles, i.e., to all things as individuals.

Major. — Since every agent acts for an end, the direction, i.e., ordering, of effects to that end extends as far as the causality of the agent. But divine providence is the plan existing in the mind of God of the order of things to their end. Therefore the extension of God's providence is equal to that of His causality.

Minor. — God is the first being, and the first efficient cause.

807. Scholia.— 1° *As for the plan of divine governance, God immediately governs all things.*— God has immediate knowledge of singular things not in as much as He knows them merely in their causes, but as they are in themselves. Moreover, it would not be fitting that God knew singular things and did not will their order, in which their principal goodness consists, since His will is the principle of all goodness. Therefore, just as God has immediate knowledge of singular things, so He must immediately determine their order ([1]).

2° *As for the execution of divine governance, God governs certain things by the intermediary agency of others.* — God, not because of any deficiency of His power, but on account of the abundance of His goodness, communicates the dignity of causality. Hence He governs inferior things by the intermediary agency of superior things ([2]), and, in particular, irrational beings by the intermediary agency of rational creatures([3]).

3° *Rational creatures are subject to divine providence in a special way*([4]).— Rational creatures, in virtue of their free will, have dominion over their acts, and therefore are subject to divine providence in a special way : they receive reward or punishment as their actions are imputable to them as deserving of reward or punishment.

(1) *Contra Gentes,* l. III, c. 76.
(2) I, q. 22, a. 3.
(3) *Contra Gentes,* l. III, c. 78.
(4) I, q. 22, a. 2, ad 5.

4° Casual and fortuitous things, which escape the ordering of a particular cause, do not escape the ordering of divine providence, for it extends to all things.

POINTS FOR REVIEW

1. Distinguish between; *a)* divine providence and the eternal law; *b)* divine providence and divine governance.
2. Prove that divine providence exists, and that it extends to all things as individuals.
3. Explain why God immediately governs all things.
4. Why are rational creatures subject to divine providence in a special way?

READING.— Dans l'ordre auquel est emprunté le langage, nous appelons providence ce rôle de la prudence humaine qui consiste, ayant le souvenir du passé et la claire notion du présent, à disposer sagement l'avenir. Pour l'appliquer à Dieu, nous devons, sans nul doute, dégager cette notion de toute attache temporelle; du moins en tant que Dieu même en devrait être affecté. C'est seulement du côté de l'objet auquel s'applique la providence que les relations temporelles peuvent être maintenues. Nous ne gardons pas moins de cette disposition tout ce qui implique disposition, ordre à introduire dans les faits, et nous disons que Dieu est providence en ce que l'ordre des choses procède de lui aussi bien que la substance des choses; que cet ordre, d'ailleurs, suppose d'une part l'orientation de chaque phénomène ou de chaque être vers les fins particulières auxquelles il doit servir, et ensuite l'orientation du tout vers la fin toute dernière; que par suite la *raison* de cet ordre (*ratio ordinis*), tout ce qu'il comporte d'intelligibilité comme tel doit trouver son équivalent supérieur dans la première cause.

Il doit paraître clair, que tout, absolument, est soumis à la Providence. Ceux qui lui ont soustrait quelque chose l'ont fait soit à cause d'objections qu'ils n'ont pas su vaincre, soit parce que, dès le principe, leur philosophie relative à Dieu était défectueuse. C'est ainsi que la considération du hasard et du mal a paru à certains incompatible avec l'idée qu'une providence régit le monde. C'est ainsi encore que le cas de la liberté dont nous portons en nous la certitude, et à laquelle d'ailleurs est suspendu l'ordre moral, a semblé impossible à concilier avec une providence universellement souveraine. D'autre part, la nécessité à laquelle obéissent les agents naturels est, aux yeux de quelques-uns, une explication suffisante de l'ordre, et ils ne sentent pas avoir le besoin de recourir à une causalité ayant celui-ci pour objet.

Cette dernière position est démontrée fautive par ce que nous avons dit en faveur de Dieu dans la 5e *voie*. Nous avons montré alors que la nécessité dont on parle n'est qu'une exécutrice, et qu'il faut supposer à son action dans le réel un antécédent idéal, à savoir une préconception, un premier établissement des faits et de l'ordre d'évolution qu'ils affectent. Quant aux difficultés énoncées, bien qu'elles ne puissent nous faire revenir sur une thèse solidement établie, il y a lieu de les résoudre.

En ce qui concerne le hasard, il ne faut pas penser que nous prétendions le nier, en lui opposant la providence. Nous le mettons seulement à son rang; nous en faisons un élément du relatif, et l'absolu qui le domine ne fait nul tort à sa nature; au contraire, il le constitue, car ce qui est voulu dans le monde par la providence, ce n'est pas uniquement des *effets*, mais aussi et surtout un *ordre*, dans lequel les justes relations des causes aux effets entrent comme élément principal. Bien loin donc que la direction imprimée par Dieu doive supprimer la contingence, elle en doit assurer le cours.— SERTILLANGES, *S. Thomas d'Aquin*, t. I, 4e édit., p. 255.

DIVINE PROVIDENCE AND EVIL

808. Statement of the question.— 1° Evil, in general, is the privation of due perfection. Evil may be physical or moral. Physical evil is the privation of a natural perfection, a privation which has no relation to the moral law ; v.g., death, blindness. Moral evil, i.e. sin, is the lack of conformity of a free act with the rule of morality ; v.g., a lie.

2° A sinful act, i.e., moral evil, is a being, i.e., an act, with a defect(1). Considered materially, moral evil is a being and an act, and hence derives from God as from its first cause ; considered formally, it is a defect.

Can God will or permit physical or moral evil ? This is the question with which we are concerned in this article.

3° To will evil directly is to be inclined to evil.

To will evil indirectly, i.e., accidentally, is to be inclined to a good to which evil is annexed.

To permit evil is not to impede evil which one can impede, but is not bound of necessity to impede.

809. Statement of the thesis.

  THESIS.— Divine providence can will no evil directly, wills physical evil indirectly, and cannot will moral evil as such even indirectly, but merely permits it ; and this permission is a good.

---

(1) I-II, q. 79, a. 2, c.

First part. — *Divine providence can will no evil directly.* — Divine providence cannot will directly what is not desirable as such, i.e., what is not the direct object of the will. But evil as such is not desirable. Therefore divine providence can will no evil directly.

Major. — To will is to desire.

Minor. — Evil is opposed to good, which is defined : that which is desirable.

Second part. — *Divine providence wills physical evil indirectly.* — To desire good to which evil is annexed in preference to a good of which the evil is the privation is to will indirectly. But divine providence desires good to which evil is annexed in preference to a good of which the evil is the privation. Therefore divine providence wills evil indirectly.

Minor. — God, in willing the moral order, v.g., justice, wills the evil of penalty, i.e., punishment ; and, in willing that the order of nature be safeguarded, He wills that certain things be naturally destroyed ; v.g., He wills the slaughtering of animals that man may have food.

Third part, — *Divine providence cannot will moral evil as such even indirectly.* — God can will no good in preference to His own goodness. But moral evil as such is opposed to God's goodness. Therefore divine providence cannot will moral evil as such even indirectly.

Major. — God's own goodness is the proper object of the divine will.

Minor. — Moral evil formally understood, i.e., as such, is a turning away from God, Who is the ultimate end.

Fourth part. — *Divine providence merely permits moral ev l as such.* — Divine providence merely permits evil which comes solely from creatures, and is not impeded by God, Who could, but is not bound, to impede it. But moral evil as such comes solely from creatures, and is not impeded by God, Who could, but is not bound, to impede it.   Therefore.

Minor. — a) *Moral evil as such comes solely from creatures.* — Moral evil as such is a privation, i.e., a defect, of a free act. But the defect of an act does not come from God, Who is the most perfect cause, but from the creature, which is an imperfect cause.   Therefore.

b) *God could impede moral evil.* — God, as the first cause, can impede any defect whatsoever of second causes, i.e., of the creature.

c) *God is not bound to impede moral evil.* — God, as the first cause, is bound to impede no defect whatsoever of second causes, but only to move them according to their condition.

Fifth part. — *The permission of moral evil is a good.* — The permission of moral evil is a good if moral evil provides opportunity for a greater participation in divine goodness and a greater manifestation of God's glory.   But moral evil provides opportunity for a greater participation in divine goodness and a greater manifestation of God's glory.   Therefore.

Minor. — It is evident from examples : a) Persecution by tyrants provided opportunities for the sufferings of the martyrs.   b) God's mercy is manifested by His forgiveness of sin, and His justice by the punishment of it.

POINTS FOR REVIEW

1. Define: physical evil, moral evil, to will evil directly, to will evil indirectly, to permit evil.

2. Prove that divine providence can will no evil directly, and cannot will moral evil even indirectly.

3. Explain why the permission of moral evil is a good.

READING.— L'univers s'établit, ainsi que nous l'avons dit, par épanouissement du Souverain Bien, et en vertu de participations échelonnées dont chacune exprime Dieu à sa manière; dont chacune est donc bonne, fût-elle même déficiente.   Mais il faut ajouter — et c'est ici que git la solution du problème: Il est meilleur qu'il y ait des natures ainsi faites.   Sans elles, la manifestation du divin serait moins riche; car nous l'avons fait voir à propos de l'inégalité, chaque nature, comme telle, quelque inférieure qu'elle soit, comporte un bien *sui generis* que nul bien ne saurait suppléer, et qui était donc dû à l'univers, étant donné le degré de bonté que lui destinait la Sagesse suprême. Souvenons-nous que les essences épanouissent l'être, et que ce serait appauvrir rcelui-ci que de lui en ravir une quelconque. Or celles qui sont déficientes de soi ou, ce qui revient au même, en raison du milieu naturel qui est comme leur prolongement, celles-là, dis-je, doivent défaillir en fait plus ou moins, et ainsi donner lieu au mal, à moins qu'on ne charge la puissance souveraine d'empêcher cet écart par une intervention permanente. Mais cette requête serait bien peu sage. Notre étude de la Providence a montré que celle-ci a pour rôle de donner les natures à elles-mêmes, non de les arracher à leur fonctionnement et à leurs tendances. Or, que serait des natures déficientes à qui Celui même dont l'influence les constitue donnerait de ne défaillir jamais ? Ce seraient des natures violentées, truquées, de fausses natures; car ce qui peut vraiment défaillir et qui est laissé à soi, de temps en temps défaille.

Et puis, dans un ordre total, fait d'êtres agissant et réagissant les uns sur les autres, le mal, bien que non-être en soi, est indirectement une condition de l'être, étant une condition de l'action. Cet argument, déjà touché à propos de l'inégalité des natures, ne vaut pas moins ici. Que deviendrait l'activité universelle, si la contrariété cessait d'y entretenir les échanges, et, matériellement ou moralement, ne faisait de la déficience des uns, êtres ou phénomènes, la rançon du devenir ou du succès des autres ? Que deviendrait la vie du lion, sans l'occision de la brebis, et que deviendrait la patience du martyr, sans les méfaits qui la suscitent ? Le bien a plus de force en bien que le mal en mal; le premier a plus de valeur que le second n'en consume. N'y a-t-il pas plus d'utilité à ce que la maison soit ferme qu'il n'y a d'ennui à enfouir ses fondements sous la terre ? Ce serait donc suggérer à la Providence d'exercer un métier de dupe, que de l'inviter à supprimer le mal. Et ce disant, on ne cherche pas à arracher le mal à lui-même. Le mal est mal; mais qu'il y ait du mal, c'est un bien, non toujours par rapport au sujet où le mal se trouve, mais en tout cas au total: en ne regardant qu'à l'ordre, et aux ultimes effets de l'ordre.

Au sujet de ces effets, serait-il nécessaire maintenant d'instituer une discussion nouvelle ? Ils profitent manifestement de ce qui vient d'être dit. Cet aboutissement dernier de toutes choses, s'il comporte un déchet, ne doit pas pour cela être jugé mauvais, puisque, premièrement, de déchet est la condition de fait imposée à l'existence et au fonctionnement des natures contingentes, et, deuxièmement, ce n'est pas un déchet brut, puisque le but tout à fait final, qui est la participation du divin, s'y retrouve sous une autre forme, à savoir, s'il s'agit du déchet matériel, par la manifestation des plus hautes lois cosmiques; s'il s'agit du déchet moral, par la manifestation de la justice, qui est la loi de l'ordre moral.

Il n'y a donc pas de motifs, à l'appui des fatales déviations que la considération du mal a imposées tant de fois à l'intelligence humaine. Il est insensé de nier Dieu pour cette raison qu'il y a le mal; on devrait plutôt arguer en sens contraire, et dire: Si le mal est, Dieu est, puisqu'il n'y aurait point de mal, s'il n'y avait d'abord le bien de l'ordre, et le bien de l'ordre aurait-il une explication, en dehors du Bien divin ? De même, il n'y a pas de raison pour écarter, de ce chef, la Providence du gouvernement immédiat de toutes choses; car si le travail qui se fait dans l'univers est bon, pris en bloc, il est bon aussi autant qu'inévitable que Dieu y collabore, ou plutôt en soit le principe. Il ne s'ensuivra pas que Dieu soit compromis dans les déficiences d'où naît le mal. En effet, ces déficiences sont le fait des agents particuliers, non le fait de la Cause Première. Nous l'avons dit plus haut, la transcendance de Dieu fait que son gouvernement laisse la nature et l'homme pleinement responsables. Les accidents de la nature sont bien à elle; le mal humain est aussi à nous. Ce qui appartient à Dieu, c'est d'être cause du bien que l'homme et la nature manifestent; c'est de permettre le mal en tant qu'il confère au bien, à savoir comme condition de fait résultant de l'établissement et du fonctionnement de natures bonnes, et aussi comme élément d'un tout qui tire parti du mal comme du bien, et qui réalise ainsi l'excellent avec plus de bonheur que ne le pourrait faire un univers figé, où le mal serait sans empire.

On le voit, dans cette doctrine, le principe de finalité est le postulat suprême. Quiconque nierait que les agents de la nature travaillent à une œuvre et s'avancent vers un but infini, ruinerait tout par la base. Mais aussi tomberait-il sous le poids des arguments qui prouvent l'ordre, sans compter que, ruinant du même coup la notion du bien, il ruinerait corrélativement celle du mal.— SERTILLANGES, *op. cit.*, pp. 320-323.

MIRACLES

810. Statement of the question. — 1° Divine providence ordinarily follows the laws of nature, but extraordinarily it can deviate from them, i.e., can operate in a miraculous manner. But can miracles be known with certainty ? It is with this question that we are concerned in this article.

2° A miracle, as the very term indicates, is something which excites wonder.

A miracle, according to its real definition, has a strict or proper meaning, and also a wide meaning. In the strict meaning of the term, a miracle is a *fact produced by God in the world which is beyond the order of action of the whole of created nature.*

a) *A fact produced in the world*, but not a doctrine ; moreover, it must be a sensible fact.

b) *Produced by God*, as the principal cause, and thus is not excluded the wonder-worker, who can act as an instrument of God.

c) *Beyond the order of action of nature :* thus is indicated that a miracle is an exception to the established order of nature. Hence, though the production of grace and the justification of the wicked can be effected only by God, they are not called miracles, because they do not take place beyond the order of nature, i.e., are not exceptions to it, since they do not appertain to the order of nature (1).

d) *Beyond the order of action of the whole of created nature*, that is to say, surpassing the power of the whole of created nature. Hence it is not sufficient that a miracle be beyond

_____

(1) I, q. 105, a. 7, ad 1.

the order of action merely of some particular created nature, for otherwise events of chance would be miracles ; and not beyond the order of action of corporal things only, but also of spiritual natures, v.g., of the angel.

A miracle is beyond the order of *action*, not of *being*, because a miracle is not entitatively and intrinsically supernatural, as is grace, but is an effect that is entitatively natural, but effectively supernatural, because it surpasses the forces of the whole of created nature ; v.g., in the resurrection of a dead person, natural life is restored to a corpse ; but such a resurrection is a miracle, because it surpasses the powers of action of the whole of created nature.

In its wide meaning, a miracle is *a fact which do s not su - pass the powers of spirits, but which, in consideration of its circumstances, is attributed either to good angels or to God ;* v. g., a holy person's walking upon water.

3° Miracles, in the strict and proper sense, are divided into three classes, corresponding to the three ways in which they surpass the powers of nature : the miracle of first order, i.e., as regards the substance of the fact ; the miracle of second order, i.e., as regards the subject in which it is wrought ; and the miracle of third order, i.e., as regards the mode in which it is wrought([1]).

a) A miracle *of first order* is a fact which so surpasses the power of created nature, that nature can in no way effect it ; v.g., the fact of two bodies being in the same place at the same time.

b) A miracle *of second order* is a fact which nature can effect, but not in the subject in which it is produced ; v g., the resurrection of the dead. Nature can cause life, but not in a dead body.

c) A miracle *of third order* is a fact which nature can effect in the subject in which it is produced, but not in the mode in

(1) I, q. 105, a. 8.— *Contra Gentes*, l. III, c. 101.

which it is produced ; v g., the sudden curing of a disease
without the usual process of nature(¹).

4° *Metaphysical certitude* is the determination of the intellect in regard to things which are absolutely necessary, and
obtains when the nexus between the subject and the predicate
is absolutely necessary ; v.g., man is rational.

Physical ce titude is the determination of the intellect in
regard to existing things which could have not existed, or could
have existed in some other way, i.e., in regard to facts ; v.g.,
Peter exists.

Probable certitude is the determination of the intellect in
regard to things which are true in the majority of cases; v.g.,
in regard to a truth asserted by a trustworthy witness. Probable certitude admits of degrees, and, in certain cases, can
have almost the same firmness as physical certitude.

5° A miracle may be considered under two aspects : a)
as a sensible fact ; and, in considering it under this aspect, we
are concerned with its *histori al* truth ; b) as a supernatural
fact ; and, in considering it under this aspect, we are concerned
with its *philosophical* truth.

811. Adversaries.— There are some authors who admit
the possibility of miracles, but yet maintain that miracles do
not exist, or, if they do, they cannot be distinguished from natural facts which are more or less extraordinary, or from feats
of magic. Such is the teaching of Rousseau, Renan, Kant,
and generally of all agnostics.

Their chief argument is as follows : we cannot know all
the forces and laws of nature ; hence what is inexplicable by

---

(1) 1° According to another classification, given by St. Thomas in *De
Potentia*, q. 6, a. 2, ad 3, miracles are *above nature,* in as much as nature can
in no way produce the effect which God produces; *against nature,* when there
remains in nature a disposition contrary to the effect which God produces;
v. g., in the resurrection of the dead; *beyond nature,* when the effect produced
by God can be produced by nature, but not in the same manner.

This division coincides with the foregoing classification. Some, however,
think otherwise.

2° Some call miracles of first order miracles in the strict sense, and
miracles of second order miracles in the wide sense.

the known laws of nature can be produced in accordance with
forces and laws of nature which we do not know([1]).

812. Statement of the thesis.

> **THESIS**.— MIRACLES, AS SENSIBLE FACTS, CAN BE
> KNOWN WITH PHYSICAL CERTITUDE ; AS
> SUPERNATURAL FACTS, SOME CAN BE
> KNOWN WITH METAPHYSICAL CERTITUDE,
> OTHERS ONLY WITH PROBABLE CERTITUDE.

First part. — *Miracles, as sensible facts, can be known with
physical certitude.* — Miracles, as sensible facts, come within
the range of our observation just as easily as do other sensible
facts.   Moverover, because they excite wonder and are wrought
in an extraordinary manner, they command more attention,
deserve and, indeed, receive more careful attention and, consequently are known with an even greater degree of physical
certitude than are ordinary sensible facts.

Second part. — *As supernatural facts, some miracles an
be known with metaphysical certitude.* — 1° Only God, as principal cause, has immediate power over being, first matter, and
the rational soul.   But it is absolutely certain that there are
some miracles of first, second, and third order whose principal
cause is an agent which has immediate power over being, first
matter, and the rational soul.   .Therefore it is absolutely certain that there are some miracles whose principal cause is God,
i.e., that some miracles, as supernatural facts, can be known
with metaphysical certitude.

Major. — Only the cause which immediately produces an
effect has immediate power over that effect ; v.g., only the

---

(1) Puisqu'un miracle est une exception aux lois de la nature, pour en
juger il faut connaître ces lois, et pour en juger sûrement, il faut les connaître
toutes: Car une seule loi qu'on ne connaîtrait pas pourrait, en certains cas
inconnus aux spectateurs, changer l'effet de celles qu'on connaîtrait.   Ainsi
celui qui prononce que tel ou tel acte est un miracle, déclare qu'il connaît
toutes les lois de la nature, et qu'il sait que cet acte en est une exception.—
J.-J. ROUSSEAU, *Lettres de la Montagne.*

legislator who immediately and directly makes a law can immediately and directly change it.   But only God, as principal cause, can produce being ; and only God can immediately produce first matter, and the rational soul, which are not produced from a preexisting subject.   Therefore.

Minor. — a) *The coexistence of two bodies in the same p'ace* must be classified as *a miracle* of first order ; v.g.   Christ's entering the cenacle after His resurrection, *the doors being shut* (John XX, 26).   Bodies cannot remain naturally distinct in being and in matter unless they remain distinct in posture and place.   Hence, if distinction according to place and posture be taken away, bodies can be conserved distinct in being and matter only by a cause which has immediate power over being and matter([1]).

b) *The resurrection of the dead* 's properly classified as a miracle of second order.   Resurrection is the immediate union of a rational soul to the first matter of a corpse, without the mediation of previous accidental dispositions.   Hence it can be effected only by a cause which has immediate power over first matter and the rational soul.

The same must be said of the restoration of sight to a man born blind.   Blindness is, as it were, a partial death.

c) The sudden changing of water into wine, without previous accidental dispositions, is a miracle of third order.

Such a change is the immediate eduction of the form of wine from first matter, and can be produced only by a cause which can immediately effect an intrinsic change in first matter.

2° *Confirmation by common sense.* — Common sense, i.e., natural reason which is, as it were, inchoative metaphysics, knows with firmest certitude that some effects are effects which are proper to God, and therefore surpass all the powers, even the unknown powers, of created nature.   Hence the man born blind of the Gospel says in defence of the reality of his cure : « From the beginning of the world it hath not been

_____
(1) *Suppl.*, q. 83, a. 3.

heard that any man hath opened the eyes of one born blind. Unless this man were of God, he could not do anything » (John IX, 32-33).

Third part. — *As supernatural facts, some miracles can le known only with probable certitude.* — Some miracles of third order, v.g., the sudden restoration to health of one afflicted with a serious disease, the elevation of a body in the air solely by the command of the voice, surpass the powers of corporal agents, but do not manifestly surpass the powers of spiritual agents. But it can be discerned whether or not a fact which is al'eged to be a miracle comes from God, at least through the mediation of angels, i.e., of good spirits. Thus miracles in the wide sense can be distinguished from feats of the devil by circumstances which produce only probable certitude.

These circumstance are enumerated by Benedict XIV ([1]), who says : «False miracles can be discerned from true miracles by their efficacy, utility, mode, end, person, and o casion.»

a) Efficacy. — Miracles are wrought, at least mediately, by divine power, as *genuine* miracles, whereas the feats of the devil are of short duration.

b) Utility. — Miracles serve some useful purpose, as in the curing of the sick and in other such things. The signs of the devil, on the contrary, are concerned with things that are deleterious or vain, as their flying through the air, their paralyzing of members of the body, and the like.

() Mode. — One who perform true miracles acts with humility, piety, and reverence. If anything dishonest, violent, cruel, or unbecoming is detected in his manner of acting, there is no miracle. Thus are eliminated many feats of magicians.

d) End — Miracles are destined to be of benefit to faith and morals ; the signs of magicians and the feats o the devil are manifestly detrimental to faith and morals.

() Person. — Miracles are wrought by persons who are noted for sanctity of life, zeal for God's glory, modesty, humility, and charity, not by persons notorious for viciousness

(1) *De Beatificatione Servorum Dei*, a. IV, c. 7, nn. 14-22.

and levity of life, and who boast of their defects. Miracles can sometimes be wrought by evil persons, but in such cases it is clear from the circumstances that they are wrought only as a confirmation of divine truth, not in approval of the life of those persons of whom God makes use in working them.

f) Occasion. — If the work performed takes place among the vain and unworthy, or if he working of a miracle is neither necessary or fitting, or if it is not wrought in the name of God the Creator, but rather by the use of base and ridiculous means, as happens in the case of feats of fakirs and spiritualists, then there is no miracle.

813. Possibility of miracles.— It is very evident that miracles are possible, because the order of nature is not absolutely necessary, but contingent, and because God, as an omnipotent free cause, can produce the effects of second causes without their help, can impede the effects of second causes, and can produce effects which surpass the power of the whole of created nature[1].

814. Difficulties.— 1° To affirm that a work of its very nature surpasses all the forces of nature, we must know all the forces of nature. But we do not know all the forces of nature. Therefore miracles, as supernatural facts, cannot be known.

Major.— We must know all the forces of nature as regards what they can do in a positive way, *I deny;* as regards what they cannot do, *I concede.*

Minor.— We do not know all the forces of nature as regards what they can do in a positive way, *I concede;* as regards what they cannot do, *I deny.*

2° Renan and others contend that miracles cannot be known with certainty unless they are performed several times before a scientific academy.

Reply: 1° If this were so, God would have to await the institution of academies, in order that He work miracles. 2° Common sense, i. e., natural reason, suffices for the knowledge of a fact which is sensible, public, and adapted to the intelligences of all. 3° There is now a scientific commission of medical doctors at Lourdes for the examination of miraculous cures; likewise, medical doctors are called together to examine the miracles proposed in cases of beatification. 4° Finally, not infrequently scientists, because of prejudice,

---

(1) Dieu peut-il faire des miracles ? C'est-à-dire peut-il déroger aux lois qu'il a établies ? Cette question sérieusement faite serait impie, si elle n'était absurde; ce serait faire trop d'honneur à celui qui le résoudrait négativement de le punir, il suffirait de l'enfermer.— J.-J. ROUSSEAU, *Troisième lettre de la Montagne.*

pride, and passion, are not capable of passing judgment on supernatural facts (1).

_____

(1) GARRIGOU-LAGRANGE, *op. cit.*, p. 101.

Poser en principe qu'un thaumaturge ne mérite crédit qu'autant qu'il comparait devant le tribunal de principaux représentants de la science du XXe siècle, et qu'il se soumet aux conditions de leur programme: c'est se moquer des siècles passés et de tout le genre humain auxquels on refuse la dose de bon sens nécessaire pour constater les faits les plus palpables; et c'est aussi se moquer de Dieu, que l'on suppose pouvoir se plier aux caprices et accepter la réglementation de sa créature au moment même où il va manifester sa plus haute puissance: c'est le condamner à ne pas agir en Dieu à l'heure où il veut prouver qu'il est Dieu.— Card. PIE, *Troisième instruction*, Oeuvres. t. V, p. 105.

END OF METAPHYSICS

ALPHABETICAL INDEX

(Numbers refer to sections)

A

Accident. Notion 643; division 644; accident and substance 645; existence of accidents without a subject 647; composition of substance and accidents in finite being 625-628.

Act. Origin of notion 545; extension of notion 546; description 548; division 550; act as it divides being 551, 552; in an order in which act is not received into potency, it is unlimited 554; act can be limited only by potency 553; act and potency are in the same genus 555; — specifies potency 556; potency can be reduced to act only by a being in act 557; opposition between potency and act 558; act is, strictly speaking, prior to potency 560; in the order of generation, potency is prior to act 559.

Analogous things. Univocal things equivocal things 505.

Analogy. Division 502, 3; abstraction 506.

Atheism. 751, 752.

B

Beauty. Definition 540; formal beauty and objective beauty 541; extension of beauty 542; powers which apprehend beauty 543; opposite of beauty 544.

Being. Cannot be defined or properly described 491; improper description 492; division 493; as signifying that which is, is an essential predicate of everything to which it is attributed 494; as signifying existence, is an essential predicate of God 495; as signifying existence, is not an essential predicate of creatures 496; being as it is first known is not known as metaphysical being 497; analogy of being 502, 503, 504; abstraction and contraction of the concept of being 506; transcendence of being 498, 499; being is the ontologically first concept 500; is the most general and simplest of predicates 501; properties of being in general 508, 509, 510, 511, 512; absolute being and absolute goodness 533; division of being by act and potency 551, 552.

Being, finite. Distinction between essence and existence 620-624; composition of substance and accidents 625-628.

C

Cause. Relations of the causes to each other 710-712; relations of the causes to their effects 713, 714; concept of cause is analogous 715.

Cause, efficient. Notion 678; division 679; constituent in first act 680; — in second act 681; efficient causality in finite beings 695-698; principle of causality 689-692, 694.

Cause, exemplar. 677.

Cause, final. Notion 699; division 700; constituent in first act 701; — in second act 702; condition required for its actual causality 704; effects 705; principle of finality 706-708; manners of acting for an end 709.

Cause, formal. Notion 671; division 672; constituent in first act 673; — in second act 674; conditions for exercise of its causality 675; effects 676.

T

U